A Checklist
of the Writings
of Daniel Defoe

A Checklist of the
Writings of Daniel Defoe

by

JOHN ROBERT MOORE

Second Edition

ARCHON BOOKS

1 9 7 1

© 1960 by Indiana University Press

Second Printing 1962

Second Edition © 1971 by John Robert Moore
Published 1971 by Archon Books, an imprint of
The Shoe String Press, Inc.,
Hamden, Connecticut 06514

Library of Congress Catalog Card No.: 70–122416
ISBN 0–208–01086–6

Printed in the United States of America

To Alice

MY FELLOW-WORKER

FOREWORD

THIS CHECKLIST has grown out of more than thirty years of sustained interest in the life and writings of Daniel Defoe.

I owe an immense debt of gratitude to William Lee, whose great pioneer work *Daniel Defoe, His Life, And Recently Discovered Writings* was based on his extensive study of Defoe's works as they could be traced through newspaper notices in the early eighteenth century. Where I have been unable to correct the dates which Lee assigned to Defoe's publications or to verify them independently, I have accepted them with grateful acknowledgment. Very rarely I have substituted later dates, on the ground that Lee misinterpreted his evidence—as when a book was advertised for sale but delayed in publication. For many other works, however, I have discovered earlier and more precise dates than his; for example, his dates (followed without question in *CBEL*) for the second, third, and fourth editions of *Robinson Crusoe* are all too late. Indeed, for the majority of the 566 items I have had no assistance from Lee; more than half of my entries were unknown to him, or at least unknown as Defoe's. To a lesser degree I am indebted to the patient researches of the late Professor W. P. Trent, whose marginalia in certain copies of Defoe's works now owned by the Indiana University Library gave me my first insight into the attribution of anonymous and pseudonymous writings. Long ago, however, I was obliged to place increasingly less reliance on an approach which was so impressionistic in method and which led so often to results which were mutually contradictory or demonstrably wrong.

My next great debt is to my contemporaries—the staffs of research libraries, antiquarian booksellers, and fellow-students of

literature and history. In more than a score of libraries in Great
Britain and the United States I have enjoyed exceptional cour-
tesies, and these have often made uncatalogued material easily ac-
cessible. When I found *A Farther Case Relating to the Poor Keel-
Men of Newcastle,* Mr. Laurence Hanson informed me that the
Bodleian owned the preliminary broadside. When I was examining
Considerations on the Present State of Great Britain, Mrs. Inez
Williams of the Huntington Library raised a question which led
to the identification of that tract under a different title (*The
Juncture*). Professor George Harris Healey of Cornell University
introduced me to *Counter Queries,* and Professor Richmond P.
Bond of the University of North Carolina led me to identify the
authorship of *A Condoling Letter.* Mr. Arnold Muirhead of St.
Albans, Hertford, called my attention to *A Hymn to the Funeral
Sermon,* and Mr. Francis F. Madan of London enabled me to date
it precisely and to clinch the attribution to Defoe. Mr. John Hayward of London offered many suggestions which have been grate-
fully accepted. The complete list would be a very long one. For
such friends one recalls the sentence which Defoe altered and
cited out of its Biblical context: "Our name is LEGION, and we
are many."

For an understanding of Defoe, we need to know what he wrote
and what he did not write. Few readers can be expected to undertake the entire corpus; but it is reasonable to expect critics, biogra-
phers, and bibliographers to realize that no "collected" edition
contains more than a very small fraction of his works. It is also
reasonable to expect that judgments of Defoe should no longer be
based on books which were not his—such as the *Prince Mirabel*
tracts or the *Short Narrative* of Count Patkul.

In its skeleton form this checklist has already been adopted as
the basis for cataloguing Defoe's works in some of the principal
British and American libraries. A great many new titles are included which can be assigned to Defoe with confidence. Many
other titles have been discarded which were previously assigned
to him for inadequate reasons. A good many others are now restored to the Defoe canon which were correctly ascribed to Defoe
by the earlier bibliographers, but which were mistakenly omitted

from the more recent lists of his writings. A considerable number
are included here in a borderland of partial uncertainty, and I
have marked each of these with a star; most of the available evidence indicates Defoe's authorship, but that evidence is not yet
adequate for complete assurance. Where such tentative assignments
are correct, they will probably be verified by further accumulation
of analogues from Defoe's other writings, relevant remarks in his
correspondence, allusions made by contemporaries, manuscript
notes in first editions, and the like.

Next after the authorship I have sought to determine the exact
date of publication. This may throw light on the significance of
the work itself. In *Memoirs of the Church of Scotland* we find
Defoe withholding a book for nine years and publishing it for a
special occasion; in *An Essay on The History of Parties* we find
him expanding a tract while it was still in the press, to keep it in
line with current events; in *A Voice from the South* we discover
a tract supposedly reprinted from articles in the *Review* which
was actually reprinted in the *Review* from the tract itself.

Dates of publication can often be determined by (and often take
special significance from) debates or legislation in Parliament,
shifts in political alignments, military events or diplomatic over-
tures, and current events of many other sorts. The two books on the
Plague Year were not unrelated to Walpole's quarantine policy,
Colonel Jack's repentance for his part in the Jacobite rising of
1715 to Atterbury's conspiracy in 1722, and the London reissue of
A History of the Union to proposed infringements by Parliament
on the terms of that Union. Dates can also be determined by careful analysis of the often-conflicting newspaper advertisements, by
manuscript notes of the first owners, by allusions in or to rival
publications, and by relationships to Defoe's other writings.

The third great question concerns the reasons for Defoe's publishing what he did. He spent much of a lifetime in accumulating
ideas and observations (beginning with his now-lost *Historical
Collections* of 1682), and he could have employed these whenever
there was occasion to draw on them. In *Moll Flanders* he used some
of the same travels which reappeared (in reverse order) in the
Tour. In the *Review* he printed one of the bills of mortality which

lay behind *A Journal of the Plague Year.* In *Some Considerations on . . . Seamen* he repeated proposals he had made twenty-three years earlier before the Select Committee of the House of Lords. In *The Commentator,* most interesting of all his works for a study of his use of source material, we find him abstracting passages from his earlier writings, referring to contemporary publications of his own, and making preliminary use of ideas and notes which he was later to develop much more extensively. In anything by Defoe we are likely to find anecdotes, economic statistics, references to his reading in history or literature, projects, or personal acquaintances and personal experiences which may appear anywhere else in his writings. Such materials seem to have been always in reserve —and always in the process of further accumulation.

The census of first editions in libraries with notable Defoe collections was not part of my original plan, but was undertaken (rather unwillingly) at the urgent request of many scholars and many libraries. It would have been impossible without extensive and exceedingly generous assistance from librarians. No doubt the margin of possible error is widened by the necessary reliance on communications from so many sources, the majority of which (so far as the ownership of first editions is concerned) I have been unable to check. No doubt, also, some of these reports have been based on card catalogues alone, with no further examination of the texts. I cannot always be sure that a copy reported by A is actually of the first issue of the first edition; or that a copy reported by B is a London original rather than an Edinburgh reprint; or that copies reported by C, D, and E are of identical rather than successive impressions (or concurrent impressions run off separately on different presses). Most of my informants, however, have shown a real understanding of the problems involved, and I have tried to do all that I could to make sure of my information when there was apparent uncertainty.

Holdings of Defoe's works in Great Britain are listed before those in America, by the use of an alphabetical key. Where a choice has been possible, I have given preference to public libraries equipped to supply reproductions. Many books in private collections have been consulted, but these have not been referred to except when they have thrown light on special problems. Basic copies have usually been chosen from the British Museum, which has the greatest single collection of Defoe's works and which is most frequented by scholars of all nations. The basic copy has been chosen from another library only when the British Museum lacks a first edition, or when its copy is imperfect or unrepresentative, or when problems have arisen at times when access to its copy was not immediately available. It is here that the Indiana University Library has proved invaluable; it has been the workshop in which much of the final checklist was assembled, and the long process of detailed checking owes much to the patient co-operation of its staff.

Except for the very few which are listed as not to be found, or which (as for some works reported to me after I had ended my travels) I have seen only in photostatic reproductions, I have inspected the original of every one of the basic copies in person, and often I have followed up this inspection by minute re-examination through photostatic copies. It is hardly too much to claim that I have read every line of Defoe's published works, in so far as these have been found and identified. In this respect I have had some advantage over Defoe himself; for it is clear that he did not reread some of his writings after they had left his hands, and that he did not see certain ones again after they had appeared in print.

It is hoped that the two indexes will prove to have special value. There has been no previous attempt to enumerate Defoe's printers and booksellers, nor any considerable attempt to list the titles and the variant titles of his works in alphabetical order (rather than by the years in which they were published).

In completing the task which most of my advisers have expected of me, I realize that a few may still wish to see a complete descriptive bibliography of Defoe. Such a proposal is not likely to come from anyone who understands the multitudinous difficulties involved; and I can only answer, with King Lear, "That way madness lies." Defoe's known works are not only more numerous than those of any other English author, and so imperfectly catalogued in all but the best libraries that a search for any one may prove as difficult as the proverbial quest for a needle in a haystack; they are scattered so widely that it has not often been possible to compare any considerable number of copies of a single work, as when several sets of the *Review* were assembled in New York for the Facsimile Text Society's reprint. Again, one can rarely be sure that one has discovered all variants of a book or tract. I have examined four variants of *An Essay upon Projects,* but the newspaper advertisements seem to indicate the existence of three others. For some months I regarded my copy of *A Hymn To The Funeral Sermon* as unique; it is now only one of the two known copies of what seems to have been the third edition. Unbound sheets of *The Memoirs Of An English Officer* were drawn on by the booksellers almost at random, so that we find a discarded leaf of the dedication of 1728 reappearing in the issue assembled fifteen years later. *A History of the Union* and *Atlas Maritimus & Commercialis* were put together almost like scrapbooks, so that in all the copies which I have examined no two are exactly alike; to insist on any one copy as the norm is to ignore the probability that many variants have equal claim to priority.

In the 566 entries here included I have sought to distinguish quartos from octavos primarily in regard to shape; the paper may have no chain lines, and as a very large proportion of the tracts were printed by half-sheet imposition the signatures cannot be relied on to distinguish between quartos and octavos. As my friends who have worked most extensively with tracts of the period are ready to admit, the conventional terminology of orthodox bibliographical description would be (all too frequently) meaningless for fugitive pamphlets which were so often printed on odd lots of paper (and sometimes in supplementary sections, on different presses) in defiance of any known rule regarding chain lines or signatures, and which have later been perhaps so frequently and so tightly rebound as to defy close inspection.

I have sought to achieve only what I could hope to finish in a single lifetime. This checklist is meant to tell *what* Defoe wrote, *when* and often *why* he wrote and published it, *who* printed and sold it, and *where* copies of first editions are to be found in accessible libraries.

Many of the relationships between Defoe's writings and his personal career are discussed at length in my recent biography,

Daniel Defoe: Citizen of the Modern World (The University of Chicago Press, 1958), and are frequently noted in this checklist.

For financial aid for travel and for the purchase of photostats necessary in preparing this checklist, I am deeply grateful to Indiana University for four sabbatical leaves and for grants from the Graduate School; to the United States Army for an appointment on the faculty of the Army University, which was for all-too-brief a time located only twenty-three miles from Oxford; to the Trustees of the Henry E. Huntington Library and Art Gallery for a Senior Fellowship; and to the American Philosophical Society for a grant-in-aid during 1955–56 for the semifinal stages of this undertaking.

CONTENTS

LIBRARY SYMBOLS

BM	British Museum
BOD	Bodleian Library
BPL	Boston Public Library
C	William Andrews Clark Memorial Library
CH	Chapin Library, Williams College
CL *	Congregational Library (Memorial Hall, Faringdon Street, London, E. C. 4)
COR	Cornell University Library
CPL *	Cleveland Public Library
CU	Cambridge University Library
DNS*	National Library of Scotland (Edinburgh)
DW	Dr. Williams's Library (London)
FFM*	Francis F. Madan's private library (present address unknown)
F	Folger Shakespeare Library
H	Library of Harvard University
HEH	Henry E. Huntington Library and Art Gallery
HW*	Williams Collection, University of Cambridge Library
I	University of Illinois Library
IU	Indiana University Library
JCB	John Carter Brown Library (See also RPB.)
JRM *	John Robert Moore's private library (Bloomington, Indiana)
LC *	Library of Congress
LEH *	Lehigh University Library
M *	University of Michigan Library
MPRL *	Manchester Public Reference Library
N	Newberry Library
NLI *	National Library of Ireland
NLS	National Library of Scotland
NO *	Naval Observatory, Washington, D. C.

NYPL	New York Public Library
P	University of Pennsylvania Library
PML	Pierpont Morgan Library
PTS *	Princeton Theological Seminary Library
R	The Philip H. & A. S. W. Rosenbach Foundation
RPB	Special Collections, Brown University Library (see also JCB.)
T	University of Texas Library
TCC *	Trinity College Library, Cambridge
UL	University of London Library (Senate House)
Y	Yale University Library

* *Library consulted for certain titles only; no complete census of the library's holdings of first editions has been attempted.*

PART ONE

Books, Pamphlets, Poems, and Manuscripts

1681

1 MEDITAC[I]ONS. 1681

Notes: Holograph poems written on the last twenty-three pages
of a 195-page manuscript, the other pages of which contain
transcripts of sermons by Mr. John Collins which Defoe heard
in London in 1681. This notebook was dated by Defoe 1681
and signed with his name and with his initials. Opposite p.
119 appears the signature of a former owner, with the name
of the town where he served as a Dissenting minister (Wimborne, Dorsetshire) and the date (April 5, 1787): "J Duncan
Wimbⁿ Apl. 5. 87." The poems alone were edited by George
Harris Healey as *The Meditations Of Daniel Defoe Now First
Published* (Cummington, Mass., 1946, pp. v–ix + 3–25). See
No. 2.

Copy: HEH

1682

**2 HISTORICAL COLLECTIONS: OR, MEMOIRS OF PASSAGES COL-
LECTED FROM SEVERAL AUTHORS. 1682**

Notes: Holograph compilation of historical notes, prepared
for the press. Last reported by Dr. J. Duncan, in his history
of his dissenting church at Wimborne, Dorsetshire, as being
in his possession together with manuscript poems by Defoe.
See No. 1. See also Walter Wilson, *Memoirs of the Life and
Times of Daniel Defoe* (London, 1830), III, 645, note (z);
Healey, *op. cit.*, pp. vi–vii. Perhaps traces of the *Historical
Collections* survive in Defoe's frequent historical parallels
(e.g., the conclusion of *Memoirs of a Cavalier*).

1

1 6 8 3

3 [PAMPHLET AGAINST THE TURKS DURING THE SIEGE OF VI-
ENNA] [1683]

Notes: Known only from a statement by Defoe in *An Appeal
to Honour and Justice* (Aitken ed., pp. 207–208): "The first
time I had the misfortune to differ with my friends was about
the year 1683, when the Turks were besieging Vienna, and
the Whigs in England, generally speaking, were for the Turks
taking it; which I, having read the history of the cruelty and
perfidious dealings of the Turks in their wars, and how they
rooted out the name of the Christian religion in above threescore and ten kingdoms, could by no means agree with. And
though then but a young man, and a younger author, I op-
posed it, and wrote against it, which was taken very unkindly
indeed."

1 6 8 7

4 [PAMPHLET AGAINST ADDRESSES TO JAMES II] [1687]

Notes: Known only from a statement by Defoe in the *Review*
(VIII, 422): "I have been early exercised with this Usage from
honest blinded Men, even from a Youth, which I am oblig'd
to expose, not to charge them, but to defend myself: I had
their Reproaches when I blam'd their Credulity and Confidence, in the Flatteries and Caresses of *Popery* under *King
James,* and when I protested openly against the Addresses
of Thanks to him, for his Illegal Liberty of Conscience, founded
upon the Dispensing Power."

1 6 8 8

5 A LETTER TO A DISSENTER FROM HIS FRIEND AT THE HAGUE,
Concerning the Penal Laws and the Test; shewing that the
Popular Plea for Liberty of Conscience is not concerned in
that Question. [1688]

4°. Pp. 1–4

Notes: No title-page. The colophon reads: "Tot de Hague, gedruckt door Hans Verdraeght, 1688." Verdraeght was a fictitious name for a Dutch printer, and the pamphlet was printed in London. Published about August 1688. First reprinted as No. IX (pp. 52–54) in *"Fourteen Papers . . . London: Printed and are to be Sold by Richard Baldwin, near the Black Bull in the Old-Bailey. 1689."* Referred to by Defoe in *An Appeal to Honour and Justice* (Aitken ed., p. 208). Sometimes confused with *A Letter to a Dissenter* (1687) by George Savile, Marquis of Halifax, and mistakenly included in the first two issues of Halifax's *Miscellanies* (1700). See *Huntington Library Quarterly*, XIV (1951), 300.

Copy: HEH. *Other copies:* BM, BOD; BPL, C, COR, F, I, R, Y

1 6 8 9

6 REFLECTIONS UPON THE LATE GREAT REVOLUTION. Written by a Lay-Hand in the Country, For the Satisfaction of some Neighbours. LONDON: *Printed for* RIC. CHISWELL, *at the Rose and Crown in St. Paul's Church-Yard.* MDCLXXXIX.

4°. Pp. 1–68

Notes: Mistakenly attributed in *State Tracts* to a Mr. Eyres.

Copy: BM. *Other copies:* BOD, CU; BPL, C, COR, F, H, HEH, I, IU, NYPL, P, Y

7 THE ADVANTAGES OF THE PRESENT SETTLEMENT, And The Great Danger Of A Relapse. Licensed, July 4. 1689. J. Fraser. LONDON: *Printed for* RIC. CHISWELL, *at the Rose and Crown in St. Paul's Church-yard.* MDCLXXXIX.

4°. Pp. 3–38

Notes: Mistakenly attributed in *State Tracts* to P. A., D. D.

Copy: BPL. *Other copies:* BM, BOD, NLS; C, COR, F, HEH, Y

1 6 9 1

8 AN ACCOUNT OF THE LATE HORRID CONSPIRACY To Depose Their Present Majesties K. William and Q. Mary, To

bring in the French and the Late King James, and ruine the City of London. With a Relation of the miraculous Discovery thereof. Also Some brief Reflections on the Trials of the Lord Preston, Major Ashton, and Mr. Elliot, who were chiefly concern'd therein, and found guilty. *By a Gentleman, who was present at their Trials.* LONDON, *Printed for* J. HUMPHRYS, 1691.

4°. Pp. [4 unnumbered] + 7–31

Notes: Very hastily written, and printed on four separate presses. Published after Lord Preston's trial 16 January 1691.

Copy: BM. *Other copies:* BOD; BPL, C, F, HEH, IU, Y

9   A NEW DISCOVERY OF AN OLD INTREAGUE: A Satyr Level'd At Treachery and Ambition: Calculated To the Nativity of the Rapparee Plott, and the Modesty of the Jacobite Clergy. Designed by Way of Conviction to the CXVII. Petitioners, and for the Benefit of those that Study the Mathematicks. Unus Nobis Cunctando Restituit.—Ennius. *Printed in the Year* MDCXCI.

4°. Pp. [2 unnumbered] + 3–36

Notes: Reprinted in *A Second Volume Of The Writings* (1705). See reprint and critical study by Mary Elizabeth Campbell: *Defoe's First Poem* (Bloomington, Indiana, 1938).

Copy: BM. *Other copies:* BOD, DW; BPL, F, H, LC, Y

1692

10 TO THE ATHENIAN SOCIETY. [1692]

Fol. P. [1 unnumbered]

Notes: Prefaced to the following work by Charles Gildon: *"The History Of The Athenian Society, For the Resolving all Nice and Curious Questions, By A Gentleman, Who Got Secret Intelligence Of their Whole Proceedings. To which are prefix'd Several Poems, Written by Mr. Tate, Mr. Motteux, Mr. Richardson, and others.* . . . London: Printed for James Dowley, and are to be Sold by the Booksellers of London and Westminster. Price 1 s." Defoe's poem was reprinted by John Dunton in successive editions of *The Athenian Oracle*.

Copy: BM. *Other copies:* BOD, CU; BPL, F, HEH, I, N, Y

1693

*12 AN ANSWER TO THE LATE K. JAMES'S LAST DECLARATION, Dated at St. Germains, April 17, S. N. 1693. LONDON, *Printed for* RICHARD BALDWIN *near the Oxford-Arms in Warwick-lane.* MDCXCIII.

4°. Pp. 1–40

Notes: DNB lists this as the second edition of Dr. James Welwood's tract of 1689, but the two occasions and the two tracts are quite different. Baldwin did not publish for Welwood, but he had issued No. 5 for Defoe and his widow long continued as one of Defoe's principal publishers. The known writings of Welwood were signed, and the preface "To the Reader" in his *Memoirs* (1700) denied his authorship of a tract attributed to him and declared his intention of signing everything that he wrote. Internal evidence is strongly in favor of an attribution to Defoe. Licensed by J. Trenchard 5 June 1693. BPL and several other copies have "N. S. 1693"; IU agrees with BM in reading "S. N. 1693."

Copy: BM. *Other copies:* BOD, NLS, UL; BPL, COR, HEH, I, IU, Y

1694

13 THE ENGLISHMAN'S CHOICE, AND TRUE INTEREST: In a
Vigorous Prosecution of the War against France; And
Serving K. William and Q. Mary, And Acknowledging
Their Right.

> Ego nec tumultum,
> Nec mori per vim metuam, tenento
> Caesare Terra. Hor.

LONDON, *Printed in the Year* 1694

4°. Pp. 3-32 (for 3-33)

Copy: BM. *Other copies:* BPL, IU, Y

1697

14 THE CHARACTER OF THE LATE DR. SAMUEL ANNESLEY, By
way of Elegy: With a Preface. *Written by one of his Hear-
ers.* LONDON: *Printed for* E. WHITLOCK, near *Stationers-
Hall,* 1697.

4°. Pp. [4 unnumbered] + 1-16

Notes: Printed by John Dunton (see *The Life and Errors of
John Dunton,* London, 1818, I, 180). Reprinted in *A True
Collection* (1703).

Copy: DW

15 SOME REFLECTIONS ON A PAMPHLET LATELY PUBLISH'D,
Entituled, An Argument Shewing that A Standing Army Is
Inconsistent with A Free Government, And Absolutely De-
structive to the Constitution of the English Monarchy.

> Hard words, Jealousies and Fears,
> Set Folks together by the Ears.
> Hudibras Lib. 1.

LONDON: *Printed for* E. WHITLOCK *near Stationers-Hall.*
1697.

4°. Pp. i–ii + 1–28

Notes: A reply to a pamphlet attributed to John Trenchard and Walter Moyle. See No. 18. 3 lines of errata at the end of the preface. In the same year the second edition corrected the signature of the preface from D. T. to D. F., dropped the list of errata, and made the corrections in the text.

Copy: BM. *Other copies:* CU, DW; BPL, COR, F, H, HEH, IU, N, P, T, Y

16 AN ESSAY UPON PROJECTS. LONDON: *Printed by* R. R. *for* THO. COCKERILL, *at the Corner of Warwick-Lane, near Pater-noster-Row.* MDCXCVII.

8°. Pp. i–xiv + 1–336

Notes: Preface signed D. F. Advertised for sale on 25 January 1696/7. Unsold sheets continued to be offered with new title-pages, as Cockerill changed his place of business. In 1702 Defoe apparently reclaimed the sheets for issue through "the Book-sellers of London and Westminster." On 26 January 1703, while Defoe was hiding from the Government after publishing *The Shortest Way with the Dissenters,* Thomas Ballard advertised this book as *Essays upon Several Subjects* "by Daniel de Fooe." Except for the title-pages, the sheets remained un-altered through at least four issues (possibly seven, to judge from the advertisements and from the publishers' known changes of address). See *Notes and Queries,* CC (1955), 109–110. The Preface (p. iii) states that the author had kept the greatest part by him for near five years.

Copy: BM. *Other copies:* BOD, DW, NLS, UL; BPL, C, COR, F, H, HEH, IU, N, NYPL, R, RPB, T, Y

1 6 9 8

17 AN ENQUIRY INTO THE OCCASIONAL CONFORMITY OF DIS-SENTERS, In Cases of Preferment. With A Preface to the Lord Mayor, Occasioned by his carrying the Sword to a Conventicle. If the Lord be God, follow him: But if Baal, then follow him, 1 Kings 18. 21. LONDON: *Printed Anno Dom.* 1697 [for 1698].

4°. Pp. [6 unnumbered] + 1–28. The BM *Catalogue* erroneously lists "pp. 26."

Notes: Preface to the Lord Mayor signed One, Two, Three, Four. In the second edition (1701, actually 1700) this Preface was replaced by a Preface to Mr. How signed D. F. According to Lee, the second edition was published 20 November 1700. It was later reprinted in *A True Collection* (1703).

Copy: BM. *Other copies:* BOD, CU, DW, UL; BPL, F, HEH, IU, NYPL, P, PML, R, T, Y

18   AN ARGUMENT SHEWING, THAT A STANDING ARMY, WITH CONSENT OF PARLIAMENT, Is not Inconsistent with a Free Government, &c. 2 Chron. 9. 25. And King Solomon had four thousand Stalls for Horses and Chariots, and twelve thousand Horsemen; whom he bestowed in the Chariot-Cities, and with the King at Jerusalem. LONDON: *Printed for* E. WHITLOCK *near Stationers.* 1698.

4°. Pp. [2 unnumbered] + 1–26

Notes: A reply to a pamphlet attributed to John Trenchard and Walter Moyle. See No. 15. Reprinted in *A True Collection* (1703), with three added footnotes.

Copy: BM. *Other copies:* BOD, DW, UL; BPL, C, F, H, N, NYPL, R, T, Y

19   A BRIEF REPLY TO THE HISTORY OF STANDING ARMIES IN ENGLAND. With some Account of the Authors. LONDON: *Printed in the Year* 1698.

4°. Pp. [2 unnumbered] + 1–25

Notes: A reply to John Trenchard's *A Short History of Standing Armies in England.* The second edition was advertised 8 December 1698.

Copy: BM. *Other copies:* BOD, CU, UL; BPL, C, COR, F, H, HEH, IU, N, P, R, T, Y

20   THE POOR MAN'S PLEA, In Relation to all the Proclamations, Declarations, Acts of Parliament, &c. Which have

been, or shall be made, or published, for a Reformation of Manners, and suppressing Immorality in the Nation. LON-DON: *Printed in the Year* MDCXCVIII.

4°. Pp. [2 unnumbered] + 1–31

Notes: The Second Edition Corrected (BOD) attributed the preface to D. F., reset the pages as [2 unnumbered] + 1–28 in 4°, changed the first part of the title to read *The Poor Man's Plea To all the Proclamations,* and named the publisher: "Printed for A. Baldwin, near the Oxford-Arms in Warwick-Lane." According to Lee, the first edition was published 31 March 1698. The second edition was advertised 24 May 1698; the third 26 March 1700. Reprinted with the preface in *A Collection* (1703), and without the preface in *A True Collection* (1703).

Copy: BM. *Other copies:* CU, UL; BPL, F, H, HEH, IU, P, T, Y

21 THE INTERESTS OF THE SEVERAL PRINCES AND STATES of Europe Consider'd, with respect to the Succession Of The Crown of Spain. And The Titles of the several Pretenders thereto, Examin'd. LONDON: *Printed in the Year* MDCXCVIII.

4°. Pp. 1–32

Notes: Published 7 April 1698. Perhaps it was a revision of this tract which Defoe announced thirteen years later as a forthcoming discussion of a proposed partition of the Spanish dominions, to be published by John Baker (*Review,* VIII, 59): "I could enlarge on this Head, but I know it is more fully handled, in a View of the Interests of the several Princes of *Europe,* on the Affair of this great Change— Which Book I am told will be Publish'd at the same Place with this Paper, in a few Days, and to which I referr the Reader for farther Satisfaction."

Copy: BOD. *Other copies:* BPL, C, COR, F, H, HEH, IU, N, Y

22 LEX TALIONIS: Or, An Enquiry Into The most Proper Ways to Prevent The Persecution Of The Protestants in

France. Matth. vii. 2. With what judgment ye judge, ye shall be judged: and with what measure ye mete, it shall be measured to you again. LONDON: *Printed in the Year* MDCXCVIII.

4°. Pp. 1–27

Notes: Advertised 13 September 1698, but perhaps published earlier. Reprinted in *A Collection* (1703). Omitted from *A True Collection* (1703), probably because Defoe considered it too similar to a later tract included in that volume, *The Danger of the Protestant Religion.*

Copy: BM. *Other copies:* BOD; BPL.

1 7 0 0

23 THE PACIFICATOR. A Poem. LONDON: *Printed, and are to be Sold by* J. NUTT, *near Stationers-Hall.* 1700.

Fol. Pp. 1–14

Notes: Published 20 February 1700. Reprinted in *A Second Volume Of The Writings* (1705).

Copy: BM. *Other copies:* BOD; BPL, C, IU, T, Y

24 THE TWO GREAT QUESTIONS CONSIDER'D. I. What the French King will Do, with Respect to the Spanish Monarchy. II. What Measures the English ought to Take. LONDON, *Printed in the Year,* 1700.

4°. Pp. [1 unnumbered] + 1–28

Notes: Advertised by A. Baldwin as published 15 November 1700. Reprinted in *A True Collection* (1703). What seems to be the second edition is sometimes listed as the first edition (Wing D850). This has five brief interpolations, inferior punctuation and some new errors (although on p. 22 "beget himself" is corrected to "forget himself"), many pages reset, and at the bottom of the title-page the following: "London, Printed by R. T. for A. Baldwin, at the Oxford-Armes, in Warwick-lane. 1700." BM has two other (and very inferior) editions of the same date: a 4° paged [1 unnumbered] + 1–24 and an 8°

(with no preface) paged 2–16 and "Printed for Charles Mount, near Holborn, 1700." The last was complained of in *The English Post,* 22 November 1700, as "a sham Edition."

Copy: BM. *Other copies:* BOD, NLS, UL; BPL, C, COR, F, H, HEH, IU, LC, N, NYPL, P, Y

25 THE TWO GREAT QUESTIONS FURTHER CONSIDERED. With some Reply to the Remarks. Non Licet Hominum Muliebriter rixare. *By the Author.* LONDON: *Printed in the Year* MDCC.

4°. Pp. [2 unnumbered] + 1–20 + 1 unnumbered page of errata

Notes: Advertised by A. Baldwin as published 2 December 1700. Reprinted with two new footnotes in *A True Collection* (1703).

Copy: BM. *Other copies:* BOD, UL; BPL, C, HEH, IU, LC, N, NYPL, R, Y ·

1701

26 THE SIX DISTINGUISHING CHARACTERS OF A PARLIAMENT-MAN. Address'd to the Good People of England—And that in Respect of some Matters of the Highest Importance to this our Kingdom, we do intend to give Directions for the calling a new Parliament, which shall begin, and be holden at Westminster, on Thursday the Sixth Day of February next. Vide Proclamation. LONDON: *Printed in the Year* MDCC [for 1701].

4°. Pp. 1–23

Notes: According to Lee, published 4 January 1701. Reprinted in *A True Collection* (1703).

Copy: BOD. *Other copies:* UL; C, H, HEH, IU, LC, N, Y

27 THE DANGER OF THE PROTESTANT RELIGION CONSIDER'D, From the Present Prospect Of A Religious War in Europe. LONDON: *Printed in the Year* 1701.

4°. Pp. [2 unnumbered] + 1–32

Notes: According to Lee, published 9 January 1701. Reprinted in *A True Collection* (1703).

Copy: BM. *Other copies:* BOD, UL; BPL, C, H, HEH, I, IU, N, P, Y

28 THE TRUE-BORN ENGLISHMAN. A Satyr. Statuimus Pacem, & Securitatem, & Concordiam Judicium & Justitiam inter Anglos & Normannos, Francos & Britones, Walliae, & Cornubiae, Pictos & Scotos, Albaniae, similiter inter Francos & Insulanos Provincias, & Patrias, quae pertinent ad Coronam nostram, & inter omnes nobis Subjectos, fermiter & inviolabiliter observi. Charta Regis Willielmi Conquisitoris de Pacis Publica, Cap. 1. *Printed in the Year* MDCC [for 1701].

4°. Pp. [2 unnumbered] + 1–71

Notes: According to Lee, published January 1701. Defoe estimated that 80,000 copies of pirated editions alone were sold. The last authorized editions in 1701 (the ninth and tenth) added a six-page explanatory preface, omitted the attack on John Tutchin as Shamwig (ll. 624–649), and blunted the attack on Duncomb by altering the title of "Sir C[harle]s D[uncom]b's Fine Speech, &c." to "His Fine Speech, &c." *A Collection* (1703) and *A True Collection* (1703) reprinted the poem from the ninth (or an even later) edition. After the accession of the House of Hanover, Defoe added a new passage of 49 lines satirizing the English temper. This "corrected" edition of 1716, although advertised as "printed upon a superfine Paper with an Elzevir Letter," was carelessly printed with many hasty errors. It was advertised by J. Roberts on 22 March 1716 as "Just publish'd"; a contemporary manuscript note in the BM copy dates it 16 March 1715/6. In *John Bull's Failings, Being Selections from Daniel Defoe's "The True-Born Englishman"* (ed. Nasarvanji Mareckji Cooper, London and Bombay, c. 1904) passages are chosen (with added subtitles) to emphasize the faults of arrogant Englishmen.

Copy: BM. *Other copies:* BOD, UL; BPL, C, CH, F, H, HEH, LC, NYPL, PML, R, T, Y

29 THE SUCCESSION TO THE CROWN OF ENGLAND, Considered.
LONDON, *Printed in the Year* 1701.

4°. Pp. [3]–38

Notes: Internal evidence dates this during the session of Parliament early in 1701. It seems to have been run off independently on different presses. There are at least two variant printings, and I am not sure which appeared first. One (BOD, JRM) has pp. 3–36, with closer punctuation and freer use of capitals, and without a statement which appears on p. 10 of the other edition: "for Victory, which *gives Crowns, takes off Attainders,* and makes any body Legitimate." *Animadversions on the Succession* (1701) identifies the printer as John Darby. This would have been either the printer who died in 1704 or his son who died in 1733.

Copy: BM. *Other copies:* BOD, NLS, UL; BPL, C, F, H, HEH, I, IU, N, NYPL, PML, R, Y

30 THE FREE-HOLDERS PLEA Against Stock-Jobbing Elections of Parliament Men. LONDON: *Printed in the Year 1701.*

4°. Pp. 1–27

Notes: According to Lee, published 23 January 1701. Second edition "with additions," pp. 1–28, with a page and a half of new text as a supplement, published 4 February 1701 and reprinted in *A True Collection* (1703). In 1719 long excerpts were printed in *The Anatomy of Exchange Alley* (No. 414).

Copy: BM. *Other copies:* BOD, UL; BPL, C, COR, F, H, HEH, IU, R, RPB, T, Y

31 A LETTER TO MR. How, By Way of Reply To His Considerations Of The Preface To An Enquiry into the Occasional Conformity of Dissenters. *By the Author of the said Preface and Enquiry.* LONDON: *Printed in the Year* 1701.

4°. Pp. 1–34

Notes: The Postscript is signed D. F. According to Lee, published by A. Baldwin 24 January 1701. Reprinted in *A Collection* (1703) and in *A True Collection* (1703).

Copy: BM. *Other copies:* BOD, DW, NLS, UL; BPL, H, HEH, LC, R, Y

32 THE LIVERY MAN's REASONS, Why he did not give his Vote for a Certain Gentleman either to be Lord Mayor; Or, Parliament Man For the City of London.

> And truly as things go, it would be Pitty,
> That such as he should represent the City.

LONDON, *Printed in the Year* MDCCI.

4°. Pp. 3–27

Notes: Published 6 February 1701.

Copy: BOD. *Other copies:* BPL, C

33 THE VILLAINY OF STOCK-JOBBERS DETECTED, And the Causes of the Late Run Upon The Bank and Bankers Discovered and Considered. LONDON, *Printed in the Year* MDCCI.

4°. Pp. 1–26

Notes: According to Lee, first edition 11 February, second edition 17 February. Reprinted in *A True Collection* (1703). Refers very favorably (pp. 5–6, 26) to *The Free-Holders Plea* (No. 30).

Copy: BM. *Other copies:* UL; BPL, CH, H, HEH, IU (lower corners imperfect), NYPL, P, R, Y

34 THE APPARENT DANGER OF AN INVASION. Briefly Represented in a Letter to a Minister of State. *By a Kentish Gentleman.* LONDON, *Printed, and sold by* A. BALDWIN, *near the Oxford-Arms in Warwick-Lane,* 1701.

4°. Pp. 1–4

Notes: Dated at the end "M——ds, Feb. 14. 1700" (i. e., 1701). Published 19 February 1701. Very probably, not certainly, Defoe's.

Copy: BM. *Other copies:* BOD, NLS; C, HEH, I, IU, Y

35 [LEGION'S MEMORIAL] [1701]

Begin: Mr. S[PEAKE]R, The Enclosed Memorial you are Charg'd with, in the behalf of many Thousands of the good People of England.

4°. Pp. 1–4

Notes: This tract is sometimes known by the title which appears near the middle of p. 1, after the address to Robert Harley: "The Memorial. To the K[night]s, C[ommon]s, and B[urgesse]s in P[arliamen]t Assembled." BM has another edition (pp. [1]–8) which is identical in text. The IU copy (pp. 1–4) omits the introductory word *Begin.* All known editions are without signatures; all lack title-pages and give no indication of place or publisher. Of the many copies I have seen, I do not know which represents the first edition. The use of multiple presses for such widely distributed pamphlets is well established; perhaps no one edition had demonstrable priority when all were rushed off the available presses as hastily as possible. The official manuscript text was "written in a hand which stood the wrong way" and was presented by Defoe in person to Robert Harley, Speaker of the House of Commons, at the door of St. Stephen's Chapel on the morning of 14 May 1701. Harley, who preserved so many papers, does not seem to have kept this.

Copy: BM. *Other copies:* BOD, DW, NLS, UL; BPL, C, H, I, IU, NYPL, R, Y

36 YE TRUE-BORN ENGLISHMEN PROCEED [first line of first stanza] [1701]

4°. Pp. 1–4

Notes: This poem appears always without a title-page, in many texts which vary considerably. It is printed (or referred to) under several other titles, such as *A Letter to a Member of Parliament, The Ballad, A Poem,* and *A Satyr upon* ——— ———. In *An Account of all the Variations Contained in the Treaty of Peace* (1730), where two stanzas are quoted, it is called *The Kentish Worthies* (the title of a very different poem by Nahum Tate). Sometimes the first word is "You" (as in HEH). Since the poem refers to *Legion's Memorial* as recently printed, and to the Kentish Petitioners as still in prison, it can be dated between mid-May and the latter part of June. A reply "Paragraph by Paragraph" was advertised on 28 June 1701 in *The Flying Post* as "sold by the Booksellers of London and Westminster." BOD has a copy of this (Pamph. 238.1701 [30]): *The Ballad, Or; Some Scurrilous Reflections In Verse, On the Proceedings of the Honourable House of Commons; Answered Stanza by Stanza. With the Memorial, Alias Legion, Reply'd to Paragraph by Paragraph.* London, Printed by D. Edwards, and Sold by the Booksellers of London and Westminster. 1701. 4°. Pp. [2 unnumbered] + 1–38. Sixteen years later Defoe quoted five lines from his ballad on the title-page of a political tract (No. 369). One line of the ballad is quoted on p. 13 (for 12) of No. 65.

Copy: BM. *Other copies:* BOD, DW, NLS; BPL, H, HEH, I, IU, NYPL, RPB

37   THE HISTORY OF THE KENTISH PETITION. LONDON, *Printed in the Year,* 1701.

4°. Pp. [4 unnumbered pages] + 1–25 + 1 page of errata

Notes: According to Lee, published in August. Reprinted 27 September in order to answer it "Paragraph by Paragraph."

Copy: BM. *Other copies:* BOD, DW, NLS, UL; BPL, COR, F, H, HEH, I, N, P, PML, R, T, Y

38   THE PRESENT STATE OF JACOBITISM CONSIDERED, In Two Querys. 1. What Measures the French King will take with respect to the Person and Title of the Pretended Prince of Wales. 2. What the Jacobites in England ought to do on the same account. LONDON: *Printed in the Year,* 1701.

4°. Pp. [2 unnumbered] + 1–22

Notes: The colophon reads: "London Printed for A. Baldwin, at the Oxford Arms in Warwick-lane. 1701." The preface is signed D. F. Internal evidence dates this tract soon after the death of James II was reported in England in September, and while the English could still suppose that Louis XIV would not attempt to set the Pretender on their throne.

Copy: BM. *Other copies:* BOD, UL; BPL, C, COR, F, H, I, N, R, T, Y

39 REASONS AGAINST A WAR WITH FRANCE, Or An Argument
Shewing That the French King's Owning the Prince of
Wales as King of England, Scotland and Ireland; is No
Sufficient Ground of A War. LONDON *Printed in the Year,*
1701.

4°. Pp. 1–30

Notes: According to Lee, published in October. Reprinted in
A True Collection (1703).

Copy: BM. *Other copies:* BOD, UL; BPL, C, COR, H, HEH, I,
IU, N, R, Y

40 LEGION'S NEW PAPER: Being A Second Memorial To the
Gentlemen of a late House of Commons. With Legion's
Humble Address to His Majesty. LONDON, *Printed; and
Sold by the Booksellers of London and Westminster.* 1702
[for 1701].

4°. Pp. 3–20

Notes: Dated 1702 on the title-page, but the Address to His
Majesty shows that it was written after William dissolved Parliament 11 November 1701 and before the new Parliament was
elected to assemble 30 December. Probably published in late
November. An edition in BOD has pp. 3–18. Y has a second
copy entitled *Legion's Second Memorial* (1702).

Copy: BM. *Other copies:* BOD, NLS, UL; BPL, C, COR, H,
HEH, IU, T, Y

41 THE ORIGINAL POWER OF THE COLLECTIVE BODY Of The
People of England, Examined and Asserted. LONDON,
Printed in the Year 1702 [for 1701].

Fol. Pp. [6 unnumbered] + 1–24

Notes: Lee dates this 27 December 1701. According to The
Conclusion, the main part of the tract was written before King
William dissolved the late parliament (11 November). In large
part a reply to Sir Humphrey Mackworth's *A Vindication of
the Commons of England* (1701). Signed D. F. Reprinted in *A
True Collection* (1703) although omitted from the table of

contents. In the *Review* for 18 January 1706/7 and 7 February 1708 (III, 654; IV, 617) Defoe referred to this tract as *The Original Right*—the title as printed after the prefatory dedications of the tract itself. Excerpts were reprinted in 1710 by Defoe's opponents in *The Modern Addresses Vindicated* (No. 177). See also the notes on No. 65.

Copy: BM. *Other copies:* CU, UL; BPL, F, H, HEH, I, N, NYPL, R, RPB, T, Y

1702

42   THE MOCK-MOURNERS. A Satyr, By way of Elegy on King William. *By the Author of the True-born Englishman.* LONDON, *Printed* 1702.

4°. Pp. [2 unnumbered] + 1–32

Notes: Reprinted in *A Collection* (1703) and in *A True Collection* (1703). According to Lee, the first edition was published about May 1702. The Second Edition Corrected, London, Printed for M. Gunne in Essex-Street, 1702, pp. [i–ii] + 1–20, was a pirated edition, retaining all faults and adding new ones. On 23 February 1703 B. Bragg was advertising the seventh edition.

Copy: BM. *Other copies:* BOD, CU, DW, NLS, UL; BPL, C, CH, COR, F, H, HEH, IU, N, P, RPB, T, Y

43   REFORMATION OF MANNERS, A Satyr. Vae Vobis Hypocritè. *Printed in the Year* MDCCII.

4°. Pp. [2 unnumbered] + 1–64

Notes: Another edition of 1702 has pp. [2 unnumbered] + 5–32. Reprinted in *A Collection* (1703) and in *A True Collection* (1703).

Copy: BM. *Other copies:* BOD, CU, UL; BPL, C, CH, COR, F, H, HEH, I, IU, N, P, R, RPB, T, Y

44   A NEW TEST OF THE CHURCH OF ENGLAND'S LOYALTY: Or, Whiggish Loyalty And Church Loyalty Compar'd. *Printed in the Year* 1702.

4°. Pp. 1–34

Notes: According to Lee, published in June 1702. Reprinted in *A Collection* (1703) and in *A True Collection* (1703). BM has another edition dated 1702 with pp. 1–32, and still another (date torn off) with pp. 1–24. NLS has an edition "Re-Printed in the Year, 1703," with pp. 3–23. In 1715 the tract was reprinted as *A Defence of Mr. Withers's History of Resistance: Or, A New Test Of The Church of England's Loyalty.* London: Printed by R. Tookey, and Sold by J. Roberts in Warwick Lane, and J. Harrison, near the Royal-Exchange. 1715 (pp. [3]–24). All these editions are in quarto and anonymous.

Copy: IU. *Other copies:* BM, BOD, DW, NLS, UL; BPL, C, COR, F, H, HEH, I, N, NYPL, P, R, RPB, T, Y

45   [QUESTIONS ON QUEEN ANNE'S SUCCESSION] [1702]

Notes: Perhaps never published. A copy (presumably in manuscript) was seized when Defoe was arrested in May 1703. The Privy Council questioned him about this. See *Review*, VII, 90–91.

46   GOOD ADVICE TO THE LADIES: Shewing, That as the World goes, and is like to go, the best way is for them to keep Unmarried. *By the Author of the True Born Englishman.* LONDON, *Printed in the Year* MDCCII.

4°. Pp. [6 unnumbered] + 1–16

Notes: The BM copy has an old manuscript note giving the date: "3. Sept." According to Lee, a second edition with additions was published in 1705. According to *CBEL*, the poem was reprinted in 1728 as *A Timely Caution: Or, Good Advice To the Ladies*. I have not seen copies of these editions.

Copy: BM. *Other copies:* CU, UL; H, HEH, IU, R, RPB, T

47   THE SPANISH DESCENT. A Poem. *By the Author of the True-Born Englishman.* LONDON, *Printed in the Year* 1702.

4°. Pp. 3–27

Notes: According to Lee, published in November. H has an edition dated 1703. Reprinted in *A Collection* (1703) and in *A True Collection* (1703).

Copy: BM. *Other copies:* BOD, CU, DW; BPL, C, HEH, IU, LC, N, T, Y

48   AN ENQUIRY INTO OCCASIONAL CONFORMITY. Shewing that the Dissenters Are no Way Concern'd in it. *By the Author of the Preface to Mr. Howe.* LONDON: *Printed in the Year* M.DCC.II.

8°. Pp. 3-31

Notes: According to Lee, published in November. Reprinted in *A Collection* (1703) and in *A True Collection* (1703). The same tract was reissued as *An Enquiry Into The Occasional Conformity Bill. By the Author Of The True-Born English-man,* LONDON. *Printed, and are to be Sold by Most Booksellers in London and Westminster.* 1704. (Some copies are dated 1703.) On p. 14 there is a marginal reference to No. 44.

Copy: BM. *Other copies:* BOD, DW, UL; BPL, C, H, IU, N, NYPL, R, Y

49   THE OPINION OF A KNOWN DISSENTER On the Bill for Preventing Occasional Conformity. 1703 [for 1702?]

Fol. half-sheet. Pp. [1-2]

Notes: The colophon reads: "London: Printed, and are to be sold by J. Nutt near Stationers-Hall. 1703." Probably published in November 1702, just before Defoe took a stand against the Occasional Conformity Bill in *The Shortest Way with the Dissenters.* This brief tract is an exceptionally able and characteristic one, largely condensed and pieced together from the most striking arguments in Defoe's previous tracts on the subject: *An Enquiry Into The Occasional Conformity of Dissenters* (1697, for 1698), *A Letter to Mr. How* (1701), and *An Enquiry Into Occasional Conformity* (1702).

Copy: HEH. *Another copy:* BOD

50   THE SHORTEST-WAY WITH THE DISSENTERS: Or Proposals For The Establishment Of The Church. LONDON: *Printed in the Year* MDCCII.

4°. Pp. 1–29

Notes: According to Lee, published 1 December 1702. T has two variants, from different settings of type. In 1703 this tract was reprinted, with Defoe's next tract serving as a supplement: *The Shortest Way With The Dissenters. [Taken from Dr. Sach[evere]ll's Sermon, and Others.] Or, Proposals For The Establishment of the Church. By the Author of the True-born English-man.* London Printed: and sold by the Booksellers. Price 3d. Pp. 1–20 in quarto, of which pp. 17–20 are a reprint of *A Brief Explanation Of A late Pamphlet, entitul'd, The Shortest Way with the Dissenters.* This expanded tract was reprinted in *A Collection* (1703) and in *A True Collection* (1703). When Defoe was indicted in Justice Hall in the Old Bailey (24 February 1703) it was alleged that copies of *The Shortest-Way* had been offered for sale on 22 December in the parish of Bow in the ward of Cheap, and that the author had sought to keep Protestant Dissenters from enjoying religious toleration and to prevent the Union of England and Scotland—as proof of which selected passages were quoted almost verbatim from certain pages (2, 3, 4, 6, 10, 11, 12, 13, 15, 16, 18, 19, and 21).

Copy: BM. *Other copies:* BOD, UL; BPL, C, COR, F, H, HEH, I, IU, NYPL, R, T, Y

1703

51 A BRIEF EXPLANATION OF A LATE PAMPHLET, Entituled, The Shortest Way with the Dissenters. [1703]

4°. Pp. [1]–4

Notes: No title-page, but London 1703. In an unsigned postscript Defoe replies to Tutchin. Published 28 February 1703. Reprinted as a supplement to *The Shortest Way with the Dissenters* in 1703 and also in *A Collection* (1703) and *A True Collection* (1703).

Copy: BOD. *Other copies:* UL; BPL, H, HEH, R

52 A DIALOGUE BETWEEN A DISSENTER AND THE OBSERVATOR, Concerning The Shortest Way with the Dissenters. LONDON, Printed in the Year, MDCCIII.

4°. Pp. 3–30

Notes: This tract, a defence of Defoe based on many of his own pamphlets, is often absurdly attributed to John Tutchin, the principal object of attack. Reprinted as Defoe's by John How (Tutchin's own publisher) in *A Collection* (1703); but omitted by Defoe from *A True Collection* (1703), presumably because it was too personal a defence to be acknowledged as his own.

Copy: BM. *Other copies:* BOD; BPL, C, IU

53   KING WILLIAM'S AFFECTION TO THE CHURCH OF ENGLAND EXAMIN'D. LONDON, *Printed in the Year* 1703.

4°. Pp. 1–26

Notes: According to Lee, the first edition was published on 25 March, the third on 3 April. On 13 April E. Mallet near Fleetbridge was advertising the fourth edition (probably pirated, for Defoe was in hiding and Mrs. Mallet was not one of his known publishers). Less than six months later Defoe satirized Elizabeth Mallet for paying Paul Lorrain ten guineas for exclusive permission to print a funeral sermon (No. 61). NLS has a fifth edition dated 1703; but on 20 January 1710 A. Bell at the Cross-Keys and Bible in Cornhill was advertising the fifth edition (perhaps unsold sheets from 1703 given new interest by the current Sacheverell controversy).

Copy: BM. *Other copies:* BOD, CU, NLS, UL; BPL, COR, F, H, HEH, I, IU, N, NYPL, P, T, Y

54   A COLLECTION OF THE WRITINGS of the Author of the True-Born English-Man. Viz. I. The True-Born English-man. A Satyr. II. The Mock Mourners. A Satyr. III. Reformation of Manners. A Satyr. IV. The Spanish Descent. A Poem. V. The Poor Mans Plea, concerning Reformation of Manners. VI. An Enquiry into the Occasional Conformity of Dissenters, in Cases of Preferment: With a Preface to Mr. How. VII. An Enquiry into Occasional Conformity: Shewing that the Dissenters are no Way Concern'd in it. VIII. A New Test of the Church of England's Loyalty. IX. The Shortest Way with the Dissenters. X. A brief Explanation of the

Shortest Way with the Dissenters. XI. A Dialogue between
a Dissenter and the Observator, concerning The Shortest
Way with Dissenters. XII. Lex Talionis: Or, An Enquiry
into the most Proper Ways to Prevent the Persecution of
the Protestants in France. XIII. A Letter to Mr. How, by
way of Reply to his Considerations of the Preface to an Enquiry into the Occasional Conformity of Dissenters. LON-
DON, *Printed in the Year* 1703.

8°. Pp. [7 unnumbered] + 289

Notes: Published 17 April 1703 by John How. After Defoe's
authorized *True Collection* appeared (22 July 1703) How continued to advertise his pirated *Collection* as a cut-price rival.
Although Defoe protested that some of the tracts were not his
and that the printing was extremely inexact, all thirteen of the
tracts in How's *Collection* are demonstrably Defoe's, and certain
ones were used as copy text by the printer of the authorized
True Collection. See Chapter IV of my *Defoe in the Pillory
and Other Studies* (Bloomington, Indiana, 1939).

Copy: IU. *Other copies:* BM, BOD, CU, UL; BPL, C, COR, F,
H, HEH, I, N, R, T, Y

55 [VERSES SATIRIZING THE KNIGHTING OF SIR DAVID HAMIL-
TON] [1703]

Notes: No copy known. See *The Republican Bullies* (1703),
p. 3. The verses were taken from Defoe's pocket (apparently in
manuscript) by Robert Stephens, the Queen's Messenger, after
Defoe's arrest on 20 or 21 May 1703. Defoe presumably regarded the knighting of Hamilton, the Queen's man-midwife,
as absurd.

56 MORE REFORMATION. A Satyr Upon Himself. *By the Author Of The True Born English-Man.* LONDON: *Printed in
the Year,* 1703.

4°. Pp. [6 unnumbered] + 1–52

Notes: The verso of the title has an "Advertisement" warning
against *A Collection* (John How's pirated edition of Defoe's

writings). Published 16 July 1703. Reprinted in *A Second Volume Of The Writings* (1705).

Copy: BM. *Other copies:* BOD, CU, UL; BPL, C, HEH, IU, N, NYPL, R, RPB, T, Y

57 THE SHORTEST WAY TO PEACE AND UNION. *By the Author of the Shortest Way with the Dissenters.* LONDON, *Printed in the Year,* 1703.

4°. Pp. 3–26

Notes: Published separately 22 July 1703, and on the same day in *A True Collection* (1703). BM has another edition (4°, pp. 3–16) which substitutes *By the Author of the True Born Englishman.* H has an edition dated 1704.

Copy: BOD. *Other copies:* CU, UL; BPL, IU, Y

58 A TRUE COLLECTION OF THE WRITINGS Of The Author of The True Born English-man. *Corrected by himself.* LONDON: *Printed, and are to be Sold by most Booksellers in London and Westminster.* MDCCIII.

8°. Pp. [22 unnumbered] + [1]–465

Notes: The verso of the title-page warns against the pirated *Collection* (No. 54). Frontispiece portrait of Defoe by J. Taverner, engraved by M. Van der Gucht. A collection of 22 poems and tracts, of which one was accidentally omitted from the Table: *The Original Power of the Collective Body of the People of England* (p. 133). This first authorized collection of any of Defoe's works was published 22 July 1703. For the second volume see No. 91.

Copy: IU. *Other copies:* BM, BOD, DW, NLS, UL; BPL, C, COR, F, H, HEH, LC, NYPL, P, R, RPB, Y

59 A HYMN TO THE PILLORY. LONDON: *Printed in the Year,* MDCCIII.

4°. Pp. 1–24

Notes: Although this poem was published without Defoe's name, its authorship was obvious. It was sold in the streets on at least one of the days while Defoe stood in the pillory (for one hour each day at noon, on 29, 30, and 31 July). According to Lee, a new edition appeared in February 1721. Reprinted in *A Second Volume Of The Writings* (1705). There are numerous minor variations in the text.

Copy: BM. *Other copies:* BOD, CU, DW; BPL, C, F, H, HEH, IU, N, PML, R, T, Y

60 THE SINCERITY OF THE DISSENTERS VINDICATED, From the Scandal Of Occasional Conformity, With Some Considerations on a late Book, Entitul'd, Moderation a Vertue. LONDON: *Printed in the Year,* MDCCIII.

4°. Pp. [2 unnumbered] 1–27

Notes: Advertised 18 September as "Sold by the Booksellers of London and Westminster."

Copy: BM. *Other copies:* DW; BPL, COR, H, N, Y

61 A HYMN TO THE FUNERAL SERMON. 1703

4°. Pp. 1–4

Notes: No title-page. No place, but London. Colophon reads: "Printed in the Year, 1703." Like all later "Hymns" by Defoe, consciously patterned after No. 59. A Pindaric ode attacking Paul Lorrain, Ordinary of Newgate, for preaching and selling a funeral sermon in the parish church of St. James, Clerkenwell, in praise of Thomas Cook [Cooke], a prize-fighter known as "the butcher of Gloucester," executed at Tyburn 11 August 1703 for murdering a constable. Mrs. Elizabeth Mallet, who had apparently pirated a tract of Defoe's on 13 April, paid Lorrain ten guineas for his exclusive permission (16 August 1703) to print his sermon *Walking with God,* a defence of Cook as a repentant sinner who (like Enoch) had been received directly into Heaven. BM has a copy of this sermon, and one of a poem expressing the supposed lament of Cook's wife: *"An Excellent New Copy of Verses, Being The sorrowful Lamentation of Mrs. Cooke, for the loss of her Husband Thomas Cooke, the Famous Butcher of Gloucester, who was Executed at Tyburn on Wednesday the 11th of August 1703. London 1703."* Of the four copies

of the *Hymn* which I have seen the first seems to be BOD
⊕ 1807. BM, probably the second edition, has manuscript notes:
"1d." and "2 Octob. 1703." JRM and BOD Pamph. 323(8) probably represent the third edition. Only the first edition has a
colophon giving the date. BM has a copy of a reply to Defoe
in doggerel verse (pressmark 164.m.34) dated, in the same hand
which appears in the notes on the *Hymn:* "9. Octob. 1703." The
Hymn was an attack on the Ordinary of Newgate, written and
published while Defoe was a prisoner.

Copy: BOD. *Copies of later editions:* BM, BOD; JRM

62   THE CASE OF DISSENTERS AS AFFECTED BY THE LATE BILL
Proposed in Parliament For Preventing Occasional Con-
formity. *By a Gentleman.* LONDON: *Printed, and Sold by*
A. BALDWIN, *near the Oxford-Arms in Warwick-Lane,* 1703.

4°. Pp. 5–31

Notes: Published 18 September 1703. Advertised by A. Baldwin, then by J. Robinson at the Golden Lion in St. Paul's
Church-yard (14 October, etc.), then again by A. Baldwin (13
November, etc.). Advertised 1 December with no publisher's
name.

Copy: BM. *Other copies:* BOD, DW; BPL, HEH, T, Y

63   AN ENQUIRY INTO THE CASE OF MR. ASGIL'S GENERAL
TRANSLATION: Shewing That 'tis not a nearer way to
Heaven than the Grave. *By the Author of the True Born
English-Man.* 2 Thess. 2. 11. And for this cause God shall
send them strong delusions. LONDON: *Printed and Sold by*
J. NUTT, *near Stationers-Hall.* 1704 [for 1703].

8°. Pp. 1–48

Notes: According to Lee, published 4 November 1703. Asgil's
book had been condemned by the Irish House of Commons 11
October. There are three prefaces: 1 page giving "Votes of the
House of Commons in the Kingdom of Ireland," 3 pages addressed "To the Honourable The Commons of Ireland Assembled in Parliament" and signed Daniel de Foe, and 3
prefatory pages signed D. F. In his address to "The Commons
of Ireland" Defoe says: "These Sheets have not only been Writ-

ten, but Printed also Three Years ago, but were reserv'd by Providence to be now Address'd to You. . . . But while the Book was in the Press, I found the Notion dy'd in the Embrio, and as it shockt Peoples Reason more than their Faith, so it began to be laid by, and the Danger, I apprehended, from it to Religion vanish'd. Wherefore, as I would never be guilty of Writing to no purpose, I supprest those Sheets, as things the World had no occasion for, and in this Silence they had perish'd had not the Author of the Argument took care to spread his fine spun Notion in the Kingdom of *Ireland*."

Copy: BM. *Other copies:* BOD, DW, NLS, UL; BPL, H, R, RPB, T, Y

64 A CHALLENGE OF PEACE, Address'd to the Whole Nation. With an Enquiry into Ways and Means for bringing it to pass. *Printed in the Year,* 1703.

4°. Pp. [4 unnumbered] + 1–24

Notes: Published 23 November. On 5 January 1704 it was advertised under the title *A Challenge to Peace and Union.* Reprinted with the original title in *A Second Volume Of The Writings* (1705). Pp. 7 and 15 contain quotations from No. 28.

Copy: BM. *Other copies:* BOD, UL; BPL, C, F, H, HEH, IU, NYPL, P, T, Y

65 SOME REMARKS ON THE FIRST CHAPTER IN DR. DAVENANT'S ESSAYS. LONDON: *Printed and Sold by* A. BALDWIN, *near the Oxford-Arms in Warwick Lane.* MDCCIV [for 1703].

4°. Pp. 1–30

Notes: According to Lee, published 10 December 1703. On pp. 17–19 and 23–26 there are long quotations from an earlier tract (No. 41) and on p. 13 (for 12) a line is quoted from No. 36. The second edition (1704) was entitled *Original Right: Or, The Reasonableness of Appeals to the People.* This is not to be confused with No. 41, *The Original Power Of the Collective Body of the People of England,* which was frequently called *The Original Right, etc.*

Copy: BM. *Other copies:* BOD, UL; H, Y

66 PEACE WITHOUT UNION. By way of Reply, to Sir H[um-
phrey] M[ackworth']s Peace at Home. LONDON, *Printed in
the Year*, MDCCIII.

Fol. Pp. 1–14

Notes: First edition December 1703; second 5 January 1704;
third 7 March 1704; according to Lee, the fourth sometime in
May 1704. The fourth edition (reprinted in *A Second Volume
Of The Writings* [1705]) added a new preface of two unnumbered pages which was signed De Foe.

Copy: BM. *Other copies:* BOD, NLS, UL; BPL, F, IU, LC, T,
Y

1704

67 THE DISSENTERS ANSWER TO THE HIGH-CHURCH CHAL-
LENGE. LONDON, *Printed in the Year* 1704.

4°. Pp. 3–55

Notes: Published 5 January and reprinted in *A Second Volume
Of The Writings* (1705). A reply to Charles Leslie, sometimes
advertised as *The Dissenters Answer to the Woolf stripp'd, or,
The High Church Challenge.*

Copy: BM. *Other copies:* BOD, NLS, UL; BPL, C, F, H, HEH,
IU, NYPL, R, T, Y

68 AN ESSAY ON THE REGULATION OF THE PRESS. LONDON,
Printed in the Year, 1704.

4°. Pp. [2 unnumbered] + 3–22

Notes: Published 7 January 1704. The manuscript was apparently divided into four parts and the tract was rushed through
on four different presses, in order to anticipate the first reading of the Licensing Bill in the House of Commons (13 January). See my introduction to the edition published by the
Luttrell Society (No. 7, Oxford, 1948). Since that was published
BOD has acquired one copy by purchase and has found another which had been overlooked because it was catalogued
under a long-disused heading.

Copy: IU. *Other copies:* BOD; BPL, H, Y. Also imperfect copies
in HEH and Y.

69 A SERIOUS INQUIRY INTO THIS GRAND QUESTION; Whether
a Law to prevent the Occasional Conformity of Dissenters,
Would not be Inconsistent with the Act of Toleration, And
a Breach of the Queen's Promise. LONDON: *Printed in the
Year* 1704.

4°. Pp. 3–28

Notes: Reprinted in *A Second Volume Of The Writings* (1705).

Copy: BM. *Other copies:* BOD, UL; BPL, C, HEH, I, Y

70 THE PARAL[L]EL: Or, Persecution Of Protestants The
Shortest Way to prevent the Growth of Popery In Ireland.
DUBLIN: *Printed in the Year* 1705 [1704?]

Fol. Pp. [3 unnumbered] + 1–26

Notes: This tract was reprinted with unusual fidelity in *A Second Volume Of The Writings* (1705). It is closely related to
Defoe's biography of Dr. Daniel Williams (1718); one important passage, telling of Nottingham's insertion in the bill
to prevent the growth of Popery in Ireland of a passage which
incapacitated Irish Protestant Dissenters from holding public
office, is almost identical in the two accounts (*Second Volume,*
pp. 377–380; *The Memoirs of the life . . . of . . . Daniel
Williams, D. D.,* pp. 27–30).

In *The Paralel* Defoe denied explicitly that the Protestant
Dissenters in Ireland were responsible for his tract (although
it was written in their behalf). It was probably printed in London rather than in Dublin, and its preface to the Queen and
its unusually fine paper and printing suggest that it was not
meant for commercial distribution. The tract must have been
subsidized by someone—presumably the wealthy and devoted
Dr. Williams, whose special information it employs and whose
views it expresses throughout.

Copy: BM

71 THE LAY-MAN'S SERMON UPON THE LATE STORM; Held

Forth at an Honest Coffee-House-Conventicle. Not so much a Jest as 'tis thought to be. *Printed in the Year* 1704.

4°. Pp. 1–24

Notes: According to Lee, published 24 February.

Copy: UL. *Other copies:* BPL, N, R

72   ROYAL RELIGION; Being some Enquiry After The Piety of Princes. With Remarks on a Book, Entituled, A Form of Prayers us'd by King William. LONDON: *Printed in the Year* MDCCIV.

4°. Pp. 3–27

Notes: According to Lee, published 18 March 1704, and a second edition published later in the same year. Reprinted in *A Second Volume Of The Writings* (1705).

Copy: BM. *Other copies:* BOD, UL; BPL, C, HEH, IU, R, T, Y

73   MODERATION MAINTAIN'D, In Defence Of A Compassionate Enquiry Into The Causes Of The Civil War, &c. In a Sermon Preached the Thirty-first of January, at Aldgate-Church, by White Kennet, D. D. Arch-Deacon of Huntingdon, and Minister of St. Botolph, without Aldgate. LONDON, *Printed in the Year*, MDCCIV.

4°. Pp. [2 unnumbered] + 1–28 (misnumbered 22)

Notes: Published 27 March. Preface "To Dr. Kennet" signed D. F.

Copy: BM. *Other copies:* CU; BPL, H, IU, Y

74   LEGION'S HUMBLE ADDRESS TO THE LORDS. [1704]

4°. Pp. 1–4

Notes: No title-page. IU copy has two unnumbered pages. According to Lee, published in April. The tract praises the House of Lords for affirming (28 March 1704) the right of freeholders to vote in the controversial Aylesbury election. In June and again in September efforts were being made to prosecute Defoe for this address (*H. M. C. Portland*, IV, 93, 138).

Copy: BOD. *Other copies:* NLS, UL; BPL, F, IU, NYPL, T, Y

75 THE CHRISTIANITY OF THE HIGH-CHURCH CONSIDER'D. Dedicated to a Noble Peer. LONDON, *Printed in the Year,* MDCCIV.

4°. Pp. [8 unnumbered] + [1]–20

Notes: Published 12 April "precisely at 12 a Clock." On 13 April it was advertised in *The Daily Courant:* "Yesterday was publish'd, The Christianity of the High-Church consider'd. Dedicated to a Noble Peer. Written by the Author of Moderation Maintain'd; . . . Price Six-Pence. Sold by B. Harris at the Golden Boar's-head in Gracious-street."

Copy: BM. *Other copies:* BOD, UL; BPL, H, IU, LC, R, Y

76 MORE SHORT-WAYS WITH THE DISSENTERS. LONDON: *Printed in the Year* 1704.

4°. Pp. 1–24

Notes: According to Lee, published 28 April. Reprinted in *A Second Volume Of The Writings* (1705).

Copy: BM. *Other copies:* BOD, DW, UL; BPL, C, COR, H, IU, N, NYPL, R, Y

77 THE ADDRESS. [1704]

4°. Pp. 1–4

Notes: No title-page, but London 1704. This poem, an attack on the outgoing House of Commons, begins "Ye Men of Might, and Muckle Power."

Copy: BM. *Another copy:* BOD

78 THE DISSENTER[S] MISREPRESENTED AND REPRESENTED. [1704]

Notes: I have seen no copy of the original edition, which (according to Lee) was published in May 1704. Reprinted in *A Second Volume Of The Writings* (1705). All bibliographies have "Dissenters" in the title, and the plural seems to be implied in the tract; but the actual reading in *A Second Volume Of The Writings* is "Dissenter."

79 OF THE FLEET AND SIR GEORGE ROOK. [1704]

Notes: Manuscript pamphlet addressed to Robert Harley. First published in *H. M. C. Portland,* VIII (1907), 135–139. Healey (*Letters,* p. 18, note 2) suggests June 1704 as the probable date. Unsigned, but enclosed in a letter from Defoe to Harley, preserved in the Harley Papers of the Duke of Portland, 37ff. 279–284.

80   A NEW TEST OF THE CHURCH OF ENGLAND'S HONESTY. LONDON: *Printed in the Year* 1704.

4°. Pp. 1–24 + one unnumbered page (an advertisement ridiculing an announced book on the sufferings of the Loyal Clergy of England)

Notes: According to Lee, published 16 July. Reprinted in *A Second Volume Of The Writings* (1705) without the advertisement. The Edinburgh edition (1705) includes the advertisement and adds on the title-page: By the Author of *The True-Born English-Man.*

Copy: BM. *Other Copies:* BOD, NLS; BPL, C, COR, F, HEH, I, IU, N, P, T, Y

81   THE STORM: Or, A Collection Of the most Remarkable Casualties And Disasters Which happen'd in the Late Dreadful Tempest, Both by Sea and Land. The Lord hath his way in the Whirlwind, and in the Storm, and the Clouds are the dust of his Feet. Nah. I. 3. LONDON: *Printed for* G. SAWBRIDGE *in Little Britain, and Sold by* J. NUTT *near Stationers-Hall.* MDCCIV.

8°. Pp. [13 unnumbered] + 1–272 + folding leaf opposite p. 222

Notes: Preface signed "The Ages Humble Servant." Published 17 July. In January 1713 unsold sheets were offered: "Printed for George Sawbridge at the Three Golden Flower-de-Lys, in Little Britain, and J. Nutt in the Savoy. Price Bound 3s. 6d." This reissue was given a long title beginning *A Collection Of the most remarkable Casualties and Disasters which happen'd in the late dreadful Tempest, . . .* The R copy of the reissue has ten misnumbered pages (instead of two for the 1704 edition, or one [IU]).

Copy: IU. *Other copies:* BM, BOD, CU, NLS, UL; BPL, C, CH, COR, F, H, HEH, I, N, NYPL, P, R, RPB, T, Y

82 MAXIMS AND INSTRUCTIONS FOR MINISTERS OF STATE. [1704]

Notes: First published by G. F. Warner in *English Historical Review*, XXII (1907), 132–143. Dated by Warner in May or June; Healey (*Letters,* p. 29) places it convincingly in July or August. The manuscript (unsigned, but in Defoe's handwriting) is in the British Museum: Lansdowne MSS. 98 ff. 223–245.

83 AN ELEGY ON THE AUTHOR OF THE TRUE-BORN-ENGLISH-MAN. With An Essay on the late Storm. *By the Author of the Hymn to the Pillory.* LONDON, *Printed in the Year,* 1704.

4°. Pp. [2 unnumbered] + 1–56. Latin poem on verso of title

Notes: According to Lee, published 15 August. The two poems, *An Elegy* and *An Essay,* were reprinted in *A Second Volume Of The Writings* (1705) but without the Latin poem in honor of Defoe (signed J. L.) which had appeared on the verso of the title-page in 1704. In the IU copy the Latin poem is unsigned.

Copy: BM. *Other copies:* BOD, CU, DW, NLS; BPL, C, CH, COR, F, H, HEH, IU, R, RPB, T, Y

84 A TRUE STATE OF THE DIFFERENCE Between Sir George Rook, Knt. And William Colepeper, Esq; Together with an Account of the Tryal of Mr. Nathanael Denew, Mr. Robert Britton, and Mr. John Merriam, Before The Right Honorable Sir John Holt, Knt. Lord Chief Justice of England, On An Indictment for the Designs and Attempts therein mentioned against the life of the said William Colepeper on Behalf of the said Sir George Rook. Part I. LONDON, *Printed: And Sold by the Booksellers of London and Westminster.* MDCCIV.

Fol. Pp. [2 unnumbered] + 1–44

Notes: The prefatory address to Sir John Holt is signed W. Colepeper, and the whole tract is ostensibly Colepeper's; but it is certainly in large part (and perhaps altogether) Defoe's.

Even the record of the trial may well be Defoe's, for it is not unlikely that he was one of the shorthand writers expelled from the courtroom before the trial was ended. Charles Leslie expressed a shrewd suspicion that Defoe wrote the tract, and there is no indication that Colepeper ever wrote anything else in this style. Possibly it is a compilation, based on a preface by Colepeper and a court record kept by other hands; but the tract is certainly Defoe's work, perhaps as editor and more likely as sole author. Part I was published 18 August. Part II was promised as forthcoming, but apparently it was never published. In the autumn of 1704 Defoe was away on a long journey for Harley, and the controversy was not one which Harley's confidential agent could be expected to continue.

Copy: BM. *Another copy:* BPL

85 A HYMN TO VICTORY. LONDON, *Printed for* J. NUT, *near Stationers-Hall.* 1704.

4°. Pp. [6 unnumbered] + 1–52

Notes: The preface to the Queen is signed De Foe; the text is signed DF. According to Lee, the first edition was published 29 August, the second authorized edition 9 September. The second edition (also published by Nutt) adds on the verso of the title a Latin poem signed J. C., with Defoe's explanation: "The following lines were sent to the Author of this Poem since the Printing of the first Edition." Another early edition published by Nutt (pp. [4 unnumbered] + 1–36) has one significant correction, and it adds on the title-page: "By the Author of The True-Born English-Man." The *Hymn* was reprinted in *A Second Volume Of The Writings* (1705) with this significant correction, but with no attribution of authorship and without the Latin poem.

Copy: BM. *Other copies:* BOD, CU, DW, NLS, UL; BPL, C, COR, H, HEH, I, IU, LC, N, NYPL, PML, R, T, Y

86 METHODS OF MANAGEMENT OF THE DISSENTERS. [1704]

Notes: Fragment (without title) addressed to Robert Harley, first published by James Sutherland (*Defoe* [1937], pp. 277–282). Healey (*Letters,* p. 50), suggests a date in August or September 1704. The manuscript is in the British Museum: Harl. MSS. 6274 ff. 227–34.

87   THE PROTESTANT JESUITE UNMASK'D. In Answer to the Two
     Parts Of Cassandra. Wherein the Author and his Libels are
     laid Open. With the True Reasons why he wou'd have the
     Dissenters Humbled. Beware of false Prophets, which come
     to you in Sheeps-cloathing, Matth. 15. 7. With my Service
     to Mr. Lesley. LONDON, *Printed in the Year,* 1704.

     4°. Pp. [2 unnumbered] + 1–52

     Notes: According to Lee, published 12 September.

     Copy: BM. *Other copies:* BOD, UL; C, H, R, Y

88   GIVING ALMS NO CHARITY, And Employing the Poor A
     Grievance to the Nation, Being an Essay Upon this Great
     Question, Whether Work-houses, Corporations, and Houses
     of Correction for Employing the Poor, as now practis'd in
     England; or Parish-Stocks, as propos'd in a late Pamphlet,
     Entituled, A Bill for the better Relief, Imployment and
     Settlement of the Poor, &c. Are not mischievous to the Na-
     tion, tending to the Destruction of our Trade, and to En-
     crease the Number and Misery of the Poor. Addressed to
     the Parliament of England. LONDON: *Printed, and Sold by
     the Booksellers of London and Westminster.* MDCCIV.

     4°. Pp. 3–28

     Notes: According to Lee, published 18 November. Reprinted
     in *A Second Volume Of The Writings* (1705).

     Copy: BM. *Other copies:* UL; BPL, C, F, H, IU, T, Y

89   QUERIES UPON THE BILL AGAINST OCCASIONAL CONFORMITY.
     [1704]

     Notes: I have found no copy of this, although Dottin describes
     it as fol., pp. 1–4. It was published during the week preceding
     2 December 1704 (*Letters,* ed. Healey, p. 71) and advertised in
     The Daily Courant (13 December 1704): "Queries upon the Bill
     against Occasional Conformity: Sold by A. Baldwin near the
     Oxford Arms in Warwick-Lane. Price 2d." A dialogue inserted
     by Defoe in *The London Post* (1 January 1705) shows that there

were twenty-seven questions in the tract and that Defoe had
been attacked as its author:

"*Honesty.* One I bought for the sake of the Title, it is cal'd
*Stockings out at Heels; or a full Answer to 27 Questions,
propos'd by a Dislocated Hosier.*

"*Truth.* That's a Comical Title enough.

"*Honesty.* And the Answer's as foolish. I never read such a
Nonsensical Paper in all my Life, certainly the Author's Brains
were out at Heels, he had his Understanding dislocated before
he wrote it, and I suppose will never be set right again. The
Queries seem to have something of Force in 'em, and deserve
a better Answer than that of a Fool."

Probably this tract was not related to one advertised by John
Nutt in *The Daily Courant* more than a year earlier (7 December
1703) with a rather similar title: *Queries relating to the
Bill against Occasional Conformity.*

1705

90   THE DOUBLE WELCOME. A Poem To The Duke of Marlbro. LONDON: *Printed, and Sold by* B. BRAGG *at the Blue-
Ball in Ave-Mary Lane.* 1705.

4°. Pp. 1–30

Notes: According to Lee, published 9 January; but on 22 January
it was advertised as "This day is published" and a manuscript note in the BM copy dates it "22. January 1705/4." The
title-page of the IU copy reads somewhat differently: "The
Double Welcome. A Poem To The Duke of Marlbro'. London,
Printed in the Year 1705." Reprinted in *A Second Volume Of
The Writings* (1705).

Copy: BM. *Other copies:* BOD, CU, DW, UL; BPL, C, H,
HEH, IU, NYPL, P, R, RPB, T, Y

91   A SECOND VOLUME OF THE WRITINGS Of The Author Of
The True-Born Englishman. Some whereof never before
printed. *Corrected and Enlarged by the Author.* LONDON:
Printed, and Sold by the Booksellers. 1705. *Price 6s.*

8°. Pp. [15 unnumbered] + 1–479

Notes: According to Lee, this was published at the beginning of 1705. About the same time was published the second edition of the first authorized volume of Defoe's collected works: *"A True Collection Of The Writings Of The Author Of The True Born English-Man. The Second Edition Corrected and Enlarg'd by himself.* Printed, and are to be Sold by most Booksellers in London and Westminster. MDCCV." This second edition (8°. Pp. [22 unnumbered] + 1–470) has some new footnotes, and the type is completely reset from the first edition of 1703. But there is no evidence that new editions of the two volumes after 1705 were anything more than reissues of unsold sheets from the 1705 printing (with new title-pages and the eventual inclusion of a key to the characters). See entries for *A True Collection* in 1710 and 1713 and for *The Genuine Works of Mr. Daniel D'Foe* in 1721.

A misleading claim ("Some whereof never before printed") appears on the title-page of *A Second Volume* (1705). Every item in both volumes had been previously published except *The Shortest Way to Peace and Union*—and even this was published separately on the same day (22 July 1703) when it appeared in *A True Collection.*

Copy: BM. *Other copies:* BOD, NLS, UL; BPL, C, COR, H, HEH, I, IU, NYPL, R, RPB, T, Y

92 PERSECUTION ANATOMIZ'D: Or, An Answer To The Following Questions, Viz. I. What Persecution for Conscience sake is? II. Whether any High-Church that Promote the Occasional Bill, may not properly be called Persecutors? III. Whether any Church whatever, whilst it savours of a Persecuting Spirit, is a true Church? IV. Who are the greatest Promoters of a Nation's Welfare, the High-Church, or Dissenters? LONDON, *Printed in the Year,* MDCCV.

4°. Pp. [2 unnumbered] + 1–23

Notes: Advertised 19 February as "Sold by J. Billingsly, at the Printing-Press under the Royal-Exchange, Cornhil; and B. Bragg in Ave-Mary-Lane. Price 6d."

Copy: BM. *Other copies:* BOD, UL

93   THE CONSOLIDATOR: Or, Memoirs Of Sundry Transactions From the World in the Moon. Translated from the Lunar Language, *By the Author of The True-born English Man.* LONDON: *Printed, and are to be Sold by* BENJ. BRAGG *at the Blue Ball in Ave-mary-lane,* 1705.

8º. Pp. 1–360

Notes: According to Lee, published 26 March. The second edition was published 17 November.

Copy: BM. *Other copies:* BOD, CU, NLS, UL; BPL, C, CH, COR, F, H, HEH, I, IU, LC, N, NYPL, P, R, RPB, T, Y

94   THE EXPERIMENT: Or, The Shortest Way with the Dissenters Exemplified. Being the Case of Mr. Abraham Gill, a Dissenting Minister in the Isle of Ely, And A Full Account of his being sent for a Soldier, by Mr. Fern (an Ecclesiastical Justice of the Peace) and other Conspirators. To the Eternal Honour of the Temper and Moderation of High Church Principles. Humbly Dedicated to the Queen. LONDON, *Printed: And Sold by* B. BRAGG, *at the Blue-Ball in Ave-Mary Lane.* MDCCV.

4º. Pp. [4 unnumbered] + 1–58

Notes: According to Lee, published 27 March. BM (Ashley Library) has a variant with different printing of dedication and title-page ornament. TCC has a copy of the second edition: *"The Honesty and Sincerity Of those Worthy Gentlemen Commonly called High-Church Men: Exemplifie'd In a Modern Instance. Most Humbly Dedicated to Her Majesty, And Her High Court of Parliament. Yea, the time cometh, that whosoever killeth you will think that he doth God service, St. John. 16. 2. London, Printed, and Sold by Benj. Bragg, in Pater-Noster-Row,* 1707. *Price One Shilling."* 4º. Pp. [2 unnumbered] + 1–58. According to Lee, this second edition (dated 1707) was published 19 October 1706. The first edition is anonymous, but the dedication to the Queen concludes with an advertisement of *The Double Welcome* "By the Author of the True-Born English-man."

Copy: BM. *Other copies:* BOD, CU, NLS, UL; BPL, C, H, I, IU, Y

95 A Hint to the Blackwell-Hall Factors: Being The
    True State of the Case between Mr. Samuel Weatherhead,
    Blackwell-Hall Factor, and Mr. John Hellier, Merchant.
    London, *Printed in the Year,* MDCCV.

    4°. Pp. 1–22

    Notes: Defoe's first known championship of John Hellier, later
    a partner with Brook in the importation and sale of Portuguese
    wine.

    Copy: BOD

96 A Journey to the World in the Moon, &c. *By the Author
    of the true Born English-man.* [1705]

    4°. Pp. 1–4

    Notes: The colophon reads: "London, Printed in the Year,
    1705." An Edinburgh edition was offered by James Watson in
    the same year: 4°, pp. 1–4; and this is more commonly met
    with than the London original (e. g., BM, NLS; CH, Y). *The
    Consolidator* (No. 93) is sometimes referred to confusingly as
    A Journey to the World in the Moon.

    Copy: DNS. *Other copies:* BPL, H, CH, HEH

97 A Letter from the Man in the Moon. To the Author of
    the True Born English-Man. [1705]

    4°. Pp. 1–4

    Notes: Anonymous, but understood to be by the Author of
    the True Born English-Man. The colophon of the IU copy
    is slightly trimmed, but apparently reads: "London, printed in
    the Year 1705." A reprint is advertised on the last page of
    James Watson's Edinburgh edition of No. 96: "There is now
    in the Press, and will speedily be Published, *A Letter* from the
    Man in the Moon, *to the Author of* The True Born English-
    Man; *containing variety of Diverting News, and Comical
    Intreagues relating to the present posture of Affairs in* Europe."

    Copy: IU

98 A Second, and More Strange Voyage to the World in
    the Moon; Containing a comical Discription of that re-
    markable Country, with the Characters and Humours of

the Inhabitants, &c. *By the Author of the true born English-man.* [1705].

4°. Pp. 1–4

Notes: No title-page. Signed "The Man from the Moon." The colophon reads: "London, printed in the Year 1705." *CBEL* gives preference to a variant edition, which I have not seen: *A second and more strange Journey to the World in the Moon.* The IU copy of No. 97 ends with the following advertisement: "There will speedily be Published a Second Voyage to the *World in the Moon:* Containing the Description of that Remarkable Country, relating to the Laws and Customs of that Place; with the Characters and Humours of the Inhabitants, the like never before Published. By the Author of the *True-Born Englishman.*"

Copy: BPL

99   ADVICE TO ALL PARTIES. By the Author of The True-Born English-man. LONDON: *Printed: And are to be Sold by* BENJ. BRAGG, *at the Blue-Ball in Ave-Mary Lane.* MDCCV. *Price 6d.*

4°. Pp. [2 unnumbered] + 1–24

Notes: According to Lee, published 30 April. C has a copy of another edition of 1705 (4°. Pp. [1 unnumbered] + 3–16).

Copy: IU. *Other copies:* BM; BPL, H, HEH, N, NYPL, Y

100   THE DYET OF POLAND, A Satyr. *Printed At* DANTZICK, *in the Year* MDCCV.

4°. Pp. [2 unnumbered] + 1–60

Notes: The preface, signed "Anglipoloski, Of Lithuania," hints broadly that Defoe is the author. Dantzick is obviously London, and the Dyet of Poland is the Houses of Parliament. In a letter to Harley (June 1704?) Defoe spoke of this poem as yet unpublished (*Letters,* ed. Healey, p. 19).

Copy: IU. *Other copies:* BM, BOD, CU, NLS, UL; BPL, C, COR, F, H, HEH, LC, H, NYPL, PML, R, T, Y

*101   A LETTER FROM SCOTLAND, TO A FRIEND IN LONDON: Con-
taining A particular Narrative of the whole Proceedings
against the Worcester and her Crew, from her first Arrival
in Leith-Road, to the 20th of April 1705. In which the
Secret Intrigues, and Bloody Designs of their Prosecutors
are Detected and Expos'd. Also an Account of the Sudden
Death of the Principal Evidence of the Day Sentence was
past; the Prisoners Behaviour after Condemnation, and
their manner of Execution; with Observations and Reflections upon the whole. Publish'd by way of Requital, for
the many Scandalous Relations and Reflections publish'd
in the Flying-Post. LONDON: *Printed in the Year,* 1705.

4°. Pp. 3–32

Notes: A tract which Defoe made use of later, in Volume II
of *A General History of the Pyrates* (1728). It has striking
similarities to some of his other writings, but I am much
less sure of his authorship than I was in 1939. See my *Defoe in
the Pillory and Other Studies* (Bloomington, Indiana, 1939),
pp. 147–154, 192–211.

Copy: BM. *Another copy:* HEH (with date trimmed off)

102   THE BALLANCE: Or, A New Test Of The High-Fliers of all
Sides: Being a Short View Of The Rise of our Present Fac-
tions, With A New History of Passive-Obedience, and a
Proposal of a Bill against Occasional Conformity that may
Pass both Houses. LONDON: *Printed in the Year* 1705.

4°. Pp. [6 unnumbered] + 1–48

Notes: Published 8 June. Has very complimentary references
to Defoe (p. 8), to *The Shortest Way with the Dissenters* (p. 8),
and to *A New Test of the Church of England's Loyalty* (p. 15).

Copy: BM. *Other copies:* BOD; Y

103   THE HIGH-CHURCH LEGION: Or, The Memorial Examin'd.
Being, A New Test Of Moderation As 'tis recomended to
all that love the Church of England And the Constitution.
LONDON: *Printed in the Year* 1705.

4°. Pp. [5 unnumbered] + 1–21

Notes: BOD and IU copies read "Legeon" in the title. According to Lee, published 17 July. On 16 July Defoe sent six copies to Lord Halifax (*Letters,* ed. Healey, p. 93).

Copy: BM. *Other copies:* BOD, UL; BPL, C, F, I, IU, R, T, Y

104   A COLLECTION FROM DYER'S LETTERS, Concerning the Elections Of The Present Parliament: With An Appendix, relating to some other Publick Matters. LONDON: *Printed, and Sold by* B. BRAGG, *in Ave-Mary-Lane.* 1706 [for 1705].

4°. Pp. [1 unnumbered] + 1–20

Notes: An exposure of Dyer's methods, published sometime between 22 September 1705 (the date of the last passage cited in the Appendix) and 29 November 1705 (when Bragg advertised it in *The Flying-Post* as "Just published"). BOD has another edition, closely printed in pp. 1–4, entitled *A Collection of several Paragraphs, Out of Mr. Dyer's Letters.* This omits the preface called "Advertisement."

Copy: BOD. *Other copies:* BPL, C, HEH, IU, Y

105   PARTY-TYRANNY: Or, An Occasional Bill in Miniature; As now Practiced In Carolina Humbly offered to the Consideration of both Houses of Parliament. LONDON: *Printed in the Year,* 1705.

4°. Pp. 1–30

Notes: According to Lee, published about November.

Copy: BM. *Other copies:* BOD, DW, NLS; BPL, CH, H, HEH, JCB, LC, PML, RPB, Y

106   AN ANSWER TO THE L[OR]D H[AVER]SHAM'S SPEECH. *By Daniel D'Foe.* 1705.

4°. Pp. 1–4

Notes: This reply to Lord Haversham was published 20 November 1705 and reprinted in the *Review* 24 November 1705 (II, 449–452). The colophon reads: "London, Printed in the Year 1705." The close trimming of the BOD colophon leaves the punctuation uncertain.

Copy: BOD. *Other copies:* BPL, F, H, I, T

107 A True Relation of the Apparition of one Mrs. Veal.
[1705?]

Notes: First edition presumably published late in 1705. The first explicit date is given by an advertisement (*The Daily Courant*, 5, 6, and 8 July 1706) of Benjamin Bragg's edition (presumably pirated, like Bragg's cut-price edition of *Jure Divino* two weeks later). The early bibliographers of Defoe (Chalmers, Scott, Wilson, and Hazlitt) listed a 1705 edition, but disagreed as to whether it was in quarto or octavo. Late in 1944 Thomas Thorp sold a copy dated 1705, which I have been unable to trace.

The earliest edition which I have seen is represented by the H copy of Bragg's edition of 5 July 1706: "*A True Relation Of The Apparition Of One Mrs. Veal, The next Day after Her Death: To One Mrs. Bargrave At Canterbury. The 8th of September, 1705.* London: Printed for B. Bragg, at the Black Raven in Pater-Noster-Row, 1706." 4°. Pp. [1 unnumbered] + 1–9. At the bottom of p. 9 appears the following advertisement: "Drelincourt's Book of the Consolations against the Fears of Death, *has been four times Printed already in* English, *of which many Thousands have been Sold, and not without great Applause: And its bearing so great a Character in this Relation, the Impression is near Sold off.*" The BM copy of the fourth edition of Drelincourt is dated 1701—five years earlier; no doubt the book was already well established in the trade by 1706, but its fourth edition had not been sold off in the previous five years. The extraordinary new popularity of Drelincourt's *Consolations* was largely due to its association with Defoe's narrative. According to Dottin, *A True Relation* was attached to the fourth edition of Drelincourt on 30 September (that is, to the unsold sheets of the fourth edition, which had been published in 1701).

In *The Daily Courant* (9 April 1707) Bragg advertised what he called the third edition, the title-page of which reads (in the NLS copy): "*A True Relation Of The Apparition Of One Mrs. Veal, The next Day after her Death, To One Mrs. Bargrave, At Canterbury, The 8th of September, 1705. Which Apparition recommends the Perusal of Drelincourt's Book of Consolations against the Fears of Death. The 3d Edition.*

Printed for B. Bragg at the Black Raven in Pater-Noster-Row."
Thereafter the two books, combining piety with sensationalism,
were almost inseparable during most of the century. Even the
pirated editions of the publisher Midwinter (1724), of a plagiarist who professed to offer a new translation of Drelincourt
(J. Spavan, 1720 and 1724), and of still another plagiarist of
the authorized translation of Drelincourt in conjunction with
a piratical imitation of Defoe (J. Bromwich and the Rev.
Mr. Payne, 1766) presented the two books in one volume. BM
and Y both have Bragg's 1706 edition.

108   DECLARATION WITHOUT DOORS. [1705]

Fol. half-sheet. P. [1]

Notes: No place, no date, no publisher, but London 1705.
Apparently a variant issue of a publication advertised in the
Review for 25 (actually 24) October 1705 (II, 404): "This Day
is Publish'd; A Declaration without Doors; by the Author of,
&c. Sold by the Booksellers of London and Westminster."
The poem is in line with Harley's attack on William Bromley,
the High-Church candidate for Speaker of the House of Commons in October 1705. Like the reprint of Bromley's *Remarks
in the Grand Tour lately performed by a Person of Quality*
which Harley distributed freely, it was meant to ridicule
Bromley's visit to Rome and his alleged subservience to Roman
Catholicism.

I have found no evidence for the existence of a quarto listed
by Wilson, Hazlitt, Lee, and Dottin as *A Declaration without
Doors; By the Author of the True-Born Englishman.* Lee and
Dottin had not seen it, for they omitted their usual attempt
to give the number of pages. Dottin's explanation that this
(apparently imaginary) prose tract was a résumé of a series
of articles in the *Review* (II, 381–428) is incredible; pp. 405–
428 were published from two to seventeen days later than the
supposed *Declaration* itself. Trent omitted the title from his
list of Defoe's writings in *CHEL* (1910), but it was mistakenly
restored to the list in *CBEL* (1941).

Copy: H. *Another copy:* DW

1 7 0 6

109 A HYMN TO PEACE. Occasion'd, by the Two Houses Joining
in One Address to the Queen. *By The Author of the True-
born English-Man.* LONDON: *Printed for* JOHN NUTT, *near
Stationers Hall.* 1706.

4°. Pp. 3–60

Notes: Old manuscript notes in two BM copies date this re-
spectively 8 January and 10 January. BOD has an 8° reprint
of this poem, issued in 1709 shortly before the Sacheverell controversy brought party strife to a climax.

Copy: BM. *Other copies:* UL; BPL, C, CH, IU, N, R, Y

110 A REPLY TO A PAMPHLET ENTITULED, THE L[OR]D H[AVER-
SHAM]'S VINDICATION of his Speech, &c. *By the Author of the
Review.* LONDON: *Printed in the Year* 1706.

4°. Pp. 3–32

Notes: The conclusion is signed: "The Author of the Review."
An old manuscript note in one BM copy dates this 15 January.

Copy: BM. *Other copies:* BOD; BPL, C, F, HEH, IU, T, Y

111 THE CASE OF PROTESTANT DISSENTERS IN CAROLINA, Shewing How a Law to prevent Occasional Conformity There,
has ended in the Total Subversion of the Constitution in
Church and State. Recommended to the serious Consideration of all that are true Friends to our present Establishment.

> Mutato nomine, de te
> Fabula narratur.

LONDON, *Printed in the Year M.DCC.VI.*

4°. Pp. 3–42

Notes: Copies are found with (BM) or without (IU) a separately
printed appendix (pp. 1–67) by John Ash and others, giving the
first charters of South Carolina, the fundamental constitutions,
the present state of the colony, etc. Published 18 March.

Copy: BM. *Other copies:* BOD; BPL, CH, F, H, HEH, IU, JCB, LC, N, NYPL, RPB

112   REMARKS ON THE BILL TO PREVENT FRAUDS COMMITTED BY BANKRUPTS. With Observations on the Effect it may have upon Trade. LONDON: *Printed in the Year* 1706.

4°. Pp. 1–29

Notes: Lee dates this 18 April. An old manuscript note in one BM copy reads: "bill read 31 Oct 1705." This tract was published at some time after 19 March 1706 when (as Defoe remarks) the bill received the royal assent. In the *Review* for 14 and 16 February 1706 (III, 77–84) he had supported the bill by long quotations from his chapter "Of Bankrupts" in *An Essay upon Projects* (1697).

Copy: BM. *Other copies:* BOD; BPL, C, Y

113   REMARKS ON THE LETTER TO THE AUTHOR OF THE STATE-MEMORIAL. LONDON: *Printed in the Year* 1706.

4°. Pp. 1–32 + 1–4

Notes: The latter section is a separately paged "Conclusion to the Ministers of State." The *Letter* is ascribed to William Stephens or Thomas Rawlins, *The State-Memorial* to John Toland.

Copy: BM. *Other copies:* BOD; BPL, C, HEH, T

114   AN ESSAY AT REMOVING NATIONAL PREJUDICES AGAINST A UNION with Scotland. To be continued during the Treaty here. PART I. LONDON: *Printed in the year* 1706.

4°. Pp. 1–30

Notes: Lee dates this 4 May. See also Nos. 116, 120, 124, 138, 139.

Copy: BM. *Other copies:* BOD, NLS, UL; BPL, C, H, HEH, IU, N, P, R, T, Y

115   JURE DIVINO. A Satyr. In Twelve Books. *By the Author of The True-Born-Englishman.*

O Sanctos Gentes, quibus haec nascuntur in hostis
Numina! ——— Juv. Sat. 15. 1. 11.

LONDON: Printed in the Year, M.DCCVI.

Fol. Pp. [2 unnumbered] + i–xxviii + [4 unnumbered] + i–vii +
1–26 + 1–32 + 1–28 + 1–30 + 1–32 + 1–20 + 1–28 + 1–34 +
1–24 + 1–26 + 1–32 + 1–23

Notes: See my *Daniel Defoe: Citizen of the Modern World* (Chicago, 1958), pp. 238–239. The poem, set up in type at intervals
for about two years, falls into seventeen sections. A new portrait
of Defoe engraved by M. Van der Gucht appears as the frontispiece, the preface is signed Defoe, and the Dedication to Reason
is signed by "The True-Born Englishman." The book was first
offered for sale in the country on 24 May. Bragg's pirated edition appeared in London on 19 July. The authorized subscription edition was first available in London on 20 July.

Copy: BM. *Other copies:* BOD, CU, DW, NLS, UL; BPL, C,
CH, COR, F, H, HEH, I, IU, LC, N, NYPL, P, RPB, T, Y

116   AN ESSAY AT REMOVING NATIONAL PREJUDICES AGAINST A
      UNION with Scotland. To be continued during the Treaty
      here. PART II. LONDON: *Printed in the Year* 1706.

4°. Pp. 3–32

Notes: Lee dates this 28 May. Part I and Part II were published
separately in London to convince the English of the advantages
of a Union with Scotland. During the summer, the two parts
were reprinted together in Edinburgh by opponents of the
Union, in an attempt to show that the English would be gainers
at the expense of the Scots: (NLS) *"An Essay At Removing National Prejudices Against A Union With Scotland. To be continued. Part I.* Edinburgh Printed in the Year 1706." [Near the
bottom of p. 27] "Finis. *An Essay At Removing National Prejudices, &c.* Part II." These two parts are in small folio numbered
consecutively, pp. 2–50.

In the Advertisement at the end of *A Fifth Essay, At Removing National Prejudices* (1707) it was made clear that the London editions of the first and second essays were the correct ones:
"These are to give Notice, That the fourth Essay is to be had at

the *Caledonia* Coffee-House, over against the Cross in *Edinburgh;* where also, will be had, the First and Second Essays of the *London* Impression."

Copy: NLS. *Other copies:* BOD, UL; BPL, C, H, HEH, IU, N, Y

117   A SERMON PREACH'D BY MR. DANIEL DEFOE: On the fitting up of Dr. Burges's late Meeting-House. Taken from his Review of Thursday the 20th of June, 1706.

4°. Pp. 1–4

Notes: No title-page or imprint. No place, but obviously London. Lee dates this June 1706.

Copy: UL. *Other copies:* BPL, Y

118   [PREFACE TO] DE LAUNE'S PLEA FOR THE NON-CONFORMISTS: Shewing The True State of their Case, and how far the Conformist's Separation from the Church of Rome for their Popish Superstitions, &c. introduced into the Service of God, justifies the Non-Conformist's Separation from them. In a Letter to Dr. Benjamin Calamy, on his Sermon, called, Scrupulous Conscience, inviting hereto. To which is added, A Parallel Scheme of the Pagan, Papal, and Christian Rites and Ceremonies. With a Narrative of the Sufferings underwent for Writing, Printing and Publishing thereof. By Thomas Delaune, who died in Newgate during his Imprisonment for this Book. Printed Twenty Years ago; but being seiz'd by the Messenger of the Press, was afterwards Burnt by the Hang-Man: And now Re-printed from the Author's Original Copy. With A PREFACE *by the Author of the Review.* LONDON: *Printed for* JOHN MARSHALL *at the Bible in Grace-church-street,* 1706 *Where are Sold most Sorts of Books to learn Short-hand.*

4°. Defoe's preface, pp. i–xi; Thomas De Laune's text, pp. [3 unnumbered] + 1–66

Notes: Lee dates this 6 June. On 16 July *The Post-Man* advertised that the seventh edition would be published the next week. In 1709, apparently before Defoe's return from Edinburgh a little earlier than 1 February 1710, and possibly without his knowledge, two other publishers by the name of Marshall reissued the book as a reply to Sacheverell: (BM) *"Dr. Sacheverell's Recantation: or, The Fire of Paul's quickly Quenched. By a Plea for the Non-Conformists. Shewing The True State of their Case, and how far the Conformist's Separation from the Church of Rome for their Popish Superstitions, introduced into the Service of God, justifies the Non-Conformist's Separation from them. Wherein there is not the least personal Reflection upon the Doctor, nor bitterness upon the account of his Doctrine; and the whole Plea is unanswerable. Attested by the Royal Testimony of that learned Prince Charles the First. With a suitable Preface by a Judicious Author.* LONDON: . . . William and Joseph Marshall, . . . 1709." The preface (pp. i–ix) is signed D. Foe.

In 1720 a still later edition of De Laune, advertised by the original publisher, again reprinted Defoe's preface: (CU) *"A Plea For The Non-Conformists. In Three Parts. . . . . By Thomas De Laune. Printed from the Original Copy, and corrected from many Faults escaped in former impressions.* London: Printed for John Marshall, at the Bible in Grace-Church-Street, MDCCXX. Price One Shilling Six-pence."

Copy: BM. *Other copies:* BOD, DW; BPL, C, F, HEH, NYPL, R

119 DANIEL DEFOE'S HYMN for the Thanksgiving. 1706.

Fol. half-sheet

Notes: The colophon reads: "London: Printed for the Author. 1706." Identical with a poem published in the *Review* for 27 June 1706 (III, 307–308): "On The Victories in Flanders, And The Thanksgiving at St. Paul's." Probably the separate was printed first, but the two versions are so similar that (except for the title and the colophon) they could have been printed from the same type.

Copy: R

120 AN ESSAY, AT REMOVING NATIONAL PREJUDICES AGAINST A UNION with England. PART III. *By the Author of the two first. Printed in the Year* MDCCVI.

4°. Pp. 3–35

Notes: No place, but certainly Edinburgh. The reasons for assigning this and certain other tracts to Edinburgh rather than to London are numerous, e.g.: Defoe's letters show that many of them were first printed in Edinburgh and that he mailed copies from there to Harley in London, they were addressed primarily to Scottish readers and they were answered or mentioned (often with exact page references) in contemporary Scottish pamphlets, there is no reason to suppose that they were ever printed in London (except as obvious reprints), they were often advertised as being newly issued by Edinburgh publishers, the press-work and often the spelling and certain idioms suggest the work of Edinburgh printers, copies are likely to survive in NLS if nowhere else, and NLS copies often have significant manuscript notes written by early owners in Scotland.

Defoe sent Harley a copy of this tract from Edinburgh before 29 October (*Letters,* ed. Healey, p. 138). The first two parts, printed in London and directed toward English readers, concerned a Union with Scotland; the four later parts, printed in Edinburgh and directed toward Scottish readers, were said to concern a Union with England.

Copy: BM. *Other copies:* BOD, NLS, UL; BPL, H, HEH, IU, N, R, Y

121   A Letter from Mr. Reason, To the High and Mighty Prince the Mob. [1706]

4°. Pp. 1–8

Notes: No title-page, but certainly Edinburgh 1706. Old manuscript notes in two NLS copies attribute this to "Capt. Donaldson" and to "James Donaldson." Still another NLS copy has a manuscript note on the last page: "Nov. 7 De Foe" in the same handwriting which appears in assigning to Defoe the next tract in the same volume (*A Short Letter to the Glasgow Men,* a tract which Defoe mentioned as his own in a letter to Harley on 9 December 1706 and which he reprinted in the *Review* for 2 January 1707). The title and the tract itself are highly characteristic of Defoe.

Copy: NLS. *Other copies:* UL; Y

122 AN ANSWER TO MY LORD BEILHAVEN'S SPEECH. *By an English Gentleman. Printed in the Year* 1706. *(Price Two Pence.)*

8º. Pp. 3–16

Copy: BOD. *Other copies:* NLS, UL; C, HEH, IU

123 THE [*sic*] THE VISION, A Poem. [1706]

4º. Pp. [1]–4

Notes: No title-page, but certainly Edinburgh 1706. Sometimes mistakenly attributed to the Earl of Haddington (as in a manuscript note on the first page of BOD). On 14 November Defoe sent a manuscript copy to Harley from Edinburgh; on 28 November he wrote that it had been printed, and he jested about Lord Beilhaven's error in supposing it to be by Lord Haddington (*Letters,* ed. Healey, pp. 148, 162). Bragg's London reprint published 7 December is entitled: (BM) *The Vision, A Poem. Being an Answer to the Lord Beilhaven's Speech. By a Person of Quality.*

HEH probably represents the first state, although it inserts an extra "The" in the title. BOD and JRM (which are exactly alike) substitute open parentheses for the first "The"; and although minor differences from HEH indicate complete resetting of the type, they are printed from the same lot of type.

Copy: HEH. *Other copies:* BOD, NLS; BPL, JRM, NYPL, Y

124 A FOURTH ESSAY, AT REMOVING NATIONAL PREJUDICES; With some Reply To Mr. H[o]dges and some other Authors, Who have Printed their Objections against An Union with England. *Printed in the Year* MDCCVI.

4º. Pp. 3–[44]

Notes: In a letter to Harley on 29 October Defoe seemed to refer to this as being in press (*Letters,* ed. Healey, p. 138). NLS copy has an old manuscript note: "By Daniel de Foe Nov. 19. 1706."

Copy: NLS. *Other copies:* BM, BOD, NLS, UL; COR, H, IU, N, NYPL, R, T, Y

125   OBSERVATIONS ON THE FIFTH ARTICLE OF THE TREATY OF
UNION, humbly offered to the Consideration of the Parliament, relating to Foreign Ships. [1706]

4°. Pp. 1–4

Notes: No place, no date, but certainly Edinburgh 1706. NLS
copy has an old manuscript note on the first page: "De Foe."
The Fifth Article was read in the Scottish Parliament on 21
November.

Copy: NLS. *Other copies:* BM; BPL, HEH, IU, Y

126   CONSIDERATIONS IN RELATION TO TRADE CONSIDERED, And
a Short View of our present Trade and Taxes, compared
with what these Taxes may amount to after the Union, &c.
Reviewed. Prov. 18. 17. He that is first in his own Cause
seemeth Just; but his Neighbour cometh and Searcheth him.
Printed in the Year MDCCVI.

4°. Pp. 3–26

Notes: No place, but certainly Edinburgh. Contains some Scots
idioms, and it is said by an old manuscript note in NLS copy to
be "by Mr Donaldson." But *A Letter from Mr. Reason* had been
erroneously attributed to the same Mr. Donaldson, Defoe often
used Scots idioms when writing for Scottish readers, the two
pamphlets attacked here are the same ones which Defoe attacked in his *Fourth Essay,* and the Biblical allusion on the
title-page to the neighbour who searcheth the man who seemed
just in his own cause is an obvious and very characteristic allusion to Defoe's own position as an Englishman who wrote as
a critical observer in Scotland.

Copy: NLS. *Other copies:* UL; HEH

127   A SEASONABLE WARNING Or The Pope and King of France
Unmasked. Printed in the Year MDCCVI.

4°. Pp. [3]–16

Notes: No place, but certainly Edinburgh. NLS copy has an old
manuscript note: "Nov. 25. 2d."

Copy: NLS. *Other copies:* BM, UL

128 A REPLY TO THE SCOTS ANSWER, To the British Vision.
[1706]

Fol. half sh.

Notes: No place, no date, but certainly Edinburgh 1706. On 28
November 1706 Defoe sent Harley a copy of Lord Beilhaven's
poem in answer to his own "ballad" (*The Vision*). Presumably
No. 128, Defoe's second reply to Beilhaven, was published early
in December. In Catalogue No. 67 (Spring 1959) Peter Murray
Hill Ltd. advertised what was said to be a previously unknown
earlier edition: "A Poem To The Author of the Scots Answer
to the Brittish Vision. *Projicit Ampullas & sesquipedalia Verba,*
Hor." This is also a folio half sheet without imprint, but it is
said to have several small textual variants besides the different
title.

Copy: BM. *Other copies:* NLS; HEH

129 CALEDONIA, A Poem In Honour Of Scotland, And The
Scots Nation. In Three Parts. EDINBURGH, Printed by the
Heirs and Successors of ANDREW ANDERSON, *Printer to the*
Queen's most Excellent Majesty, *Anno. Dom.* 1706.

Fol. Pp. [8 unnumbered] + 1–60

Notes: The verso of the title-leaf gives A. Maitland's extract
from the minutes of the Scottish Privy Council (3 December)
granting Defoe exclusive right to publish the poem. The Dedication to the Duke of Queensberry [i–ii] is signed DANIEL DE
FOE. The Preface to the Parliament [i–vi] is signed DE FOE.

In the IU copy the last two pages of this Preface are printed
in reverse order. Published by subscription in Edinburgh about
the beginning of December. In the London edition of the next
year (8°. Pp. [6 unnumbered] + 1–55) the Preface to Parliament
was replaced by two unnumbered pages giving "A List of Bene-
factors and Subscribers to this Work"—that is, subscribers to
the Edinburgh edition. This cheap London reprint was not (as
Lee supposed) a subscription edition. The title-page of the BM
copy reads: "*Caledonia, A Poem In Honour of Scotland, And
The Scots Nation. In Three Parts.* London: Printed by J. Matthews, and Sold by John Morphew, near Stationers-Hall. 1707."
Lee dates the London reprint 28 January 1707. On 2 November

1706 Defoe had written to Harley that he was writing a poem in praise of Scotland (*Letters,* ed. Healey, p. 141).

In 1748 the poem was reissued in London (apparently to serve a political end by honoring the Duke of Argyll and the Scottish people) with a new title-page: "*Caledonia: A Poem In Honour of Scotland, And The People of that Nation. In Which The Scandalous and Groundless Imputations of Cowardice, Savageness, and Immorality; so much ascribed to the Inhabitants of that truly Ancient and Heroic Kingdom, are, with great Justice, confuted, and retorted upon her False and Envious Accusers. And They proved To be as Zealous, in Defence of the Protestant Religion, against the Attempts of the Church of Rome, as any other Protestants in the Three Kingdoms. Whereby Scotland Is rescued out of the Jaws of Slander, the Grave of her Character, and the Gulph of Prejudice; in which all the Great and Warlike Actions of her Nobility, Gentry, and Commanality are too much buried.* Dedicated to the Duke of Argyll.

> Friendship! The rarest plant that ever grew,
> Talk'd of by many, understood by few.

London: Printed for W. Owen, near Temple-Bar, and sold at the Pamphlet Shops at the Royal-Exchange, Ludgate-street, and Charing-Cross. MDCCXLVIII. (Price One Shilling.)"

In this reprint (4°. pp. [4 unnumbered] + 9–58?) there is no indication that Defoe was the author or that the poem had been written more than forty years earlier on a different occasion. The original prefatory material of the Edinburgh and London editions is replaced by a dedication "To His Grace the Duke of Argyll" signed by "The Editor" and by a new introduction called "The Preface." In the only copy of the 1748 reprint which I have seen (HEH) the last leaf is missing. Presumably this contained the last page and a half of the accepted text of the poem.

Copy: BM. *Other copies:* BOD, NLS; BPL, C, CH, H, HEH, IU, N, R, T, Y

*130   THE STATE OF THE EXCISE AFTER THE UNION, Compared With what it is Now. *Printed in the Year* MDCCVI.

4°. Pp. 3–8

Notes: Published in Edinburgh about 1 December; the excise on beer and ale after the Union had been discussed in the

Scottish Parliament on 28 November. The use of Scotticisms is excessive—possibly because of the Edinburgh printer, perhaps because Defoe (as often elsewhere in his Scottish tracts) was deliberately writing like a Scotsman. Very probably but not quite certainly Defoe's. An old manuscript note on the title-page of one NLS copy says "By Dan. De Foe."

Copy: BM. *Other copies:* NLS, UL; LC

*131 THE STATE OF THE EXCISE &c. VINDICATED, From the Remarks of the Author of the Short View &c. Wherein other Escapes of that Author, are likewise taken notice of. [1706]

4°. Pp. [1]–8

Notes: No place, no date, but certainly Edinburgh 1706. Excessive use of Scotticisms, as in the preceding tract. An old manuscript note on the first page of one NLS copy says "De Foe." Very probably but not quite certainly Defoe's.

Copy: NLS. *Other copies:* UL; Y

132 A SHORT LETTER TO THE GLASGOW-MEN. [1706]

4°. Pp. 1–8

Notes: No title-page, but certainly Edinburgh 1706. On 9 December Defoe wrote to tell Harley that he was printing this tract; on 12 December he enclosed a copy. One NLS copy has an old manuscript note on the first page: "By De Foe. Dec. 12." Reprinted in the *Review* for 2 January 1706/7 (III, 625–628).

Copy: NLS. *Other copies:* BPL, NYPL, Y

133 THE RABBLER CONVICTED: Or A Friendly Advice to all Turbulent and Factious Persons, From one of their own Number. [1706]

4°. Pp. [1]–4

Notes: No title-page, but certainly Edinburgh 1706. One NLS copy has an old manuscript note on the first page: "Dec. 18. Dan. de Foe."

Copy: NLS

134   THE ADVANTAGES OF SCOTLAND BY AN INCORPORATE UNION
      WITH ENGLAND, Compar'd with These [*sic*] of a Coalition
      with the Dutch, Or League with France. In Answer to a
      Pamphlet, call'd, The Advantages of the Act of Security,
      &c. To which is added, A Post-Script In Answer to The
      Letter concerning the Consequence of an Incorporating
      Union. *Printed in the Year* M.DCC.VI.

      4°. Pp. 3–35

      Notes: An old manuscript note on the title-page of the NLS
      copy reads: "By De Foe." Defoe praises this tract highly, by
      title, on p. 8 of *A Fifth Essay, At Removing National Prejudices*
      (1707).

      Copy: BM. *Other copies:* NLS, UL; C, COR, F, H, IU, N,
      NYPL, Y

135   A LETTER CONCERNING TRADE, From several Scots-Gentle-
      men that are Merchants in England, To their Country-
      Men that are Merchants in Scotland. [1706]

      4°. Pp. [1]–15

      Notes: No place, no date, but certainly Edinburgh 1706. An old
      manuscript note on the first page of the NLS copy dates this
      "Tuesday, Dec. 24, 1706." Defoe cites this tract on p. 26 of *A
      Fifth Essay, At Removing National Prejudices* (1707). On 9
      January 1706/7 the English reprint was advertised in *The
      Flying-Post:* "To morrow will be publish'd, A Letter concerning
      the Union, with relation to Trade, from several Scots Gentle-
      men, Merchants in England, to their Country-Men that are
      Merchants in Scotland. Sold by B. Bragg at the Raven in Pater-
      Noster-Row. Price Two Pence." NLS has a copy of this reprint.

      Copy: NLS. *Another copy:* UL

136   AN ENQUIRY INTO THE DISPOSAL OF THE EQUIVALENT. [1706]

      4°. Pp. 1–8

      Notes: No title-page, but apparently Edinburgh 1706. An old
      manuscript note on the first page of the NLS copy says "By De
      foe." This tract is very characteristic of Defoe, and it makes in-

credible the attribution to him (in *CBEL*) of *A Letter to a Member of Parliament, anent the Application of the 309,885 Lib: 10 Shil: Ster. Equivalent* (1706). *An Enquiry* was published very late in December, as a reply to *A Letter to a Member of Parliament* (which is dated 20 December).

Copy: NLS. *Other copies:* UL; BPL, H, HEH, N, Y

1 7 0 7

137   A SCOTS POEM: Or a New-years Gift, From A Native Of The Universe, To His Fellow-Animals in Albania.

> Sero sapiunt Phryges,
> Expectata die, tandem venit.
> Ignoti nulla Cupido.
> Quos vult perdere, Jupiter dementat,
> Sua cuique placent.

EDINBURGH, *Printed Anno Dom.* M.D.CC.VII.

8°. Pp. [4 unnumbered] + 1–30

Copy: NLS

138   A FIFTH ESSAY, AT REMOVING NATIONAL PREJUDICES; With A Reply To Some Authors, Who have Printed their Objections against An Union with England. *Printed in the Year* M.DCC.VII.

4°. Pp. [6 unnumbered] + 1–35

Notes: NLS copy has an old manuscript note on the title-page: "Jan. 6. 1707." The tract is anonymous, but the authorship is made clear by the tone of the preface and by allusions in the tract itself. P. 2 has a personal reference to D. F. and to one of Defoe's earlier tracts; on p. 8 the author cites *The Advantages of Scotland By An Incorporate Union with England* (1706) and on p. 26 *A Letter Concerning Trade* (1706).

Copy: BM. *Other copies:* BOD, NLS, UL; BPL, H, HEH, IU, N, R, T, Y

139   TWO GREAT QUESTIONS CONSIDERED, I. What is the Obligation of Parliaments to the Addresses or Petitions of the

People, and what the Duty of the Addressers? II. Whether
the Obligation of the Covenant or other national Engage-
ments, is concern'd in the Treaty of Union? Being a Sixth
Essay At Removing National Prejudices Against the Union.
Printed in the Year M.DCC.VII.

4°. Pp. 3–31

Notes: No place, but obviously Edinburgh; anonymous, but the
authorship is clearly understood. An old manuscript note on
the title-page of the NLS copy reads: "By Daniel Defoe." Published in January. On 17 January Defoe apparently promised to
send Harley a copy by the next post (*Letters,* ed. Healey, p. 194).

Copy: BM. *Other copies:* BOD, NLS, UL; BPL, COR, H, IU, T

 140   THE DISSENTERS IN ENGLAND VINDICATED from some Reflections in a late Pamphlet, Entitled, Lawful Prejudices, &c.
[1707]

4°. Pp. 1–8

Notes: No title-page, but obviously Edinburgh 1707. Old manuscript note on first page of NLS copy: "Feb. oo oi oo De Foe."
On 18 March Defoe wrote to Harley that he had sent him a
copy "Long Since" (*Letters,* ed. Healey, p. 210).

Copy: BM. *Other copies:* NLS, UL; H, HEH, N, Y

141   PASSION AND PREJUDICE, The Support of one another, And
Both destructive to the Happiness of this Nation, In Church
and State; Being A Reply to the Vindicator of Mr. W[eb-
ste]r's Lawful Prejudices. These Six things the Lord hates
—Prov. 6. 16, 19. A False Witness that speaketh Lies, and
he that soweth Discord among Brethren. These are the
things that ye shall do, speak ye every Man the Truth to his
Neighbour. Execute the Judgment of Peace and Truth in
your Gates. And let none of you imagine evil in your hearts
against his Neighbour. Zach. 8. 16, 17. EDINBURGH, *Printed
in the Year,* M.DCC.VII.

4°. Pp. 3–16

Notes: This tract is anonymous, but it includes letters signed D. F. The whole tract is called "The Preface," although it ends with "Finis." It seems intended as a preface to *The Dissenters in England Vindicated* (1707), which follows it immediately in the same bound volume of tracts, separately stitched and separately paged (NLS 3/2849). A powerful tract, highly characteristic of Defoe. Certainly the reply to the Rev. James Webster which Defoe assured Harley on 18 March he had withdrawn after it had been printed (*Letters,* ed. Healey, p. 210). The NLS copy is probably unique.

Copy: NLS

142 PROPOSALS FOR PRINTING BY SUBSCRIPTION A compleat History Of The Union. *By the Author of the True-Born-Englishman.* [1707]

Fol. half-sheet

Notes: No place, no date, but apparently London 1707. The proposals are anonymous. On 29 March 1707 the *Review* (IV, 84) had advertised that the proposals *"will be published in a very few Days, and in the mean Time Subscriptions are taken in at* John Matthews, *Printer hereof."* The unique copy (UL) is dated in the handwriting of Narcissus Luttrell: "1. May. 1707." See *The Library* for September 1956 (Fifth Series, XI, 202–206).

Copy: UL

*143 THE FIFTEEN COMFORTS OF A SCOTCH-MAN. Written by Daniel D'Foe in Scotland. LONDON: *Printed in the Year,* MDCCVI.

8°. Pp. 2–8

Notes: Attributed to Defoe on the title-page, and from internal evidence probably his, although the title seems quite uncharacteristic of him and the tract itself is inferior in composition to any known to have been written by him. A hasty and bald restatement of the terms of the Union in exceedingly ragged verse. Ostensibly by a Scot, writing about February 1707, after the Union had been accepted by the Scottish Parliament and while the author was waiting hopefully for its ratification by the English Parliament. Clearly the work of an English observer who interprets the Union as favorable to the interests of Scotland.

Copy: BOD

144   A DISCOURSE UPON AN UNION OF THE TWO KINGDOMS Of England and Scotland. LONDON: *Printed for* A. BALDWIN, *near the Oxford-Arms in Warwick-Lane.* 1707.

8°. Pp. 5–47

Notes: The tract was written by Defoe after the Scottish Parliament passed the Act of Union, but apparently before it was ratified in London.

Copy: C. *Other copies:* BOD, NLS, UL; HEH, IU, N, Y

145   REMARKS UPON THE LORD HAVERSHAM'S SPEECH in the House of Peers, Feb. 15, 1707.

4°. Pp. 1–8

Notes: No title-page, but almost certainly Edinburgh 1707. In several places Defoe deliberately used Scotticisms (or else his printer mistook his spelling).

Copy: NLS. *Another copy:* UL

146   A SHORT VIEW OF THE PRESENT STATE OF THE PROTESTANT RELIGION In Britain, As It is now profest in the Episcopal Church in England, the Presbyterian Church in Scotland, and the Dissenters in Both. EDINBURGH, Printed in the Year, M.DCC.VII.

8°. Pp. 3–48

Notes: One NLS copy has an old manuscript note on the title-page: "By Dan. de Foe." On p. 18 Defoe refers explicitly to another of his tracts: "what I said in the sixth Essay . . ." On 18 March he wrote to Harley that he had sent him a copy "Enclosed by this post" (*Letters,* ed. Healey, p. 210). Lee dates the first edition (Edinburgh) in March, the second edition (London) in April.

The second edition has a new title-page and a new preface: *The Dissenters Vindicated: Or, A Short View Of The Present State Of The Protestant Religion in Britain, As It is now profess'd in the Episcopal Church in England, the Presbyterian Church in Scotland, and the Dissenters in Both. In Answer to some Reflections in Mr. Webster's Two Books Publish'd in Scotland.* London: Printed in the Year MDCCVII." 8°. Pp. [7 unnumbered] + 3–48. This is otherwise a literal reprint of the Edinburgh first edition, except for a few minor changes of spelling and punctuation, the omission of two paragraphs (pp. 44–45) in which Defoe had defended his private character, and the change from "Persons, whose ill treatment I complain of" (p. 47) to "Persons, who I complain of" (p. 46).

Copy: BM. *Other copies:* CU, NLS, UL; BPL, HEH, N, P, T, Y

147 THE TRUE-BORN BRITAIN. *Written by the Author of the True-Born Englishman.* LONDON: *Printed in the Year,* MDCCVII.

8°. Pp. 2–8

Notes: Attributed to Defoe on the title-page, and from internal evidence certainly his. In some respects apparently a companion poem to No. 143, but much more carefully written. It presents the point of view of an Englishman shortly after the ratification of the Union by the English Parliament.

Copy: BOD

148 A VOICE FROM THE SOUTH: Or, An Address from some Protestant Dissenters in England to the Kirk of Scotland. [1707]

4°. Pp. 1–8

Notes: No title-page, but Edinburgh 1707. Usually considered to be a reprinting of articles published in the *Review* on 10 and 15 May; but an old manuscript note on the first page of the NLS copy reads: "De foe. ap. 10. 1707." Apparently the tract was published in Edinburgh in April and reprinted one month later in two numbers of the *Review*. See *Letters* (ed. Healey), p. 214.

Copy: NLS. *Another copy:* BPL

149   A MODEST VINDICATION OF THE PRESENT MINISTRY: From the Reflections publish'd against them in a late Paper, Entitled, The Lord Haversham's Speech, &c. With a Review and Ballance of the Present War. Evincing, That We are not in such a Desperate Condition as that Paper insinuates. Humbly submitted to the Consideration of all, but especially the Right Ho[n]ourable and the Honourable, the North-British Lords and Commons. *By a Well-Wisher to the Peace of Britain.* LONDON: *Printed in the Year* MDCCVII.

4°. Pp. [1 unnumbered] + 1–14

Notes: Apparently written in great haste by Defoe in Edinburgh, printed in London, and proofread in Edinburgh (with an added preface). An answer to Lord Haversham's speech in the House of Lords on February 15, 1707. Refers to the completion of the Union and to the controversy over the importation of French wines into Scotland before the Union became effective. Probably published in the early summer of 1707 as an authorized defence of the Ministry. The preface on the verso of the title-leaf concludes: *"I foresee one Objection that may possibly be made to this Discourse: 'Tis like the Enemies of the* Ministry *may impute it to some Emissary of theirs. To which I shall only Answer, That the thing is owing meerly to my own Inclination, and the due sense I have of the great Obligations we are under, to those noble Persons in whose Hands the Administration is so happily and prosperously lodged."*

Copy: BOD. *Other copies:* UL; BPL, HEH

150   THE TRADE OF BRITAIN STATED; Being The Substance of two Papers published in London On Occasion of the Importation of Wine and Brandy from North-Britain. [1707]

4°. Pp. 1–8

Notes: No place, no date, but Edinburgh 1707. Reprinted from the *Review* for 10 and 12 June 1707 (IV, 205–212).

Copy: BM

151 AN HISTORICAL ACCOUNT OF THE BITTER SUFFERINGS, and Melancholly Circumstances of the Episcopal Church in Scotland, Under the Barbarous Usage and Bloody Persecution of the Presbyterian Government. With an Essay on The Nature and Necessity of a Toleration to the North of Britain. EDINBURGH, *Printed in the Year, M.DCC.VII.*

8°. Pp. 3–40

Notes: See No. 152.

Copy: BM. *Other copies:* BOD, DW, NLS, UL; BPL, F, H, Y

152 PRESBYTERIAN PERSECUTION EXAMINED. With An Essay On The Nature and Necessity of Toleration in Scotland. EDINBURGH, *Printed in the Year,* M.DCC.VII.

8°. Pp. 3–40

Notes: Identical with the preceding tract except for the difference in the title-page and in one head-title. If No. 151 is the earlier issue, probably its ironical title was replaced to avoid the misunderstanding which so often resulted from Defoe's use of irony. HEH reports that there is no indication that the title-leaf of No. 152 is a cancel. Dr. William Beattie, Librarian of NLS, reports: "There is no trace of a cancel in the title-leaf of either of the two tracts in question. It is quite clear from typographical blemishes, etc., that the same setting was used for both, with alterations to the title-page and to the head-title as given on the top of p 3 (Sig A2). The ornament and imprint at the foot of the title-page are the same in both. Your view that *Presbyterian Persecution Examined* appeared slightly later within the year 1707 may possibly be deemed to derive some slight support from the fact that the word 'December' has been written below the date of printing on the title-page of that tract in what looks like a contemporary hand."

This tract is quoted approvingly in No. 368 (pp. 315–316, for 411–412). As early as 1705, in an advertisement at the end of the Edinburgh reprint of *A New Test of the Church of England's Honesty,* Defoe had announced that he had a manuscript ready to reply to the High Church charge of persecution.

Copy: NLS. *Other copies:* UL; F, HEH, R

153   DE FOE'S ANSWER TO DYER'S SCANDALOUS NEWS LETTER. [1707]

4°. Pp. 1–3

Notes: No title-page, no place, no date, but Edinburgh 1707. Lee dates this in August 1707.

Copy: NLS. *Other copies:* BPL, T

154   DYERS NEWS EXAMINED as to His Sweddish Memorial against the Review. [1707]

4°. Pp. 1–4

Notes: No title-page, no place, no date, but Edinburgh 1707. Anonymous, but obviously meant to be understood as Defoe's own defence of his *Review*. Dottin dates this in September 1707.

Copy: BM. *Other copies:* BPL, IU

1 7 0 8

155   REFLECTIONS ON THE PROHIBITION ACT, Wherein The Necessity, Usefulness and Value of that Law, are Evinced and Demonstrated. In Answer to a Letter on that Subject, From a Gentleman concern'd in Trade. LONDON, *Printed in the Year,* MDCCVIII.

8°. Pp. 3–22

Notes: Ostensibly a letter dated "London, Jan. 10, 1707/8."

Copy: BM. *Other copies:* BOD, CU, UL; BPL, C, F, H, HEH, IU, Y

156   ADVICE TO THE ELECTORS OF GREAT BRITAIN; occasioned by the intended Invasion from France. 1708.

4°. Pp. 1–4

Notes: No title-page. The colophon reads: "Printed in the Year 1708." Published by J. Morphew in London 19 April, and apparently reprinted in Edinburgh not long afterward. The BM copy of the Edinburgh edition (4°, 1708) has part of the title-page and part of the imprint torn away, but it names the publisher: "Heirs & Successors of Andrew Anderson: Edinburgh, [1708]." One of the NLS copies has an old manuscript note below the colophon: "By D. De foe May 11. 1708."

Copy: NLS. *Other copies:* BOD, CU; BPL, C, F, H, HEH, N, Y

157 A MEMORIAL TO THE NOBILITY OF SCOTLAND, Who are to Assemble in order to Choose the Sitting Peers for the Parliament of Great Britain. EDINBURGH, *Printed by the Heirs and Successors of* ANDREW ANDERSON, *Printer to the Queens most Excellent Majesty, Anno Dom,* 1708.

4°. Pp. 3–16

Copy: C

158 SCOTLAND IN DANGER, Or, A Serious Enquiry into the Dangers which Scotland has been in, is now in, or may be in since the Union; With some Humble Proposals for the Remedy. [1708]

4°. Pp. 1–8

Notes: No title-page. The colophon reads: "Edinburgh, Printed by the Heirs and Successors of Andrew Anderson, Printer to the Queens Most Excellent Majesty."

Copy: NLS. *Other copies:* UL; N

159 AN ANSWER TO A PAPER CONCERNING MR. DE FOE, against his History of the Union. 1708.

4°. Pp. 1–8

Notes: No title-page. The colophon reads: "Edinburgh, Printed by the Heirs and Successors of Andrew Anderson, Printer to the Queens most Excellent Majesty, 1708."

Copy: NLS. *Other copies:* BOD, UL; HEH, R, Y

1 7 0 9

160 THE SCOT'S NARRATIVE EXAMIN'D; Or, The Case Of The
Episcopal Ministers in Scotland Stated, And the late Treatment of them In The City of Edinburgh Enquir'd Into:
With a Brief Examination, into the Reasonableness of the
Grievous Complaint of Persecution in Scotland, and a Defence of the Magistrates of Edinburgh, in their Proceedings
there: Being some Remarks on a late Pamphlet, Entitled,
A Narrative, of the late Treatment of the Episcopal Ministers within the City of Edinburgh, &c. LONDON: *Printed
in the Year,* 1709.

4°. Pp. i–[x] +1–41

Notes: Lee dates this 19 February.

Copy: BM. *Other copies:* BOD, NLS, UL; BPL, F, HEH, IU, R,
RPB, Y

161 THE HISTORY OF THE UNION Of Great Britain. EDINBURGH,
Printed by the Heirs and Successors of ANDREW ANDERSON,
Printer to the Queen's most Excellent Majesty, Anno Dom.
1709.

Fol. No two copies seem to be exactly alike, but the pagination
of one typical copy (BM) is as follows: Pp. [i–x] Dedication to
the Queen (signed DANIEL DEFOE) + [i–iv] Dedication to the
Duke of Queensberry (signed D. DE FOE) + i–xxxii The Preface (signed D. F.) + 1–31 A General History of Unions in Britain + 32–60 Of Affairs In Both Kingdoms + 1–116 Of the Last
Treaty + 1–76 Of The Carrying on of the Treaty in Scotland
+ 1–273 An Abstract Of the Proceedings + [i] Errata + 1–38
Appendix Part I + 1–131 Appendix Part II.

Notes: The sheets seem to have been printed at intervals for
nearly two years, so that as early as 1708 there was some public
controversy regarding certain statements in the text. Most of
the sections were separately printed, and in the copies I have
seen the Dedication to the Duke of Queensberry appears in
three different places. In one copy the Dedication to the Queen
is omitted. Dottin describes a copy with a portrait; I recall no

copy with this feature except that in the Huntington Library—
a tipped-in variant of the *Jure Divino* portrait, with "Probitas
Laudatur et Alget" inscribed in the panel at the base around
the coat of arms, and with the original inscription in the panel
at the base changed from "Laudatur et Alget/ Juven. Sat. I." to
"M^r. Daniel De Foe/ Author of the True Born Englishman."

In 1712, when there was some fear that the conditions of the
Union might be violated by the British Parliament, sheets of
The History of the Union were reissued in London as a re-
minder of the terms on which the Union had been accepted by
Scotland. This London reissue was advertised 26 April 1712 in
the *Review* (VIII, 688): "The History of the Union in Folio
Dedicated to Her Majesty, Printed in Edinburgh, and never yet
Publish'd in London; written by the Author of the Review, and
sold only by John Baker, at the Black-Boy in Pater-Noster-Row,
and by J. Matthews, Printer in Little-Britain, and at no other
place." The Dedication to the Queen, although mentioned in
the advertisement, was not included in the London reissue, the
title-page of which read: "*A Collection of Original Papers And
Material Transactions, Concerning the late Great Affair Of The
Union Between England and Scotland. Also An Exact Journal
Of The Proceedings Of The Treaty As well at London as in
Edinburgh. Wherein the Privileges of the Presbyterian Kirk,
and the Case of the Toleration of Episcopal Dissenters there,
are very clearly stated. In Five Parts.* Faithfully Collected from
the Records and Registers; by a Person Concern'd in the said
Treaty, and present in both Kingdoms at the Time of its Trans-
acting. London: Printed for J. Knapton at the Crown in St.
Paul's Church-Yard; N. Cliff, at the Bible and Three Crowns
near Mercers Chapell; and J. Baker, at the Black-Boy in Pater-
Noster-Row. MDCCXII."

NYPL has a variant reissue of the Edinburgh edition which
is unexplained as yet. It has two title-pages, the first that of
Edinburgh in 1709, the second identical with that of Baker and
Matthews in 1712 except for the concluding lines: "London:
Printed for E. Curll, at the Dial and Bible against St. Dunstan's
Church; and R. Gosling at the Mitre . . . 1711." I have had
no opportunity to examine this copy since it was reported by
the NYPL staff. Curll was an unscrupulous publisher, and the
statement that the book was printed for him is obviously false;
but it is not clear why he would have been interested in so huge

a book which had not sold out its first Edinburgh edition of two years earlier. Presumably he secured unsold sheets from Edinburgh, retained the Edinburgh title-page as a proof that he was offering the original history, and predated his reissue 1711 (instead of 1712) as a deliberate falsification to establish it as the original London reissue. Defoe did not know of any previous London publication when he advertised (26 April 1712) that the book had never yet been published in London; but possibly his fear of a rival and unauthorized publication explained his insistence that his London issue was "sold only by John Baker, at the Black-Boy in Pater-Noster-Row, and by J. Matthews, Printer in Little-Britain, and at no other place."

Copy: BM. *Other copies:* BOD, NLS, UL; BPL, C, COR, F, H, HEH, IU, N, P, R, T, Y. *Copies of the authorized London reissue of 1712:* HEH, Y (Law Library). *Copy of London reissue with Curll's imprint and the date 1711:* NYPL

162   A COMMENDATORY SERMON PREACH'D NOVEMBER THE 4TH, 1709. Being the Birth-Day of King William, Of Glorious Memory. By Daniel de Foe. LONDON: *Printed by* J. DUTTON, *near Fleet-street.* [1709]

8°. Pp. 2–8

Notes: Reprinted from the *Review* of 5 November 1709 except for the insertion of a text from Samuel and the omission of one quotation from *The Mock Mourners* and one paragraph of the *Review's* text.

Copy: BM

163   PARSON PLAXTON OF BARWICK. [1709]

Notes: This verse lampoon is known only by a four-page MS transcript entitled *Defoes Satyr/ Par[so]n Pl[ax]ton of Barwick in ye County of York turnd inside out.* The text of this transcript (HEH, HM 20340) has been published by Spiro Peterson in *The Huntington Library Quarterly*, XIX (1955), 71–73. See also Defoe's very similar attack on Plaxton in No. 207 (pp. 35–36).

164   A LETTER TO MR. BISSET, Eldest Brother of the Collegiate Church of St. Catherines; In Answer to his Remarks On

Dr. Sacheverell's Sermon. LONDON; *Printed for* J. BAKER, *at the Black-Boy in Pater-Noster-Row.* MDCCIX. (*Price 1d.*)

8°. Pp. 3–15

Notes: Signed *"Your most gentle Reprover, AMICUS."* Advertised in *The Post-Boy* 22 December 1709 as "published this day." The manuscript must have been sent from Edinburgh, as Defoe did not return to London until late in January 1710. On 8 July 1710 John Moncur was offering an edition in Edinburgh. BM has also a copy of a Dublin edition for P. Campbell (1710).

Copy: BM. *Other copies:* BOD, NLS; F

1710

165 A LETTER FROM CAPTAIN TOM TO THE MOBB, Now Rais'd for Dr. Sacheverel. [1710]

8°. Pp. 1–8

Notes: No title-page. The colophon reads: "London, Printed for J. Baker at the Black Boy in Pater-noster-Row, 1710." Lee dates this 11 March.

Copy: BM. *Other copies:* BOD, CU, UL; BPL, C, H, HEH, I, IU, P, T, Y

166 A REPROOF TO MR. CLARK, And a brief Vindication of Mr. De Foe. [1710]

4°. Pp. 1–8

Notes: No title-page. The colophon reads: "Edinburgh, Printed and sold by John Moncur at the foot of the Bull-Closs forgainst the Trone. Anno 1710." Like some other tracts which Defoe published in Edinburgh, this has several Scotticisms. The tract states that Defoe is out of the kingdom, which dates it before November 1710.

Copy: BM. *Other copies:* NLS; BPL, R, T

167 ADVERTISEMENT FROM DANIEL DE FOE, To Mr. Clark. [1710?]

4°. Pp. [i]–4

Notes: Signed D. F. No title-page, but Edinburgh and probably 1710. Later than *A Reproof to Mr. Clark,* to which it refers as the work of an unknown hand. The tract says that the author is not now in Scotland, and this dates it before November 1710.

Copy: NLS. *Other copies:* BPL, HEH

168 A SPEECH WITHOUT DOORS.

> Sibi id Negotî creditit solum dari,
> Populo ut placerent quos fecisset Fabulas.
> > Terent.

LONDON, *Printed for* A. BALDWIN *near the Oxford-Arms in Warwick-Lane.* M.DCC.X. *Price Two Pence.*

8°. Pp. 3–20

Notes: Advertisement on verso of title-leaf. Lee dates the tract 19 April.

Copy: BM. *Other copies:* BOD, CU, DW, NLS, UL; BPL, C, CH, COR, F, H, HEH, I, IU, N, NYPL, P, R, RPB, T, Y

169 THE AGE OF WONDERS: To the Tune of Chivy Chase. 1710.

Fol. half-sheet

Notes: The colophon reads: "Printed in the Year M.DCC.X." The poem attacks the Sacheverellites, and it begins "The Year of Wonders is arriv'd." Reprinted in Edinburgh in 1710 by John Reid Junior.

Copy: BM. *Other copies:* BOD, NLS; IU

170 GREENSHIELDS OUT OF PRISON And Toleration settled in Scotland, Or The Case Of Mr. Greenshields, Farther Examin'd. With Some Enquiry into the Mistakes about that Affair, which have so much impos'd upon the Present Age. LONDON: *Printed for* N. CLIFF, *at the Golden Candlestick in Cheapside near Mercers Chapel.* MDCCX.

Fol. Pp. 3–20

Notes: Published 24 April 1710.

Copy: BPL. *Another copy:* H

171   A VINDICATION OF DR. HENRY SACHEVERELL; *By D. D'F.
      Esq; Or, Otherwise, &c.* [1710]

8°. Pp. 1–8

Copy: Y. TCD has a copy omitting "By D. D'F. Esq;"

172   INSTRUCTIONS FROM ROME, In Favour of the Pretender, In-
      scrib'd to the most Elevated Don Sacheverellio, and his
      Brother Don Higginisco. And which All Perkinites, Non
      Jurors, High-flyers, Popish Desirers, Wooden Shoe Ad-
      mirers, and absolute Non Resistance Drivers, are obliged
      to pursue and maintain (under pain of his Unholinesses
      Damnation) in order to carry on their intended Subversion
      of a Government, fix'd upon Revolution Principles. LON-
      DON, *Printed and Sold by* J. BAKER, *at the Black Boy in
      Pater Noster Row. Price Two Pence.* [1710]

8°. Pp. 1–16

Notes: Entered at Stationers' Hall 10 May. One BM copy has
an old MS note on the title-page: "11. May. 1710."

Copy: BM. *Other copies:* NLS; BPL, C, IU, R, T, Y

173   THE BANBURY CONVERT: Or, Daniel De Foe's Address to
      Her Majesty. 1710.

Fol. half-sheet

Notes: Reprinted with slight changes from the *Review* of 16
May 1710 (VII, 81–84). The colophon reads: "Printed for J.
Baker, at the Black Boy in Pater-Noster-Row, 1710."

Copy: NLI. *Other copies:* R, Y

174   THE RECORDER OF B[ANBU]RY'S SPEECH To Dr. Sach[eve]r-
      ell. 1710.

Fol. half-sheet

Notes: Colophon reads: "London: Printed in the Year 1710."
Advertised by A. Baldwin in *The Post-Man* for 1–4 July, 1710.

Copy: FFM

175 THE BAN[BUR]Y APES: Or, The Monkeys Chattering to the Magpye. In a Letter to a Friend in London. Nunc aut Nuncquam. LONDON, *Printed, and are to be Sold by* R. MAWSON *at the Bible and Star in Ave-Mary-Lane.* [Entered in the Hall-Book.] *Price 1d.* [1710]

4°. Pp. 3–8. The chain lines are vertical, but the pages are quarto in shape.

Notes: The only copy of the first edition which I have examined (IU) is defective at the foot of the title-leaf. Its readings have been supplemented from a photostat of the BOD copy. On 8 July the tract was entered at Stationers' Hall by Thomas Darrack. Later in the same month most of its material reappeared as part of *A New Map.*

Copy: IU. *Other copies:* BOD, DW, NLS

176 A COLLECTION OF THE SEVERAL ADDRESSES in the late King James's Time: Concerning the Conception and Birth of the pretended Prince of Wales. [1710]

Fol. Pp. 1–16

Notes: No title-page. Announced by Defoe in the *Review* for 4 July 1710 (VII, 166–167) as "a Book I purpose to give you a view of in a few Days," a counterblast to a volume of Sacheverellite addresses to the Queen advertised in *The Post-Boy.* No. 176 was answered by No. 177, a tract based on modified quotations from Defoe himself. No. 188 reprints (pp. 18–48) fifteen of these addresses to James II and parallels them with fifteen almost identical addresses to Queen Anne.

Copy: IU. *Other copies:* BOD; HEH, Y

177 THE MODERN ADDRESSES VINDICATED, And the Rights of the Addressers, asserted, *By D. De Foe.* Extracted out of his Book, Intituled, The Original Right of the People of England Examined and Asserted. 1710.

8°. Pp. 1–8

Notes: No title-page. The colophon reads: "London: Printed for J. Morphew near Stationers-Hall, 1710. Price 1d." Condensed and excerpted from *The Original Power of the Collective Body of the People of England, Examined and Asserted* (an early tract of Defoe's, better known by its subtitle *The Original Right, etc.*) which had appeared in 1701 (dated 1702) as a defence of the Whig addresses to King William. The High Church party altered these excerpts and adapted them to the reign of Queen Anne, thereby making Defoe appear to favor the Sacheverellites.

Copy: BPL. *Other copies:* BOD; C

178 [A HISTORY OF THE MOB] [1710]

See notes for *A Hymn to the Mob,* No. 324.

179 [A HYMN TO THE RABBLE] [1710]

See notes for *A Hymn to the Mob,* No. 324.

180 DR. SACHEVERELL'S DISAPPOINTMENT AT WORCESTER. Being A True Account of his cold Reception there. In *A Letter From A Gentleman in that City to his Friend in London.* LONDON *Printed, and Sold by* J. BAKER, *at the Black-Boy in Pater-Noster-Row,* 1710.

8°. Pp. 3–7

Notes: Reprinted *in toto* in *A New Map* (1710). A jesting abridgment of a genuine communication dated 15 July which was advertised in *The Post-Man* (25 July): *The Worcester Triumph: Or a True Account of Dr. Sacheverell's Entrance and Reception in that City, on Friday, July the 14th, 1710. Being part of a Letter from a Gentleman in Worcester to a Friend in London.*

Copy: FFM

181 A NEW MAP OF THE LABORIOUS AND PAINFUL TRAVELS Of our Blessed High Church Apostle. Giving a True Account of the many Strange, Miraculous Cures and Wonders that he has perform'd both on Dumb and Blind Persons throughout the Countreys wheresoever he went. Set forth to Illustrate his mighty Cavalcading. With the extraordinary Offer made to the High Church Priest by his most Christian

Majesty the French King, That his Noble Statues should be set up in all Market-places, and Venerable Picture in all Parish Churches in Albion, if he would but undertake to muster great Numbers of Foot and Horse in his Progress, and perswade 'em to enter into the Pretender's Pay, in order to restore the Chevalier de St. George. Also the many fruitless Attempts and Miscarriages of the Paganites and Lewissites, set forth from Time to Time, how they would have impos'd the Tiler's son upon the Albionites. And lastly, how this cunning stratagem was hatch'd and contriv'd betwixt the Perkinites and the Sacheverellites, to restore the said Chevalier de St. George, and how providentially it was happily discover'd. Entered in the Hall Book, according to Order. Printed in the Year, MDCCX.

8°. Pp. 2–16

Notes: Published in late July, this tract incorporates material from *The Banbury Apes* and from *Dr. Sacheverell's Disappointment at Worcester,* and it is closely analogous to passages in the *Review* for 13 and 27 July 1710 (VII, 184 and 206).

Copy: NLS. *Other copies:* CL; HEH, IU

*182   HIGH-CHURCH MIRACLES, Or, Modern Inconsistencies. 1710.

Fol. half-sheet

Notes: The colophon reads: "London, Printed and Sold by A. Baldwin, at the Oxford Arms in Warwick-Lane, 1710." The tract is in ragged heroic verse, with footnote explanations. Very probably, not certainly, Defoe's.

Copy: BOD

183   A SHORT HISTORICAL ACCOUNT Of the Contrivances and Conspiracies of the Men of Dr. Sacheverell's Principles, in the late Reigns. [1710]

8°. Pp. 1–8

Notes: No title-page. The colophon reads: "London, Printed and are to be sold by A. Baldwin in Warwick-Lane. 1710."

Copy: UL. *Other copies:* NLS; IU, R

184 FOUR LETTERS TO A FRIEND IN NORTH BRITAIN, Upon the Publishing The Tryal of Dr. Sacheverell.

This is not a Controversy of Reason against Reason, but of downright Impudence against all the Sense and Reason of Mankind.

Archbishop *Tillotson.*

Protect us mighty Providence,
    What wou'd these Madmen have?
First they wou'd bribe us without Pence,
Deceive us without common Sense,
    And without Power enslave.

Earl of *Dorset.*

LONDON, *Printed in the Year* M.DCC.X.

8°. Pp. 3–35. In some copies the last page is numbered 34.

Notes: Another BM edition (pressmark 4106.b.84) has pp. 1–27 in 4° (in double columns, whereas this is in single column). Claimed for Arthur Maynwaring (by John Oldmixon) and for Robert Walpole (by Horace Walpole). Possibly it passed through the hands of Maynwaring when he was supervising much of the Whig pamphleteering; but it is vastly superior to anything known as his, and internal evidence establishes it as Defoe's. The stanza quoted from "The Young Statesman" by the Earl of Dorset was a favorite of Defoe's. The main part of the tract concludes with the date "July 5. 1710." The two-page postscript is dated "July 23."

Copy: BM (pressmark E.1990.10). *Other copies:* BOD, NLS; HEH, IU

185 SELDOM COMES A BETTER: Or, A Tale Of A Lady And Her Servants. Qui capit ille facit. LONDON, *Printed in the Year* M.DCC.X. *Price Two Pence.*

8°. Pp. 3–16

Notes: Advertised on 7 August 1710 as sold by B. Bragge; but Benjamin Bragg had died in July, and Sarah Popping had taken over his *Observator.*

Copy: BOD. *Other copies:* BM, BOD, CU; BPL, C, F, HEH, IU

186   A LETTER FROM A DISSENTER IN THE CITY To A Dissenter
      In The Country: Advising him to a Quiet and Peaceable
      Behaviour in this present Conjuncture. LONDON: *Printed
      for* A. BALDWIN, *in Warwick-lane.* MDCCX. *Price 2d.*

      8°. Pp. 3–16

      Notes: Internal evidence dates this after the fall of Godolphin's
      Ministry (8 August 1710).

      Copy: IU. *Other copies:* N, T

187   AN ESSAY UPON PUBLICK CREDIT: Being An Enquiry How
      the Publick Credit comes to depend upon the Change of the
      Ministry, or the Dissolutions of Parliaments; and whether
      it does so or no. With an Argument, Proving that the Pub-
      lick Credit may be upheld and maintain'd in this Nation;
      and perhaps brought to a greater Height than it ever yet
      arriv'd at; Tho' all the Changes or Dissolutions already
      Made, Pretended to, or now Discours'd of, shou'd come to
      pass in the World. LONDON: *Printed, and Sold by the Book-
      sellers,* MDCCX. *Price, Three Pence.*

      8°. Pp. 5–28

      Notes: Published 23 August by J. Morphew, the tract soon
      reached a third edition. It has often been attributed (without
      the slightest probability) to Robert Harley. On 5 September
      1710 Defoe wrote to Harley: ". . . The Town does me too
      much Honour, in Supposeing it well Enough done to be your
      Own. I mean the Essay Upon Credit." (*Letters,* ed. Healey, pp.
      276–277.)

      Copy: BM. *Other copies:* BOD, NLS, UL; BPL, COR, F, H,
      HEH, IU, NYPL, P, R, Y

188   A NEW TEST OF THE SENCE OF THE NATION: Being a Mod-
      est Comparison Between The Addresses To The Late King
      James, And Those to Her Present Majesty. In Order to
      Observe, How far The Sence of the Nation may be judg'd
      of by either of them. LONDON, *Printed in the Year* 1710.

8°. Pp. 1–91

Notes: An old manuscript note on the title-page of the BM copy dates this "3 August 1710." The tract includes (p. 65) an address to the Queen from Shrewsbury on August 3, but it includes one from the clergy of London (pp. 57–58) dated August 26. Publication can hardly be dated earlier than September 1. The fifteen addresses to King James are identical with fifteen of the forty-two included in No. 176, although arranged in a different order. Six of the addresses to Queen Anne are repeated in condensed form in No. 212 (pp. 7–9).

Copy: BM. *Other copies:* BOD, NLS, UL; BPL, C, H, HEH, I, IU, N, NYPL, Y

189 A LETTER FROM A GENTLEMAN AT THE COURT OF ST. GER-MAINS, To One of his Friends in England; Containing A Memorial about Methods for setting the Pretender on the Throne of Great Britain. Found at Doway, after the Taking of that Town. *Translated from the French Copy, Printed at Cologne by Peter Marteau.* LONDON, *Printed in the Year* 1710.

8°. Pp. 5–8 + 9–47

Notes: There are numerous variants, besides ostensible later editions; the above seems to be probably the first issue of the first edition. Advertised 5 September as "Sold by the Booksellers of London and Westminster." By 16 September it was being advertised by J. Baker, whose name also appeared on the second edition. John Oldmixon was inclined to claim it (with many other tracts) for Arthur Maynwaring. After Defoe's death it was claimed by Pierre Des Maizeaux in applying to Walpole for a pension. But the tract (which Defoe cited very frequently as "the Doway Letter") was one of Defoe's own favorites. Possibly Des Maizeaux made the French translation for circulation on the Continent, which might be supposed by some readers to be the original. The tract itself was one of Defoe's best and most characteristic writings, and it could have been written only by one who was intimately acquainted with English affairs.

Copy: BM. *Other copies:* CU, NLS; BPL, C, COR, HEH, IU, N

190   A CONDOLING LETTER TO THE TATTLER: On Account of the Misfortunes of Isaac Bickerstaff, Esq; A Prisoner in the [Gatehouse] On Suspicion of Debt. LONDON: *Printed and Sold by* S. POPPING, *at the Black Raven, in Pater-noster-Row.* [1710]

8°. Pp. 3–16

Notes: No place, no date, but London 1710. Signed Censor Censorum. Published sometime between 5 and 26 September. Defoe's first attack on Steele, it may have been prompted in part by the notoriety of Steele's lack of financial integrity, but more directly by Steele's refusal to support the coalition Ministry which Harley still hoped to form after the overthrow of Godolphin on 8 August.

Copy: BM. *Another copy:* BOD

191   QUERIES TO THE NEW HEREDITARY RIGHT-MEN. *Printed and Sold by the Booksellers of London and Westminster.* 1710. *Price Two Pence.*

8°. Pp. 3–15

Notes: This quotes with high approval (pp. 13–14) a recent tract by Defoe: *A Letter From A Gentleman At The Court Of St. Germains* (No. 189). Advertised by S. Popping in *The Flying-Post* on 7 October 1710 as "published this day."

Copy: BM. *Other copies:* BOD, CU, NLS; BPL, C, F, IU, N, T

192   AN ESSAY UPON LOANS: Or, An Argument Proving That Substantial Funds settled by Parliament, with the Encouragement of Interests, and the Advances of Prompt Payment usually allow'd, will bring in Loans of Money to the Exchequer, in spight of all the Conspiracies of Parties to the Contrary; while a Just, Honourable, and Punctual Performance on the Part of the Government supports the Credit of the Nation. *By the Author of the Essay upon Credit.* LONDON: *Printed, and Sold by the Book-sellers,* MDCCX.

8°. Pp. 3–27

Notes: Advertised by J. Morphew. Lee dates the London publication 21 October; but the tract probably appeared some days earlier, for it was being offered for sale in Edinburgh by Mrs. McKay on 24 October. On 5 September 1710 Defoe had proposed writing such a tract (*Letters,* ed. Healey, p. 277).

Copy: BM. *Other copies:* BOD, NLS, UL; BPL, HEH, I, IU, N, NYPL, P, R, Y

193   A WORD AGAINST A NEW ELECTION. That The People of England May See the Happy Difference between English Liberty And French Slavery; And May Consider Well, before they make the Exchange. *Printed in the Year* 1710.

8⁰. Pp. 3–23

Notes: Published in London in October. Mrs. McKay was offering the tract for sale in Edinburgh by 31 October. HEH has two copies, identical except that in one the second line of the title-page has been reset to read "About A" for "Against A."

Copy: BM. *Other copies:* DW, NLS; BPL, H, HEH, Y

194   A SUPPLEMENT TO THE FAULTS ON BOTH SIDES: Containing the Compleat History Of The Proceedings of a Party ever since the Revolution: In a Familiar Dialogue between Steddy and Turn-Round, Two Displac'd Officers of State. Which may serve to Explain Sir Thomas Double: And to show How far the Late Parliament were Right in Proceeding against Dr. Sacheverell, by way of Impeachment. LONDON: *Printed for* J. BAKER, *at the Black-Boy in Pater-Noster-Row,* 1710. (*Price 1s.*)

8⁰. Pp. [2 unnumbered] + 3–76

Notes: Published 21 October 1710. There are five known editions, which seem to have been hastily printed on several different presses. The norm for this tract is perhaps the IU Copy 2 and the JRM copy, perhaps also the BM copy with the pressmark E. 1988. (5.), although this could be established only by a minute examination of the third with the two others. BM has two other variants: 101.c.55, in which pp. 49–76 are misnumbered 41–68; and E. 2190 (I *.), in which sig. D is of a different setting of type.

In the IU Copy 1 sig. A is somewhat different from what appears to be the norm in spelling, capitalization, punctuation, and syllabification. In almost every one of these details this signature resembles the corresponding section of a fifth variant, the BPL 4° with pp. [1 unnumbered] + 3–32 which has a different and less complete title-page: *"Faults on Both Sides: The Second Part: Containing the Compleat History of Proceedings Ever-since the Revolution: In a Familiar Dialogue between Steddy and Turn-Round, two displac'd Officers of State. Which may serve to Explain Sir Thomas Double;* London: Printed for J. Baker; at the Black-Boy in Pater-noster-Row, 1710. (Price 1s.)." I know of only two other copies of the fifth variant (F and Y), which appears to have been a very hasty reprint.

Both before and after publication the tract was advertised with the more usual title (although in the first advertisement Steddy was called Steady and Turn-Round was called Turn-coat). On 21 October 1710 it was announced in *The Daily Courant:* "This Day is Publish'd, A Supplement to the Faults on both Sides; containing the Compleat History of the Proceedings of a Party ever since the Revolution: In a familiar Dialogue between Steady and Turn-coat, two Displaced Officers of State, which will serve to explain Sir Tho. Double, and to shew how far the last Parliament were right in Proceeding against Dr. Sacheverell by way of Impeachment. Pr. 1s. Sold by J. Baker in Pater-Noster-Row." On 14 May 1711 the same publisher advertised the tract in the unnumbered pages attached to Defoe's *Eleven Opinions About Mr. H[arle]y.*

The tract contains significant references to Defoe's sufferings for writing *The True-Born Englishman* (p. 31) and *The Shortest Way with the Dissenters* (p. 37) and an approving citation (p. 62) from his recent *Letter From A Gentleman At The Court Of St. Germains.* On p. 4 there is a characteristic bantering allusion to his own recent *Essay upon Loans:* "We shall bring our Two Gentlemen to speak directly to Things, without spending Eleven or Twelve Pages about Introductions to Discourse, and saying something or other, which signifies nothing, of their Grand-Fathers, their Great Estates, &c."

Copy: IU (Copy 2). *Other copies:* BM, BOD, DW, NLS; BPL, C, COR, F, H, HEH, I, IU (Copy 1), JRM, N, P, Y

195   THE BRITISH VISIONS. [1710, 1711]

Notes: Of the original Newcastle tract the printer Joseph Button sent 400 copies to Defoe in Edinburgh sometime before 23
December 1710 (*Letters,* ed. Healey, p. 304). In the *Review* for
21 April 1711 Defoe puffed this as a little book he had seen
at Newcastle. In the *Review* for 26 April he wrote: "I saw it in
Manuscript in *November* last, and in Print in Newcastle some
short Time after; . . ."

It has sometimes been supposed that the BM copy (conjec-
turally dated 1711) represents the Newcastle first edition. According to the BM *Catalogue* this is in 12mo, according to Teerink
(1028) and the Rothschild *Catalogue* (751) it is in 16mo. The
Rothschild *Catalogue* quotes Freeman as authority for saying
that it was written by Defoe at Newcastle on his way back to
London in 1711. We do not know where it was written; Defoe
stated that he saw the manuscript in November 1710; and Defoe
was in Edinburgh in December 1710 when Button sent him 400
printed copies.

HEH has a copy (differing only slightly from that of UL)
which may represent the first London edition: *"The British
Visions: Or, Isaac Bickerstaff, Sen. Being Twelve Prophesies for
The Year 1711.* Enter'd into the Hall-Book of the Company of
Stationers. Printed in the North, and Reprinted at London,
and Sold by J. Baker at the Black-Boy in Pater-Noster-Row,
1711. (Price 2d.)" This is in 8º, with pp. [3] + 4–16. On 24
April 1711 Baker advertised the tract in the *Review* as having
been published "yesterday." On 26 April Baker was advertising
in *The Post-Boy* against pirated copies: "The British Visions,
or, Isaac Bickerstaff's 12 Prophecies for the Year 1711. Printed
above 6 months past, and now reprinted and sold by J. Baker
in Pater-Noster-Row, Price 2d. This is the Prophecy mention'd
in Saturday's Review. N. B. The Genuine Copy is to be had
only of J. Baker, all others must be Spurious; the True One
being enter'd according to Act of Parliament, no other dare
print it."

The tract was known by still another title; in the *Review* for
2 April 1711 Defoe called it *British Visions, or Twelve new
Prophesies for the Year 1711.*

IU has a crudely printed copy (n.d., 8º, pp. [1 unnumbered] +
4–15) which is perhaps either a pirated London reprint or the

otherwise unidentified Newcastle original. The title-page reads: *The British Visions: or, Isaac Bickerstaff's Twelve Prophecies.*

Copies of various editions or reissues: BM, NLS, UL; BPL, H, HEH, IU, NYPL, T

196   ATALANTIS MAJOR. *Printed in* OLREEKY, *the Chief City of the North Part of Atalantis Major. Anno Mundi* 1711 [for 1710].

8°. Pp. 1–46

Notes: Published before 26 December 1710 (*Letters,* ed. Healey, p. 307).

Copy: BM. *Other copies:* BOD, NLS; BPL, C, H, HEH, IU, N, NYPL, T, Y

197   A TRUE COLLECTION OF THE WRITINGS of the Author of the True-Born Englishman. [1710]

Notes: Advertised on 28 December 1710 in the *Review* (VII, 476): "This Day is Publish'd, the Third Edition of A True Collection of the Writings of the Author of the True-born English-Man, Corrected and Enlarg'd by himself; in two Volumes in 8vo. Price 12s. Sold by John Morphew near Stationers Hall, and most Booksellers in England." It is sometimes supposed that this edition was entitled *The Genuine Works of Mr. Daniel DeFoe* and that it contained a key to the characters alluded to in the text. One of the JRM copies has this new title but lacks the key. I have found no indication from newspaper advertisements that the new title or the key appeared before 1721, nor do the available copies give evidence of any resetting of the type after 1705 (except for the title-page and the key). This is a difficult matter to be certain of, because no edition seems to have borne a date on the title-page.

1 7 1 1

198   R[OGUE]'s ON BOTH SIDES. In Which are the Characters Of Some R[ogue]'s not yet describ'd; With a true Description of An Old Whig, and a Modern Whig; an old Tory, and a Modern Tory; High-flyer, or Motly; As also of a Minister

of State. *By the same Author.* LONDON, *Printed for* JOHN
BAKER, *at the Black-Boy in Pater-noster-Row,* 1711. *Price
6d.*

8°. Pp. [i–ii] + 1–36

Notes: The BM copy, pressmark 8132.aaa.1(4), is defective, giving an entirely different tract after p. 8.

Copy: BOD. *Other copies:* NLS; BPL, C, H, HEH, IU, RPB,
T, Y

199 A SHORT NARRATIVE OF THE LIFE AND ACTIONS OF HIS
GRACE JOHN, D. OF MARLBOROUGH, From The Beginning
of the Revolution, to this present Time. With some Re-
marks on his Conduct. *By an Old Officer in the Army.*
LONDON, *Printed for* JOHN BAKER, *at the Black-Boy in
Pater-noster-Row,* 1711. *Price Six-Pence.*

8°. Pp. 3–45

Notes: Published 20 February.

Copy: BM. *Other copies:* BOD, NLS, UL; BPL, F, HEH, IU

200 COUNTER QUERIES. [1711?]

Fol. half-sheet. Pp. 1–2

Notes: No place, no date, but probably London early in 1711.

Copy: BM

201 CAPTAIN TOM'S REMEMBRANCE TO HIS OLD FRIENDS THE
MOBB of London, Westminster, Southwark, and Wapping.
[1711]

Fol. half-sheet. Pp. [1–2]

Copy: H. *Another copy:* HEH

202 A SEASONABLE CAUTION TO THE GENERAL ASSEMBLY. In A
Letter From A Member Of Parliament Of North-Britain,
To A Minister in Scotland: Occasioned by The House of
Lords Reversing the Sentence of Mr. Greenshiels. *Printed
in the Year,* 1711.

8º. Pp. 3–31

Notes: Published about March 1711, and probably in Edinburgh. Defoe mentioned the reversal of Greenshields' sentence in the *Review* for 8 March 1711 (VII, 593).

Copy: C. *Another copy:* BPL

203   A Spectators Address to the Whigs, On The Occasion Of The Stabbing Mr. Harley. *Printed in the Year* 1711. *Price Two-Pence.*

8º. Pp. 3–15

Notes: Published 17 March. Later advertised as "Sold by the Booksellers of London and Westminster."

Copy: BM. *Other copies:* BOD; BPL, C, COR, H, I, IU, P, T

204   The Secret History of the October-Club: From its Original to this Time. *By a Member.* London: *Printed in the Year,* 1711. *Price 1s.*

8º. Pp. 1–86

Notes: Published 19 April; second edition 10 May. For Part II see No. 207.

Copy: BM. *Other copies:* BOD, CU, NLS; BPL, C, F, H, IU, NYPL, P, T

205   The Succession of Spain Consider'd: Or, A View Of the several Interests Of The Princes and Powers Of Europe, As they Respect the Succession of Spain and the Empire. London, *Printed, and Sold by* J. Baker, *at the Black-Boy in Pater-Noster-Row,* 1711. *(Price 6d.)*

8º. Pp. 1–45

Notes: Published 2 May 1711.

Copy: IU. *Other copies:* BPL, COR, H, HEH, Y

206   Eleven Opinions about Mr. H[arle]y; With Observations. London, *Printed for* J. Baker, *at the Black-Boy in Pater-noster-Row,* 1711.

8°. Pp. 3–89

Notes: Lee dates this 14 May.

Copy: BM. *Other copies:* BOD, CU, DW, NLS, UL; BPL, C, CH, COR, H, HEH, I, IU, N, NYPL, R, RPB, T, Y

207 THE SECRET HISTORY OF THE OCTOBER CLUB, From Its Original to this Time. *By a Member.* PART II. LONDON: *Printed for* J. BAKER, *at the Black-Boy in Pater-noster-Row,* 1711. (*Price 1s.*) *Where may be had the First Part. Price 1s.*

8°. Pp. 1–93

Notes: Published 23 June. Referred to in No. 206 (p. 55) as forthcoming.

Copy: BM. *Other copies:* BOD, CU, NLS; BPL, C, COR, HEH, I, IU, N, NYPL, P, T, Y

208 THE REPRESENTATION EXAMINED: Being Remarks On The State Of Religion In England. LONDON: *Printed for* A. BALDWIN, *at the Oxford-Arms-Inn, in Warwick-Lane, 1711. Price Sixpence.*

Fol. Pp. 3–12

Notes: Reprinted in Edinburgh in 1711 by J. Moncur with a fuller and more explanatory title which reads: (BM) *The Representation Of The Lower House of Convocation of the English Clergy Examined: Being Remarks On The Present State of Religion Now in England.*

Copy: BM. *Other copies:* BOD, NLS; HEH

209 REASONS FOR A PEACE: Or, The War At an End. LONDON: *Printed in the Year,* 1711.

8°. Pp. 2–8

Notes: Reprinted in Edinburgh in 1711 by John Reid Junior.

Copy: IU

210 AN ESSAY UPON THE TRADE TO AFRICA. In Order to set the Merits of that Cause in a true Light And Bring the Dis-

putes between the African Company and the Separate Traders into a narrower Compass. *Printed in the Year* 1711.

8°. Pp. 3–48

Copy: BM. *Other copies:* BOD, UL; IU, LC, NYPL

211 THE SCOTCH MEDAL DECIPHER'D, And The New Hereditary-Right Men display'd: Or, Remarks On The late Proceedings of the Faculty of Advocates at Edinburgh, upon receiving the Pretender's Medal. With an Account of the Laws which make those Proceedings High-Treason. To which the said Proceedings are prefix'd. Gens in servitutem nata. LONDON: *Printed for* S. POPPING *at the Black Raven in Pater-noster-Row.* 1711. (*Price Three Pence.*)

8°. Pp. 3–24

Notes: Pp. 3–6 give "Minutes *of the Advocates at* Edinburgh. *July* 30." This is an obvious misprint for June 30. Dundasse's speech and Defoe's account of the affair in the *Review* for 31 July 1711 (VII, 224) date the meeting of the Advocates on 30 June. Pp. 7–21 give "Remarks," a vigorous and very characteristic exposure of the sophistry underlying the Advocates' acceptance of a Jacobite medal at such a time and under such conditions. Pp. 22–24 give a postscript: "P. S. *An Account of the Laws which make the Proceedings of the* Scotch *Advocates High–Treason; by way of Caveat to our* English *Highfliers.*" The tract was probably published early in August.

Copy: IU. *Other copies:* C, CPL

212 A SPEECH FOR MR. D[UNDA]SSE YOUNGER OF ARNISTOWN, If he should be impeach'd of H[igh] T[reaso]n for what he said and did about the Pretender's Medal, lately sent to the Faculty of Advocates at Edinburgh. LONDON; *Printed for* J. BAKER *in Pater-noster-Row.* M.DCC.XI. (*Price Two Pence.*)

8°. Pp. 3–15

Notes: Published 30 August. Pp. 7–9 restate (in condensed form) six of the addresses to Queen Anne given in No. 188 (pp. 18–48).

Copy: BM. *Other copies:* BOD, NLS, UL; BPL, C, COR, F, HEH, I, IU, LC, N, NYPL, Y

213 A TRUE ACCOUNT OF THE DESIGN, AND ADVANTAGES OF THE SOUTH-SEA TRADE: With Answers to all the Objections rais'd against it. A List of all the Commodities proper for that Trade: And the Progress of the Subscription towards the South-Sea Company. LONDON: *Printed, and Sold by* J. MORPHEW, *near Stationers-Hall, 1711. Price Six Pence.*

8°. Pp. 3–38

Notes: Published on or before 8 September. As early as 28 June *The Examiner* had published a preliminary notice of the plan for a somewhat similar publication: "There is now prepairing for the Press, A General and particular Account of the Advantages of a South-Sea Trade, as limited by the late Act of Parliament, for the Erecting a Company to make Settlements in those Parts. Illustrated with several new and accurate Maps and Draughts, by Herman Moll, Geographer. A more particular Account of which Design, will be publish'd in a few Days: and those Gentlemen that have any thing to communicate, useful to this Design, are desir'd to send it speedily to John Morphew near Stationers Hall."

However, it is clear that Defoe had not given active support to Harley's South Sea project as early as June 1711, and no maps or draughts by Herman Moll appear in Defoe's tract as actually published.

Copy: BM. *Other copies:* UL; C, H, IU, NYPL, P, Y

214 AN ESSAY ON THE SOUTH-SEA TRADE. With An Enquiry into the Grounds and Reasons of the present Dislike and Complaint against the Settlement of a South-Sea Company. *By the Author of the Review.* LONDON: *Printed for* J. BAKER, *at the Black-Boy in Pater-Noster-Row.* 1712 [for 1711].

8°. Pp. 5–47

Notes: Published 13 September 1711; second edition 30 October.

Copy: BM. *Other copies:* BOD, NLS, UL; BPL, COR, H, HEH, IU, N, P, R

215   THE TRUE STATE OF THE CASE Between The Government And The Creditors of the Navy, &c: As it Relates to the South-Sea-Trade. And the Justice of the Transactions on either Side Impartially enquired into. LONDON: *Printed, and Sold by* J. BAKER *at the Black-Boy in Pater-Noster-Row,* 1711. *(Price 2d.)*

8°. Pp. 3–15

Notes: Published in late September. Baker's advertisement on the back page lists No. 214 as "Just published."

Copy: UL. *Other copies:* BPL, F, HEH, IU, P, Y

216   REASONS WHY THIS NATION OUGHT TO PUT A SPEEDY END TO THIS EXPENSIVE WAR; With a Brief Essay, at the Probable Conditions On Which the Peace Now Negotiating, may be Founded. Also An Enquiry into the Obligations Britain lies under to the Allies; and how far she is obliged not to make Peace without them. [A quotation from Judges VI, 24, and one from Psalms CXX, 6, 7.] *Printed for* J. BAKER *at the Black Boy in Pater-Noster-Row,* 1711.

8°. Pp. 3–47

Notes: Published 6 October; second edition 11 October; third edition 18 October. An earlier date of publication than 6 October is indicated by the reference to this tract in the title of No. 217, but I have found no other authority for this, Defoe alludes to this tract in *Minutes Of The Negotiations Of Monsr. Mesnager* (1717), where the French envoy is represented as saying (pp. 108–109): ". . . a certain Person, who the *Swedish* Resident, Monsieur *Lyencroon,* recommended, and who wrote an excellent Tract in our Interest, entituled, *Reasons why this Nation* (meaning *England*) *ought to put an End to this expensive War,* &c. I was extremely pleased with that Piece, tho' I could not read it distinctly, and for that Reason had it translated into *French,* and caused it to be Printed at St. *Omer* in *Flanders,* and dispersed thro' the *Low Countries,* and at *Paris,* for the publick Information of our own People. Monsieur *Lyencroon* used his Endeavour to bring this Author into my Measures; and to facilitate the Thing, I caused an hundred Pistols to be conveyed to him, as a Compliment for that Book, and let him know, it came from a Hand that was as able to treat him honourably, as he was sensible of his Service; But I missed my Aim in the Person, tho' perhaps the money was not wholly lost; for I afterwards understood that the Man was in the Service of the State, and that he had let the Queen know of the hundred Pistols he had received; so I was obliged to sit still, and be very well satisfied that I had not discovered my self to him, for it was not our Season yet."

Copy: BM. *Other copies:* BOD, CU, NLS, UL; BPL, COR, F, H, I, N, NYPL, P, R, RPB, T, Y

217 REASONS WHY A PARTY AMONG US, and also among the Confederates Are obstinately bent against a Treaty of Peace with the French at this time. *By the Author of the Reasons for putting an end to this Expensive War.* But the Unbelieving Jews stirred up the Gentiles, and made their Minds evil affected: And the Multitude of the City was divided. Acts. XIV. Vers. 2. 4. *Printed for* JOHN BAKER, *at the Black-Boy in Pater-Noster-Row,* 1711. *Pr. 6d.*

8°. Pp. 3–48

Notes: Published in early October, immediately after *Reasons Why This Nation Ought to put a Speedy End to this Expensive War;* but as late as 29 November it was still advertised "This day is Publish'd." Second edition 9 October; third edition 18 October.

Copy: BM. *Other copies:* BOD, UL; BPL, C, H, HEH, I, IU, P, Y

218 ARMAGEDDON: Or, The Necessity Of Carrying on the War, If Such a Peace cannot be obtained as may render Europe safe, and Trade secure. [Quotations of five Scriptural verses: Jeremiah 6. 14, Deut. 23. 6, Jeremiah 14. 19, and 2 Kings 9. 22, 23.] LONDON: *Printed for* J. BAKER, *at the Black Boy in Pater-Noster Row. Price Six Pence.* [1711]

8°. Pp. 3–47

Notes: Published 30 October.

Copy: BM. *Other copies:* BOD, CU, NLS, UL; BPL, COR, H, HEH, I, IU, N, P, R, T, Y

219   THE BALLANCE OF EUROPE: Or, An Enquiry into The Respective Dangers Of giving the Spanish Monarchy To The Emperour As well as to King Philip, With the Consequences that may be expected from either. *Printed for* JOHN BAKER, *at the Black-Boy in Pater-Noster-Row,* 1711. *Price 6d.*

8°. Pp. 3–48

Notes: Published 1 November.

Copy: IU. *Other copies:* BM, BOD, CU, DW, NLS, UL; BPL, C, H, HEH, N, P, T, Y

220   WORCESTERSHIRE-QUERIES ABOUT PEACE. *By Tom Flockmaker, Clothier Of Worcester.* LONDON: *Printed for* S. POPPING *at the Raven in Pater Noster-Row,* 1711. *Price Two Pence.*

8°. Pp. 3–15

Copy: BOD. *Another copy:* CU

221   AN ESSAY AT A PLAIN EXPOSITION Of That Difficult Phrase A Good Peace. *By the Author of the Review. Printed for* J. BAKER *at the Black-Boy in Pater-Noster-Row.* 1711. *(Price 6d.)*

8°. Pp. 3–52

Notes: Published 8 November.

Copy: BM. *Other copies:* CU, NLS, UL; BPL, H, HEH, IU, N, P, R, T, Y

222   THE FELONIOUS TREATY: Or An Enquiry Into The Reasons Which moved his late Majesty King William of Glorious Memory, To enter into a Treaty at Two several Times with the King of France for the Partition of the Spanish

Monarchy. With An Essay, Proving that it was always the Sense both of King William, and of all the Confederates, and even of the Grand Alliance it self, That the Spanish Monarchy should never be United in the Person of the Emperor. *By the Author of the Review.* LONDON *Printed and Sold by* J. BAKER, *at the Black-boy in Pater-Noster-Row,* 1711. *Price 6d.*

8°. Pp. 3–48

Notes: Published 6 December.

Copy: BM. *Other copies:* NLS, UL; BPL, C, H, HEH, IU, N, P, T, Y

223 [A SPEECH OF A STONE CHIMNEY-PIECE] [1711]

Notes: I have not found the original lampoon. In *The Present State of the Parties in Great Britain* (1712) Defoe states (p. 102) that this was "a little short paper which was handed about at that Time in Manuscript." Part of the lampoon is quoted carefully, as if from the written text, in *The Present State of the Parties* (pp. 102–104), published 17 May 1712. This passage, obviously imitated from the famous speech of Lord Belhaven (Beilhaven) in the last Scottish Parliament, represents the stone as making a passionate remonstrance from the well-known chimney in the House of Lords.

The latter part of the passage had been printed in the *Review* for 25 December 1711 (but there from memory alone, and with the inconsistency of being addressed "to a Person of Honour"—whereas the central point of the speech is that the stone chimney-piece supposedly uttered it in the House of Lords, as a rebuke to those lords who had remained silent when the Dissenters were betrayed by the Whigs who supported the Occasional Conformity Bill in order to secure an alliance with Lord Nottingham). Quite possibly Defoe avoided so direct a rebuke to the House of Lords in his own *Review* while the issue was still highly controversial.

The lampoon can be dated immediately after 18 December 1711, when the Occasional Conformity Bill was passed by the House of Lords. See *Boston Public Library Quarterly,* IX (1957), 137–142.

224 AN ESSAY ON THE HISTORY OF PARTIES, And Persecution In
Britain; Beginning, With a brief Account of the Test-Act,
and an Historical Enquiry into the Reasons, the Original,
and the Consequences of the Occasional Conformity of
Dissenters. With some Remarks on the several Attempts
already made, and now making for an Occasional Bill.
Enquiring how far the same may be esteem'd a Preservation to the Church, or an Injury to the Dissenters. LONDON:
Printed for J. BAKER *at the Black-Boy in Paternoster-Row,*
1711. (*Price 6d.*)

8°. Pp. 3–48

Notes: This tract can be dated with considerable precision, and
its contents fall into two distinct groups. The title-page and
most of the text were written (and probably set up in type)
before 18 December (when the Occasional Bill was passed by
the House of Lords). But on p. 42 Defoe refers explicitly to
the votes *"Die Lunae Decemb.* 18. 1711*."* On 20 December the
Bill was passed by the House of Commons. In the conclusion
of the tract (pp. 43–48) Defoe refers to it as a Bill from which
only the Queen can now grant relief. In the *Review* for 22
December he suggests an appeal from the Dissenters to the
Queen, and in the same issue appeared an advertisement:
"This Day is publish'd, An Essay on the History of Parties"
followed by the full title of the tract. But on the same day any
hope of relief from the Queen was ended when the Bill became
an Act through the royal assent.

Copy: BM. *Other copies:* BOD, UL; BPL, H, HEH, IU, N, Y

1 7 1 2

225 A DEFENCE OF THE ALLIES and the Late Ministry: Or,
Remarks On The Tories New Idol. Being A Detection Of
the Manifest Frauds and Falsities, in a late Pamphlet, Entituled, The Conduct of the Allies and of the late Ministry,
in the Beginning and Carrying on the War. LONDON:
Printed, and Sold by J. BAKER, *at the Black-Boy in Pater-
Noster-Row.* 1712. *Price 6d.*

8°. Pp. 1–46

Copy: BM. *Other copies:* DW; BPL, C, H, HEH, T, Y

226 A JUSTIFICATION OF THE DUTCH From several late Scandalous Reflections: In which is shewn the Absolute Necessity
of Preserving a Strict and Inviolable Friendship betwixt
Great-Britain and the States-General: With the Fatal Consequences that must attend a War with Holland.

Semper ego Auditor tantum? Nunquàmne reponam
Vexatus toties————

Juven. Sat.

———— Quid demum decimo nisi Dedecus Anno?

Vir. AEneid.

Justum & tenacem propositi virum
Non Civium Ardor prava jubentium,
Non Vultus instantis Tyranni.
Mente quatiet solida.

Hor:

LONDON: *Printed for* J. BAKER, *at the Black-Boy in Pater-
noster-Row.* 1712. *Price Six-pence.*

8°. Pp. 3–48

Copy: HEH. *Other copies:* BM, BOD, NLS, UL; C, HEH, IU,
N

227 NO QUEEN: OR, NO GENERAL. An Argument, Proving The
Necessity Her Majesty was in, as well for the Safety of Her
Person as of Her Authority, to Displace the D[uke] of
M[arl]borough. LONDON: *Printed, and Sold by the Book-
sellers of London and Westminster.* 1712.

8°. Pp. 1–52

Notes: Published 10 January, "Sold by the Booksellers of London and Westminster." Second edition 23 January. In some
copies (IU, JRM) the last four pages are misnumbered 41–44.

Copy: BM. *Other copies:* BOD, DW; BPL, COR, F, H, HEH,
IU, NYPL, P, R, T, Y

228   THE CONDUCT OF PARTIES In England, More especially of those Whigs Who now appear Against the New Ministry, And A Treaty of Peace. *Printed in the Year* 1712.

8º. Pp. 3–42

Notes: Published 24 January. Pp. 20–25, 28, 31–33, and 36–38 contain long quotations (with some modifications and rearrangement) from No. 204 (pp. 16–20, 20, 23–25, and 23–26), introduced by the statement (p. 20): "that you may have this from a Second Authority, and an Author, who, as it should be seen was in the Secret, we corroborate our Evidence by giving you this Part by Quotation, the Tract and its Author well known."

Copy: BM. *Other copies:* BOD, NLS, UL; BPL, C, COR, F, H, HEH, IU, NYPL, P, T, Y

229   PEACE, OR POVERTY. Being A Serious Vindication of Her Majesty and Her Ministers Consenting to a Treaty for a General Peace. Shewing The Reasonableness, and even Necessity, there was for such a Procedure. LONDON: *Printed, and Sold by* JOHN MORPHEW, *near Stationers-Hall.* 1712. *Price 2d.*
8º. Pp. 3–16

Notes: Published 29 January.

Copy: NLS. *Other copies:* BOD, CU; BPL, H, HEH, IU, P, RPB, Y

230   THE CASE OF THE POOR SKIPPERS AND KEEL-MEN OF NEW-CASTLE. [1712?]

Fol. half-sheet

Notes: Not for sale, but prepared for presentation to members of the House of Commons. Drawn up by Defoe on behalf of the keel-men (coal barge-men) of Newcastle, showing how their employers (the hoast-men) had confiscated and misappropriated the funds which the keel-men had contributed to relieve their own poor. BM has a hostile tract (*The Case of the Poor Skipper Keel-men of New-Castle, Truly Stated*) in which this petition is attacked and its author (fairly obviously Defoe) is referred to as a mercenary writer. See notes on No. 231.

Copy: BOD

231 A FARTHER CASE RELATING TO THE POOR KEEL-MEN OF NEWCASTLE. [1712]

Fol. half-sheet

Notes: Not for sale, but prepared for presentation to members of the House of Commons. Closely related to articles in the *Review* for 12, 14, and 17 February 1712 (VIII, 560, 563–572), and to Defoe's letters to Harley on 19 June 1711 and 14 February 1712 (*Letters,* ed. Healey, pp. 332 and note, 369 and note). See No. 230.

Copy: BM

232 THE HISTORY OF THE JACOBITE CLUBS: With the Grounds of their Hopes from the P[resen]t M[inistr]y: As also a Caveat against the Pretender.

Nostra dabunt alios hodie Convivia Ludos:
Conviviae miseri interea, Somnoque Famaeque Urgentur.

Juvenal.

LONDON: *Printed for* J. BAKER, *at the Black-Boy in Pater-Noster-Row,* 1712. *Price Six-Pence.*

8⁰. Pp. 3–40
Copy: BM. *Other copies:* DW, NLS; BPL, Y

233 IMPERIAL GRATITUDE, Drawn from a Modest View Of The Conduct Of The Emperor Ch[arl]es VI, And the King of Spain Ch[arl]es III: With Observations on the Difference, &c. Being a farther View of the Deficiencies of our Confederates. LONDON: *Printed in the Year* 1712.

8⁰. Pp. [2 unnumbered] + 1–76

Notes: The Preface is signed "Philopax." Published before 28 February, and "Sold by the Booksellers of London and Westminster." In *Reasons Against Fighting* (7 June 1712) Defoe refers to *Imperial Gratitude* as lately published. In No. 488 (pp. 40–46) Defoe cites it very approvingly and quotes it at length.

Copy: BM. *Other copies:* CU; BPL, C, F, HEH, IU

234 THE HIGHLAND VISIONS, Or The Scots New Prophecy: Declaring in Twelve Visions what Strange Things shall come to Pass in the Year 1712. *Entered in the Hall Book, according to Act of Parliament.* LONDON, *Printed for* J. BAKER *in Paternoster Row.* 1712.

8°. Pp. 3–16

Notes: Published 12 March 1712 for 2*d.* The imprint in the BOD copy (which appears to be a pirated edition) is *Printed in the Year 1712.*

Copy: HEH. *Other copies:* BPL, H, Y

*235 PLAIN ENGLISH, with Remarks And Advice To Some Men who need not be Nam'd. LONDON, *Printed and Sold by* J. WOODWARD, *in Scalding-Alley over against Stocks Market,* 1712. *Price Three Pence.*

8°. Pp. 5–21

Notes: Very probably Defoe's, although Woodward was not one of his usual publishers and the tract is so badly spelled by the printer that attribution of authorship is not quite certain.

Copy: BM. *Other copies:* BOD, NLS; C, H, I, IU, Y

236 WISE AS SERPENTS: Being An Enquiry Into The Present Circumstances Of The Dissenters, And What Measures they ought to take in Order to Disappoint the Designs of their Enemies. Prov. xix. 25. Smite a Scorner, and the Simple will beware; and reprove one that hath Understanding, and he will understand Knowledge. LONDON: *Printed, and Sold by* J. BAKER, *at the Black-Boy in Pater-Noster-Row.* 1712.

8°. Pp. 1–46

Notes: Published 13 May.

Copy: Y. *Other copies:* COR, T

237 THE PRESENT STATE OF THE PARTIES IN GREAT BRITAIN: Particularly An Enquiry into the State of the Dissenters in England, and the Presbyterians in Scotland; their Religious and Politick Interest consider'd, as it respects their Circumstances before and since the late Acts against Occasional Conformity in England; and for Tolleration of Common Prayer in Scotland. [Long Latin quotation about the Inquisition in Belgium.] LONDON *Printed, and Sold by* J. BAKER *in Pater-Noster-Row,* 1712. *Price Five Shillings.*

8°. Pp. [6 unnumbered] + 1–352

Notes: Published 17 May.

Copy: BM. *Other copies:* CU; BPL, H, HEH, R, Y

238 REASONS AGAINST FIGHTING. Being An Enquiry into this Great Debate, Whether it is Safe for Her Majesty, or Her Ministry, to Venture an Engagement with the French, considering the Present Behaviour of the Allies. [Quotes the Resolution of the House of Commons on Wednesday 28 May 1710 and the Queen's answer on 30 May.] *Printed in the Year* 1712. *Price 6d.*

4°. Pp. 1–38 (Some copies, including IU, number the last page 28 by mistake.)

Notes: Published 7 June. P. 31 refers to No. 233: "that very New and Unknown Thing, of which Authors have lately endeavoured to make some Description, called *Imperial Gratitude.*"

Copy: BM. *Other copies:* BOD, UL; BPL, COR, H, HEH, I, IU, P, T

239 THE PRESENT NEGOTIATIONS OF PEACE VINDICATED from the Imputation of Trifling. LONDON: *Printed and Sold by the Booksellers.* 1712. *Price 6d.*

8°. Pp. 3–40

Notes: Advertised 7 June by J. Baker.

Copy: BM. *Other copies:* BOD; BPL, HEH, IU

240   THE VALIDITY OF THE RENUNCIATIONS Of Former Powers, Enquired into, And The Present Renunciation Of The Duke of Anjou, Impartially Considered. With A Preface, relating to the Guarantee for the Protestant Succession. LONDON: *Printed, and Sold by* J. MORPHEW, *near Stationers-Hall.* 1712.

8°. Pp. [4 unnumbered] + 1–35

Copy: Y. *Other copies:* CU; C, H, HEH, Y

241   AN ENQUIRY INTO THE DANGER AND CONSEQUENCES OF A WAR With the Dutch. LONDON: *Printed for* J. BAKER, *at the Black-Boy in Pater-Noster-Row.* 1712.

8°. Pp. 3–40

Copy: BM. *Other copies:* BOD, NLS, UL; BPL, C, COR, F, H, HEH, IU, N, NYPL, P, Y

242   A FURTHER SEARCH INTO THE CONDUCT OF THE ALLIES, And The Late Ministry, As To Peace And War. Containing also A Reply to the several Letters and Memorials of the States-General. With a Vindication of the British Parliament in their late Resolves and Address relating to the Deficiencies of the Dutch. LONDON: *Printed for* JOHN MORPHEW, *near Stationers-Hall.* 1712.

8°. ·Pp. 3–77

Notes: The BOD and IU copies read *A Farther Search.*

Copy: BM. *Other copies:* BOD; BPL, C, COR, HEH, IU

243   THE JUSTICE AND NECESSITY OF A WAR with Holland, In Case the Dutch Do not come into Her Majesty's Measures, Stated and Examined. LONDON: *Printed, and Sold by the Booksellers of London and Westminster.* 1712.

4°. Pp. 3–36

Notes: Published 26 July.

Copy: BM. *Other copies:* BOD, DW, NLS; BPL, C, COR, F, H, HEH, I, IU, Y

244 AN ENQUIRY INTO THE REAL INTEREST OF PRINCES In The
Persons of their Ambassadors, And How far the Petty Quarrels of Ambassadors, or the Servants and Dependents of
Ambassadors one among another, ought to be Resented by
their Principals. With an Essay on what Satisfaction it is
necessary to Give or Take in such Cases. Impartially Ap-
plied to the Affair of Monsieur Mesnager, and the Count
Rechteren, Plenipotentiaries at Utrecht. LONDON: *Printed,
and Sold by* J. BAKER, *at the Black-Boy in Pater-Noster-
Row.* 1712. *Price 3d.*

8°. Pp. 3–23

Notes: Lee dates this 18 September.

Copy: BOD. *Another copy:* Y

245 A SEASONABLE WARNING AND CAUTION Against the Insinua-
tions Of Papists and Jacobites In Favour of the Pretender.
Being a Letter from an English-Man at the Court of Han-
nover. [Quotations from Deut. VI. 9 and Rev. I. 11.] LON-
DON: *Printed for* J. BAKER *at the Black-Boy in Pater-noster-
Row.* 1712.

8°. Pp. 3–24

Copy: BM. *Other copies:* NLS; BPL, HEH, IU

246 HANNIBAL AT THE GATES. Or, The Progress Of Jacobitism.
With The Present Danger Of The Pretender.

Pene occupatem Seditionibus
Delevit Urbem Dacus & Aethiops.

Hor.

LONDON: *Printed for* J. BAKER, *at the Black-Boy in Pater
Noster-Row.* 1712. *Price 6d.*

8°. Pp. 3–40

Notes: Lee dates this 30 December. The second edition, pub-
lished 10 April 1714, was considerably expanded as a reply to
Hannibal not at our Gates: (BM) *Hannibal* at the Gates: Or,
The Progress of Jacobitism, With The Present Danger Of The

Pretender: And Remarks on a Pamphlet now Publish'd, In-titul'd, Hannibal not at our Gates, &c. The Second Edition. London. Printed for J. Baker at the Black-Boy in Pater-Noster-Row. 1714. Price 6d.

8°. Pp. 3–48

Copy: BM. *Other copies:* BOD, DW, UL; BPL, C, COR, HEH, IU, N, R, Y

1713

247   A STRICT ENQUIRY INTO THE CIRCUMSTANCES OF A LATE DUEL, With some Account of the Persons Concern'd on Both Sides. Being, A Modest Attempt to do Justice to the Injur'd Memory of a Noble Person Dead, and to the Injur'd Honour of an Absent Person Living. To which is added, The Substance of a Letter from General Mac Cartney to his Friend. LONDON: *Printed for* J. BAKER, *at the Black-Boy in Pater-Noster-Row.* 1713. (*Price 6d.*)

8°. Pp. 3–30 (for 46)

Copy: BM. *Other copies:* BOD, NLS, UL; BPL, H, HEH, IU, Y

248   REASONS AGAINST THE SUCCESSION OF THE HOUSE OF HANOVER, With An Enquiry How far the Abdication of King James, supposing it to be Legal, ought to affect the Person of the Pretender. Si Populus vult Decipi, Decipiatur. LONDON: *Printed for* J. BAKER, *at the Black-Boy in Pater-Noster-Row.* 1713. (*Price 6d.*)

8°. Pp. 1–45

Notes: Published 21 February. Lee dates the fourth edition in April.

Copy: BM. *Other copies:* BOD, CU, DW, NLS, UL; BPL, C, CH, COR, F, H, HEH, I, IU, LC, NYPL, P, R, T

249   NOT[TINGH]AM POLITICKS EXAMIN'D. Being An Answer To a Pamphlet lately Publish'd, Intitul'd, Observations Upon

The State of the Nation. LONDON: *Printed for* J. BAKER, *at the Black-Boy in Pater-Noster-Row.* 1713. (*Price 6d.*)

4°. Pp. 3–34

Notes: Published 21 February. Unusual among Defoe's writings for its extremely long paragraphs; apparently written in great haste and in anger.

Copy: BM. *Other copies:* BOD; BPL, H, IU, P, Y

250   THE SECOND-SIGHTED HIGHLANDER: Or, Predictions And Foretold Events: Especially about the Peace. *By the famous Scots Highlander.* Being Ten New Visions for the Year 1713. *Printed for, and Sold by* J. BAKER *in Pater-noster-Row,* LONDON.

8°. Pp. [i] + 4–23

Copy: BPL. *Other copies:* BOD, UL; BPL, HEH

251   AND WHAT IF THE PRETENDER SHOULD COME? Or, Some Considerations Of The Advantages and Real Consequences Of The Pretender's Possessing the Crown Of Great Britain. LONDON: *Printed, and Sold by* J. BAKER, *at the Black Boy in Pater-noster-row.* 1713. (*Price 6d.*)

8°. Pp. 3–40

Notes: Old manuscript notes in BM copy: "by Daniel de Foe" and "23. March. 1713/2."

Copy: IU. *Other copies:* BM, BOD, DW, NLS, UL; BPL, COR, F, H, HEH, P, R, Y

252   AN ANSWER TO A QUESTION THAT NO BODY THINKS OF, Viz. But what if the Queen should die? LONDON, *Printed for* J. BAKER, *at the Black Boy in Pater-noster Row.* 1713. *Price Six Pence.*

8°. Pp. 3–45

Notes: Published in April. The NYPL copy is dated 1712.

Copy: BM. *Other copies:* BOD, DW, UL; BPL, C, COR, F, HEH, I, IU, N, NYPL, PML, R, Y

253　AN ESSAY ON THE TREATY OF COMMERCE With France: With necessary Expositions. Prov. xviii. 13. He that Judgeth a Matter before he Heareth it, 'tis Folly and Shame unto him. LONDON: Print[ed] for J. BAKER, at the Black-Boy in Pater-Noster-Row, 1713. (Price 6d.)

8°. Pp. 3–44

Notes: Published 23 May. Lee dates the second edition in May.

Copy: BM. Other copies: DW, NLS, UL; BPL, C, COR, F, H, HEH, IU, NYPL, P, R, Y

254　AN ACCOUNT OF THE ABOLISHING OF DUELS IN FRANCE: Being Extracts out of the Edicts of the Kings, the Regulations of the Marshals, and the Records of the Parliaments of France, with the Resolutions of the Archbishops, Bishops, and the Clergy there, in relation to that Matter. LONDON: Printed for JOHN MORPHEW, near Stationers-Hall, 1713. Price 1s.

8°. Pp. [i–xiv] + 1–67

Notes: Defoe compiled and translated this work. He had long anticipated nearly all the points included in it. He had apologized to readers of the Review on 16 May 1704 (I, 97) for his inability to procure in England (during the war with France) a copy of the ordinance erecting a Court of Honor to prevent duelling. When he did secure a copy late in 1704, he published it as he had promised to do (as a 14-page appendix to Vol. I of the Review) in exactly the same translation which reappears here eight years later on pp. 34–56. He had shown personal concern in the attempt to interest Parliament in the prevention of duels; and when this book was advertised in The Guardian (1 June 1713) it was said to be "Humbly offered to the Consideration of the House of Commons." The book contains material which Defoe knew in the French originals before 1704, which he translated in part about the beginning of 1705, and which he published in 1713 in an appeal to the House of Commons.

Copy: BOD. Another copy: NLS

255   UNION AND NO UNION. Being an Enquiry Into the Griev-
      ances of the Scots. And How far they are right or wrong,
      who alledge that the Union is dissolved. LONDON; *Printed,
      and Sold by* JOHN BAKER *at the Black-Boy in Pater-Noster-
      Row.* 1713. *Price 3d.*

      8°. Pp. 3–24

      Notes: Published 2 June. Pp. 18–21 draw on No. 161 as evi-
      dence for the terms of the Union.

      Copy: BM. *Other copies:* BOD, NLS, UL; BPL, C, COR, H,
      HEH, IU, NYPL, R, Y

256   CONSIDERATIONS UPON THE EIGHTH AND NINTH ARTICLES
      Of The Treaty Of Commerce and Navigation, Now pub-
      lish'd by Authority. With some Enquiries into the Dam-
      ages that may accrue to the English Trade from them.
      LONDON, *Printed for* J. BAKER, *at the Black Boy in Pater-
      Noster-Row,* 1713. *Price 6d.*

      8°. Pp. 3–40

      Notes: Published 2 June.

      Copy: BM. *Other copies:* UL; H, HEH, IU, R, Y

257   SOME THOUGHTS UPON THE SUBJECT OF COMMERCE WITH
      FRANCE. *By The Author of the Review.* Job. 21. 2. Suffer
      me that I may speak, and after that I have spoken, Mock
      on. LONDON: *Printed for* J. BAKER, *at the Black-Boy in
      Pater-Noster-Row,* 1713. (*Price 6d.*)

      8°. Pp. 3–48

      Notes: Lee dates this in June. A statement on pp. 46–47 dates
      it after Defoe discontinued the *Review* (11 June 1713) and
      while he was still out on bail. Not a résumé of articles pub-
      lished in the *Review,* as has sometimes been said, but an argu-
      ment in favor of reopening trade with France—buttressed by
      references to Defoe's previous statements on the subject in the
      Review (I, IV, and VI).

      Copy: UL. *Other copies:* BPL, C, H

258   A TRUE COLLECTION OF THE WRITINGS of the Author of the True-Born Englishman. [1713].

Notes: On 25 June 1713 *The Daily Courant* carried this advertisement: "To Morrow will be Publish'd, A True Collection of the Writings of the Author of the True-Born English-Man, containing these following Treatises. . . . Vol. I. The 3d Edition, corrected and enlarged by the Author. London, Printed and Sold by the Author. Price bound 6s. The 2d Vol. will be published next week. Price bound 6s." Lee dates both volumes 1 July and calls this the 4th edition. See entries above for *A Second Volume of the Writings* (1705) and for *A True Collection Of The Writings* (1710) and below for *The Genuine Works Of Mr. Daniel D'Foe* (1721).

259   THE TRADE OF SCOTLAND WITH FRANCE, CONSIDER'D; In Two Letters directed to the Author of the Mercator. EDINBURGH: *Printed by* JAMES WATSON. *Sold at his Shop opposite to* the Lucken-booths. 1713.

4°. Pp. 3–8

Notes: I reports copies of this both in 4° and in 8°. Also printed in *Mercator* for 7 and 9 July 1713 (Nos. 19 and 20). Presumably the letters appeared first in *Mercator* and they were reprinted in Scotland as a tract, to give them currency where the periodical itself was little known.

Copy: UL. *Other copies:* I, IU, Y

260   A GENERAL HISTORY OF TRADE. 1713

Notes: Issued in four instalments, ostensibly for the months of June, July, August, and September. The first part was advertised 21 July; the first three parts (separately) 21 November; the fourth part 17 December. The titles of the four parts vary considerably, according to the share Defoe was taking in the current controversy over the commercial articles of the Treaty of Utrecht:

[JUNE] *A General History Of Trade, And Especially Consider'd as it Respects The British Commerce, As well at Home, as to all Parts of the World. With Essays upon the Improve-*

ment of Our Trade in Particular. To be Continued Monthly.
LONDON: *Printed for* J. BAKER, *at the Black-Boy in Pater-Noster-Row,* 1713. *Price 6d.* 8°. Pp. 3–45.

[JULY] *A General History Of Trade, And Especially Consider'd as it Respects The British Commerce, As well at Home, as to all Parts of the World. With a Discourse of the Use of Harbours and Roads for Shipping, as it relates particularly to the filling up the Harbour of Dunkirk. This for the Month of July.* LONDON: *Printed for* J. BAKER, *at the Black-Boy in Pater-Noster-Row,* 1713. *Price 6d.* 8°. Pp. 3–48.

[AUGUST] *A General History Of Trade, And Especially Consider'd as it Respects The British Commerce: In which are Particularly Described,* 1. *The History and Reason of Commerce in England.* 2. *The Decay of Commerce in Scotland, and Methods of Recovering it.* 3. *The Original of the Dutch Fishery, and How they got it from the Scots. With other Accounts of those Matters both Profitable and Diverting. This for the Month of August.* LONDON: *Printed for* J. BAKER, *at the Black-Boy in Pater-Noster-Row,* 1713. Price 6d. 8°. Pp. 3–48.

[SEPTEMBER] *A General History of Trade, And Especially Consider'd as it Respects The British Commerce: In which an Attempt is made to State, and Moderate the present Disputes, about Settling a Commerce between Great-Britain and France. This for the Month of September* [.] *Printed for* J. BAKER, *at the Black-Boy in Pater-Noster-Row,* 1713. Price 6d. 8°. Pp. 3–40.

Copy: UL. *Other copies:* H, HEH, Y

261　THE HONOUR AND PREROGATIVE OF THE QUEEN'S MAJESTY Vindicated and Defended Against The Unexampled Insolence of the Author of the *Guardian: In a Letter From a Country Whig to Mr. Steele.* LONDON: *Printed for* JOHN MORPHEW, *near Stationers-Hall,* 1713. *Price 3d.*

8°. Pp. 2–23

Notes: Sometimes mistakenly attributed to Mrs. Manley. Published 13 August as a reply to *The Guardian* of 7 August—an example of the speed of some of Defoe's best writing. Second edition 25 August.

Copy: BM. *Other copies:* BOD, CU; BPL, C, N

262 MEMOIRS OF COUNT TARIFF, &c.

> Omnibus in terris, quae sunt à Gadibus usque
> Auroram, & Gangem pauci possunt
> Vera bona, atque illis multum remotâ
> Erroris Nebulâ

Juv. Sat. 10

LONDON: *Printed for* JOHN MORPHEW, *near Stationers-Hall.*
1713. *Price 1s.*

8°. Pp. 3–95

Notes: Published 20 August.

Copy: BM. *Other copies:* BOD, CU, UL; BPL, C, COR, F, H,
I, IU, NYPL, P, T, Y

263 A BRIEF ACCOUNT OF THE PRESENT STATE OF THE AFRICAN
TRADE. LONDON: *Printed for* J. BAKER, *at the Black-Boy in
Pate[r]-Noster-Row.* 1713.

8°. Pp. 7–55

Copy: BM. *Other copies:* BPL, Y

264 REASONS CONCERNING THE IMMEDIATE DEMOLISHING OF
DUNKIRK: Being A Serious Enquiry Into The State and
Condition of that Affair.

> O miseri, quae tanta Insania, Cives?
> Creditis avectos hostes?

Virg.

LONDON: *Printed for* JOHN MORPHEW, *near Stationers Hall.*
1713. *Price 6d.*

8°. Pp. 3–48

Notes: Published 12 September.

Copy: BM. *Other copies:* BOD, CU; BPL, HEH, IU, N

265 A LETTER FROM A MEMBER OF THE HOUSE OF COMMONS To His Friend in the Country, Relating to the Bill of Commerce. With A True Copy of the Bill, and an Exact List of all those who voted for and against Engrossing it. LONDON: *Printed and Sold by* J. BAKER *at the Black-Boy in Pater-Noster-Row.* 1713.

8°. Pp. 1–46

Notes: IU has a second copy which represents a different setting throughout, although it differs only in a few minute particulars (such as having a comma after "Printed" on the title-page, an ornament instead of parallel lines at the top of p. 1, and a lower case initial letter in "Impartial" [p. 23, l. 19]). I do not know which issue is the earlier one. The NLS copy resembles this second IU copy.

Copy: BM. *Other copies:* BOD, CU, DW, NLS, UL; BPL, C, COR, F, H, HEH, IU, N, NYPL, P, R, RPB, T

266 WHIGS TURN'D TORIES, And Hanoverian-Tories, From their Avow'd Principles, prov'd Whigs: Or, Each Side in the Other Mistaken. Being A plain Proof, that each Party deny that Charge which the other bring against them: And that neither Side will disown those Principles, which the other profess. With an Earnest Exhortation to all Whigs, as well as Hanoverian-Tories, to lay aside those Uncharitable Heats amongst such Protestants, and, seriously to consider, and effectually provide against those Jacobite, Popish, and Conforming Tories; whose Principal ground of Hope to Ruine all Sincere Protestants, is from those Unchristian and Violent Feuds amongst our selves. LONDON: *Printed for* J. BAKER, *at the Black-Boy, in Pater-Noster-Row,* 1713. (*Price 6d.*)

8°. Pp. [6 unnumbered] + 1–40

Copy: NLS. *Other copies:* BOD, DW, UL; BPL, C, F, H, IU, N, Y

267 A VIEW OF THE REAL DANGERS OF THE SUCCESSION, From

The Peace with France: Being A sober Enquiry into the Securities proposed in the Articles of Peace, And Whether they are such as the Nation ought to be satisfy'd with or no. LONDON: *Printed for* J. BAKER, *at the Black-Boy in Pater-Noster-Row,* 1713. *Price Six-Pence.*

8°. Pp. 3–44

Notes: Reissued in 1714 as *A View Of The Real Danger Of The Protestant Succession.* See No. 274.

Copy: CU. *Other copies:* NLS; BPL, HEH, IU, T, Y

268   EXTRACTS FROM SEVERAL MERCATORS; Being Considerations On the State of the British Trade. DUBLIN: *Printed and Sold by* EDWARD WATERS *at the New Post-Office Printing-House in Essex-Street, at the Corner of Sycamore-Ally,* 1713. *(Price 6d.)*

4°. Pp. [3]–27

Notes: It seems probable that this cheaply printed collection of excerpts from *Mercator* was published only in Dublin, for circulation where *Mercator* was not easily accessible.

Copy: BM. *Another copy:* UL

269   A LETTER TO THE DISSENTERS. LONDON: *Printed for* JOHN MORPHEW, *near Stationers Hall.* 1713. *Price 6d.*

8°. Pp. 3–48

Notes: Published 3 December; second edition (with an entirely new preface) 29 May 1714. For a different tract with the same title see No. 413.

Copy: BM. *Other copies:* BOD, CU, DW, NLS, UL; BPL, C, COR, F, H, HEH, I, IU, N, T, Y

270   PROPOSALS FOR IMPLOYING THE POOR In and about the City of London, Without any Charge to the Publick. LONDON,

Printed for J. BAKER *at the Black-Boy in Pater-noster-Row.*
M.DCC.XIII. *Price Three Pence.*

8°. Pp. 3–22

Copy: Y

1 7 1 4

271 A LETTER TO THE WHIGS, Expostulating with Them upon
Their Present Conduct: Wherein, The Grounds and Reasons of the Present Allarm about the Pretender are Enquir'd into, Examin'd, and Impartially Stated. LONDON:
Printed for E. SMITH, *at the Royal-Exchange Gate, Cornhill,* 1714. (*Price 6d.*)

8°. Pp. 3–48

Copy: BOD. *Other copies:* DW; BPL, C, H, HEH, IU, Y

272 MEMOIRS OF JOHN, DUKE OF MELFORT; Being an Account
of the Secret Intrigues Of The Chevalier de S. George, Particularly relating to the Present Times. Published from the
original Papers found in the Closet of the said Duke since
his Death. LONDON, *Printed for* J. MOOR, *near St. Paul's,*
MDCCXIV. *Price Six-Pence.*

8°. Pp. 3–40

Notes: Published 6 February 1714. The second edition is identical, aside from an additional line on the title-page: "The Second Edition." As the second edition is much less scarce than
the first, it was presumably a much larger printing from standing type—a practice for which there is considerable evidence
for other political tracts which proved their effectiveness. Only
five copies of the first edition are known, of which NLS has
three.

Copy: N. *Other copies:* NLS; BPL

273 THE SCOTS NATION AND UNION VINDICATED; From the Reflections cast on them, In An Infamous Libel. Entitl'd, The

Publick Spirit of the Whigs, &c. In which the most Scandalous Paragraphs contain'd therein are fairly Quoted, and fully Answer'd. LONDON: *Printed for* A. BELL *at the Cross-Keys and Bible in Cornhill; And Sold by* J. BAKER, *at the Bla[c]k-Boy in Pater-Noster-Row,* 1714. (*Price 6d.*)

4°. Pp. 3–28

Notes: Published 23 February 1714.

Copy: BM. *Other copies:* BOD, NLS, UL; BPL, COR, HEH, N, T, Y

274   A VIEW OF THE REAL DANGER OF THE PROTESTANT SUCCESSION. LONDON: *Printed for* J. BAKER, *at the Black-Boy in Pater-Noster-Row.* 1714. [*Price Six-Pence.*]

8°. Pp. 3–44

Notes: Published 10 April. See No. 267, *A View of the real Dangers of the Succession* (1713).

Copy: BOD. *Other copies:* DW; BPL, COR, H, HEH, IU

275   REASONS FOR Im[PEACHING] THE L[OR]D H[IGH] T[REASURE]R, And some others of the P[resent] M[inistry] [.] *Printed and Sold by* J. MOORE *near St. Paul's. Price Six-pence.* [1714].

8°. Pp. 3–39

Notes: Published 16 April.

Copy: NLS. *Other copies:* BOD; BPL, C, F, H, HEH, IU, NYPL, P, Y

276   A LETTER TO MR. STEELE, Occasion'd by his Letter to a Member of Parliament, Concerning The Bill for preventing the Growth of Schism. By a Member of the Church of England. LONDON: *Printed for* J. BAKER, *at the Black-Boy in Pater-Noster-Row,* 1714. *Price 6d.*

8°. Pp. 3–40

Notes: Published in June.

Copy: DW. *Other copies:* BPL, C, T

277 THE REMEDY WORSE THAN THE DISEASE: Or, Reasons
Against Passing the Bill for Preventing the Growth of
Schism. To which is added, A Brief Discourse of Toleration
and Persecution, Shewing, Their Unavoidable Effects good
or bad; and Proving that neither Diversity of Religions, nor
Diversity in the same Religion, are Dangerous, much less
Inconsistent with good Government. *In a Letter to a Noble
Earl.*

Haec sunt enim Fundamenta firmissima nostrae Libertatis,
sui quemque juris & retinendi & dimittendi esse Dominum.
Cic. in Orat. pro Balbo.

LONDON: *Printed for* J. BAKER, *at the Black-Boy in Pater-
Noster-Row.* 1714. *Price 6d.*

8°. Pp. 3–48

Notes: Published 9 June.

Copy: BM. *Other copies:* BOD, NLS, UL; BPL, COR, F, H,
HEH, N, T, Y

278 THE WEAKEST GO TO THE WALL, Or The Dissenters Sacri-
fic'd by All Parties: Being A true state of the Dissenters
Case, as it respects either High-Church or Low-Church.
LONDON: *Printed for* J. BAKER, *at the Black-Boy in Pater-
Row* [sic]. MDCCXIV. (*Price 6d.*)

8°. Pp. 3–40

Notes: Published shortly after 3 June. On pp. 37–39 it quotes
a passage from *Faults on both Sides* which had been quoted in
The Flying-Post for 3 June.

Copy: BOD. *Other copies:* BPL, C, COR, H, HEH

279 A BRIEF SURVEY OF THE LEGAL LIBERTIES OF THE DIS-
SENTERS: And How far the Bill now Depending consists
with Preserving the Toleration Inviolably. Wherein The
present Bill is Published; and also the Toleration Act at

large, that they may be compar'd with One Another. London: *Printed for* J. Baker, *at the Black Boy in Pater-Noster-
Row.* 1714. *Price 6d.*

8°. Pp. 3–39

Notes: Advertised 20 July, but probably published about two
months earlier. An attack on the Schism Bill which had been
introduced in the House of Commons on 12 May and was still
being debated in Parliament. The Bill became an Act when it
received the royal assent on 25 June.

Copy: BM. *Other copies:* BOD, NLS; BPL, F, H, HEH, Y

280   The Secret History of the White Staff, Being An Account of Affairs under the Conduct of some late Ministers,
and of what might probably have happened if Her Majesty
had not Died. London: *Printed for* J. Baker *at the Black-
Boy in Pater-Noster-Row.* 1714. *(Price One Shilling.)*

8°. Pp. 3–71

Notes: Four editions appeared before 27 October, the second of
which was advertised on 2 October by J. Baker and B. Berington. A pirate was offering a pretended continuation of the book
before 27 October. See Nos. 282 and 298.

Copy: BM. *Other copies:* BOD, CU, DW, NLS; BPL, C, F, H,
HEH, IU, N, P, R, RPB, T, Y

281   Advice to the People of Great Britain, With Respect to
Two Important Points of Their Future Conduct. I. What
they ought to expect from the King. II. How they ought to
behave by him. London: *Printed for* J. Baker *in Pater-
Noster-Row,* 1714. *Price Six-pence.*

8°. Pp. 3–40

Notes: Lee dates this 7 October.

Copy: BOD. *Other copies:* BM, CU, DW, UL; BPL, C, F, H,
HEH, IU, P, R, RPB, T, Y

282   The Secret History of the White Staff, Being An Account of Affairs Under the Conduct of some Late Ministers,
And of what might probably have happen'd if Her Majesty

had not Died. PART II. LONDON: *Printed for* J. BAKER *at the Black-Boy in Pater-Noster-Row.* 1714. (*Price One Shilling.*)

8º. Pp. 3–71

Notes: Published 27 October. For Parts I and III see Nos. 280 and 298.

Copy: BM. *Other copies:* BOD, NLS, UL; BPL, F, H, HEH, IU, N, NYPL, R, T, Y

283 A SECRET HISTORY OF ONE YEAR. LONDON: *Sold by* A. DODD *at the Peacock, without Temple-Bar, Pr. 6d.* MDCCXIV.

8º. Pp. [3]–40

Notes: Sometimes mistakenly attributed to Robert Walpole.

Copy: BM. *Other copies:* BOD, CU, UL; BPL, F, H, HEH, I, IU, N, NYPL, R, RPB, T, Y

284 TORIES AND TORY PRINCIPLES RUINOUS to both Prince and People. Being A Specimen of the Inconsistency of their Pretended Principles and Real Practices. [Six-line quotation from Dryden's translation of the second satire of Persius.] LONDON: *Printed for* J. BAKER *in Pater-Noster-Row,* 1714. *Price One Shilling.*

8º. Pp. 3–96

Notes: Sometimes advertised as "Printed for A. Bell in Cornhill and J. Baker in Pater-Noster-Row."

Copy: BOD. *Other copies:* NLS, UL; BPL, IU

285 IMPEACHMENT, OR NO IMPEACHMENT: Or, An Enquiry how far the Impeachment of certain Persons, at the present Juncture, would be consistent with Honour and Justice. LONDON: *Printed for* J. MORE, *and are to be Sold by the Booksellers.* 1714. (*Price Three-Pence.*)

8º. Pp. [i]–ii + 5–23

Copy: BM. *Other copies:* BOD, NLS; BPL, C, COR, H, HEH, IU, N, P, Y

*286 THE BRISTOL RIOT. Containing, I. A Full and Particular Account of the Riot in General, with several Material Circumstances Preceding, and Contributing to it. II. The whole Proceedings relating to the Tryal of the Rioters, before Judge Powys, Judge Tracey, and Mr. Baron Price. *By a Gentleman who attended the Commission.* LONDON: *Printed for J.* ROBERTS, *near Oxford-Arms in Warwick-Lane,* 1714. *(Price 6d.)*

8°. Pp. 1–31

Notes: Very probably, not quite certainly, Defoe's. Published 4 December. The postscript is dated "Novemb. 29." See also No. 288.

Copy: BM. *Other copies:* BOD; HEH, IU

287 THE PERNICIOUS CONSEQUENCES OF THE CLERGY'S INTERMEDLING with Affairs of State. With Reasons Humbly offer'd for passing a Bill to incapacitate them from the like Practice for the future. LONDON: *Printed for J.* BAKER, *at the Black Boy in Pater Noster-Row. (Price 6d.)* [1714?].

8°. Pp. [3]–39

Notes: This tract appeared shortly after the Bristol riot, to which it refers (pp. 38–39).

Copy: BPL. *Other copies:* C, HEH

*288 A FULL AND IMPARTIAL ACCOUNT OF THE LATE DISORDERS IN BRISTOL. To which is Added the Compleat Tryals of the Rioters Before Mr. Justice Powys, Mr. Justice Tracey and Mr. Baron Price. LONDON: *Printed for J.* ROBERTS, *near the Oxford-Arms in Warwick-Lane.* 1714. *(Price 6d)*

8°. Pp. 1–34

Notes: Certainly by the author of *The Bristol Riot* (No. 286), who was very probably Defoe. Published in early December, sometime after 4 December.

Copy: BOD. *Another copy:* IU

1 7 1 5

289 THE SECRET HISTORY OF THE SECRET HISTORY OF THE
WHITE STAFF, PURSE AND MITRE. *Written by a Person of
Honour* [.] LONDON: *Printed and Sold by* S. KEIMER, *at the
Printing-Press in Pater-Noster-Row.* 1715. (*Price Six Pence.*)

8°. Pp. 3–40

Notes: Published 4 January.

Copy: BM. *Other copies:* BOD, UL; BPL, C, COR, F, H, IU,
N, P, T

290 STRIKE WHILE THE IRON'S HOT, Or, Now is the Time To Be
Happy. Humbly propos'd, upon His Majesty's Late Most
Gracious Injunction. LONDON: *Printed and Sold by* S.
KEIMER, *at the Printing Press in Pater-Noster-Row,* 1715.
(*Price Six Pence.*)

8°. Pp. 5–43

Notes: Published 4 January.

Copy: BM. *Other copies:* BOD, NLS; BPL, C, HEH, IU, N, P

291 MEMOIRS OF THE CONDUCT OF HER LATE MAJESTY AND HER
LAST MINISTRY, Relating to the Separate Peace with France.
By the Right Honourable the Countess of ————[.] LON-
DON: *Printed, and Sold by* S. KEIMER, *at the Printing-House
in Pater-Noster-Row.* 1715. (*Price One Shilling.*)

8°. Pp. 3–80

Notes: Published 6 January.

Copy: BM. *Other copies:* BOD, NLS; BPL, C, COR, F, HEH,
I, IU, N, NYPL, P, Y

292 TREASON DETECTED, In An Answer To That Traiterous and
Malicious Libel, Entitled, English Advice to the Free-
holders of England Humbly offer'd to the Consideration
of all those Freeholders who have been poyson'd with that

Malignant Pamphlet. LONDON: *Printed, and Sold by* S. KEIMER, *at the Printing-Press in Pater-Noster-Row,* 1715. [*Price Six Pence.*]

8°. Pp. 3–35

Notes: Published 22 January. Dottin dates the second edition in February.

Copy: DW. *Other copies:* BM; BPL, N, Y

293   THE IMMORALITY OF THE PRIESTHOOD: Being An Historical Account Of the Factious and Insolent Behaviour Of The Inferior Clergy, Ever since the Reformation. Shewing, How Troublesome and Dangerous they have been to the State, and the many Mischiefs that have happen'd for want of a due Restraint of the Licentiousness of the Pulpit. LONDON, *Printed for* J. ROBERTS, *in Warwick-Lane.* 1715. *Price 1s.*

8°. Pp. [4 unnumbered] + 1–2 + 1–70

Notes: The tract includes remarks first printed in *The Flying-Post* on 22 January, and it was probably published soon afterwards. See the notes for No. 294.

Copy: BM. *Another copy:* N

294   THE JUSTICE AND NECESSITY OF RESTRAINING THE CLERGY In Their Preaching. Wherein is shown, That the Licentiousness of the Pulpit, and the Pride and Ignorance of the Inferior High-Flying Clergy, have Occasion'd the late Disorders in the State, and the Contempt of that Venerable Body. With a short Historical Account of their Seditious and Insolent Preaching and Practices from the Reformation to the present Times; and of the Trouble and Confusions that have happen'd thereupon. To which is added, The Bishop of Salisbury's New Preface to the Third Volume of his History of the Reformation, concerning the late Reviv'd Controversies, Viz. I. The Sacraments being an Expiatory Sacrifice. II. The Necessity of Secret Confession and Absolution. III. The Church's Authority acting in an Independence on the Civil Powers. IV. That singular and

extravagant Conceit on the Invalidity of Lay-Baptism.
LONDON, *Printed for* J. ROBERTS *in Warwick-Lane.* 1715.
Price One Shilling.

8⁰. Pp. 1–70

Notes: This tract is identical with the preceding, the same
sheets being used, except that it lacks the Preface and The
Royal Injunction to Convocation.

Copy: BM. *Another copy:* BOD

295 THE SECRET HISTORY OF THE SCEPTER, Or The Court Intrigues In the Late Reign. Accipitus pugnant dulce loquun-
tur aves. LONDON: *Printed and Sold by* S. KEIMER, *at the
Printing-Press in Pater-Noster-Row.* 1715. (*Price One Shilling.*)

8⁰. Pp. 3–67

Notes: Published 27 January. See No. 296; I do not know which
was published first.

Copy: BM

296 THE SECRET HISTORY OF STATE INTRIGUES In the Management of the Scepter, In the late Reign. LONDON: *Printed
and Sold by* S. KEIMER, *at the Printing-Press in Pater-
Noster-Row.* 1715. (*Price One Shilling.*)

8⁰. Pp. 3–67

Notes: Concludes with an advertisement: "Just Publish'd,
Strike while the Iron's Hot: Or, now is the Time to be Happy.
Humbly propos'd upon His Majesty's most Gracious late Injunction. Price 6d." See No. 295; I do not know which was
published first.

Copy: BM. *Other copies:* BOD; BPL, COR, F, H, HEH, IU, N,
P, Y

297 THE CANDIDATE: Bring a Detection of Bribery and Corrup-
tion As it is just now in Practice all over Great Britain, In
order to make Members of Parliament. Humbly Recom-

mended To all those who are now keeping Christmas at the Expence of their Representatives. They that will Buy, will Sell. LONDON: *Printed and Sold by* S. KEIMER, *at the Printing-Press in Pater-Noster-Row.* 1715. (*Price One Shilling.*)

8°. Pp. 3–72

Notes: Published 27 January; second edition 19 March.

Copy: CU. *Other copies:* BM; BPL, Y

298 THE SECRET HISTORY OF THE WHITE STAFF, Being An Account Of Affairs Under the Conduct of some Late Ministers, And of what might probably have happen'd if Her Majesty had not died. PART III. LONDON: *Printed for* J. BAKER *at the Black-Boy in Pater-Noster-Row.* 1715. (*Price One Shilling.*)

8°. Pp. 3–80

Notes: Lee dates this 29 January. Subsequently the three parts were issued together as one pamphlet. See Nos. 280, 282.

Copy: BM. *Other copies:* BOD; BPL, C, F, H, IU, N, R

299 A REPLY TO A TRAITEROUS LIBEL, Entituled, English Advice to the Freeholders of Great Britain. LONDON: *Printed for* J. BAKER *at the Black-Boy in Pater-Noster-Row.* 1715. (*Price Six-pence.*)

8°. Pp. [3]–40

Notes: Lee dates this 29 January.

Copy: NLS. *Other copies:* BOD, BM; BPL, C, COR, H, HEH, IU, NYPL, P, Y

300 THE PROTESTANT JUBILEE. A Thanksgiving Sermon On That Doubly remarkable Day The 20th of January; Appointed for Celebrating the Praises of God, for our Wonderful Deliverance, by the Happy Accession of His Most Gracious Majesty King George, To the Throne of Great Britain, When we were just at the Brink of Ruin. And it came

to pass the self same Day—Exod. xii. 51. LONDON: *Printed, and Sold by* S. KEIMER, *at the Printing-Press in Pater-Noster-Row.* [Date obliterated by a manuscript correction to 1714; it should read 1714/5 or 1715.] *Price 6d.*

8⁰. Pp. 5–27

Notes: Published 8 February 1715.

Copy: IU. *Another copy:* BPL

301 A LETTER TO A MERRY YOUNG GENTLEMAN, Intituled, Tho. Burnet, Esq; In Answer to One writ by him to the Right Honourable the Earl of Halifax; by which it plainly appears, the said Squire was not awake when he writ the said Letter. LONDON, *Sold by* J. MORPHEW *near Stationers Hall,* 1715. (*Price Four-pence.*)

8⁰. Pp. 3–24

Notes: Published 12 February; second edition 17 February. BOD and IU have a very cheap reprint (probably pirated) by D. Brown, 1715. The tract is sometimes attributed to William Oldisworth.

Copy: BM. *Other copies:* BOD, NLS, UL; BPL, C, COR, F, H, HEH, I, IU, N, P, Y

302 BURNET AND BRADBURY, Or The Confederacy Of The Press and the Pulpit For The Blood Of The Last Ministry. LONDON: *Printed and Sold by* S. KEIMER, *at the Printing-Press in Pater-Noster-Row,* 1715. (*Price Six Pence.*)

8⁰. Pp. 5–34

Notes: Published 16 February; second edition sometime in the same year.

Copy: BM. *Other copies:* NLS, UL; BPL, IU, Y

303 A VIEW OF THE PRESENT MANAGEMENT OF THE COURT OF FRANCE, And what new Measures they are like to take. LONDON, *Printed for* J. BAKER, *in Pater-Noster-Row.* 1715. *Price Six-pence.*

8⁰. Pp. 3–40

Copy: BPL. *Other copies:* BPL, HEH

304 THE FEARS OF THE PRETENDER TURN'D INTO THE FEARS OF DEBAUCHERY. Propos'd, without Ceremony, to the Consideration of the Lords Spiritual and Temporal; with a Hint to Richard Steele, Esq; LONDON: *Printed and Sold by* S. KEIMER, *at the Printing-Press in Pater-Noster-Row,* 1715. (*Price Six Pence.*)

8⁰. Pp. 5–38

Notes: CBEL states that this tract reached a third edition in 1715.

Copy: BM. *Other copies:* NLS; C, HEH, IU, Y

305 A FRIENDLY EPISTLE BY WAY OF REPROOF From one of the People called Quakers, To Thomas Bradbury, A Dealer in many Words. LONDON: *Printed, and Sold by* S. KEIMER, *at the Printing-Press in Pater-Noster-Row.* 1715. (*Price Sixpence.*)

8⁰. Pp. 5–39

Notes: Lee dates this 19 February. The third edition was published 5 March. BOD has a copy of the sixth edition which indicates that the Quakers had been disturbed by the implication that one of their own number had written the book, and which makes considerable alterations to soften references to the evil influence of the Court and the courtiers, of stage plays, etc. The title-page of this sixth edition reads: "*A Friendly Epistle By Way of Reproof From one of the People called Quakers, To Thomas Bradbury, A Dealer in many Words. To which is added a Letter from the Author to the Publisher, relating to the Threats and Menaces of several of the People called Quakers, for publishing the said Book.* The Sixth Edition, Corrected and Amended. London: Printed, and Sold by S. Keimer, at the Printing-Press in Pater-Noster-Row; 1715. (Price Six Pence.)" Pp. 5–24 are identical with the corresponding pages in the earlier editions. Pp. 25, 26, 28, 29, and 34 are softened by

considerable alterations or omissions. P. 39 has been reset to add
the catch words "A Letter" (and accidentally it has been misnumbered 4). P. [40] has been added, ostensibly as a letter from
the author to warn Keimer to make *the Amendments herein
marked*: "*so snall thy Enemies be ashamed of their Design to
hurt thee.*" Probably someone at Court had objected to the
broad attack on the bad influence of the courtiers on public
morals, a subject which Defoe had taken up even more boldly
in *The Fears of the Pretender turn'd into the Fears of Debauchery* (No. 304).

Copy: BM. *Other copies:* UL; BPL, F, IU, N, T, Y

306   REFLECTIONS UPON SACHEVERELL'S SERMONS OF JANUARY
20 AND 31, 1715. A Sermon Preach'd January 11. 1714/5.
By Henry Sacheverell, D. D. Rector of St. Andrew's Holborn. As it was taken in Short Hand by one of his Parishioners. To which is added, A Postscript containing Notes of
another Sermon, preach'd on the Twentieth of the same
Month. With proper REFLECTIONS upon each Discourse.
LONDON: *Printed and sold by* A. BOULTER *without Temple-
Bar, and* J. HARRISON *at the Royal-Exchange.* 1715. (*Price
4d.*)

8°. Pp. [2 unnumbered] + 5–28

Notes: Defoe was responsible only for the Remarks, the Postscript, and probably the Preface: Pp. [2 unnumbered] + 12–28.
On 5 March the tract was advertised with a warning against
"Grubstreet Copies of the sermon which are being printed,
without the Remarks, and sold about the streets for One
Penny"—in other words, Sacheverell's sermon without Defoe's
remarks.

Copy: BM

307   AN APPEAL TO HONOUR AND JUSTICE, Tho' it be of His
Worst Enemies. *By Daniel De Foe.* Being A True Account
of his Conduct in Publick Affairs. Jerem. xviii. 18. Come
and let us smite him with the Tongue, and let us not give
heed to any of his Words. LONDON: *Printed for* J. BAKER,
at the Black Boy in Pater-Noster-Row. 1715.

8⁰. Pp. 1–57 + 58

Notes: Published 24 February. The "Conclusion by the Publisher" (p. 58) was probably written by Defoe.

Copy: BM. *Other copies:* UL; BPL, F, H, I, N, R, T, Y

308   SOME REASONS OFFERED BY THE LATE MINISTRY In Defence of their Administration. LONDON: *Printed for* J. MORPHEW, *near Stationers Hall, 1715. (Price One Shilling.)*

8⁰. Pp. [3]–78

Notes: Published 3 March.

Copy: BM. *Other copies:* BOD, CU; BPL, C, COR, F, H, HEH, I, IU, N, NYPL, P, Y

309   THE FAMILY INSTRUCTOR. In Three Parts. With a Recommendatory Letter By the Reverend Mr. S. Wright. LONDON: *Sold by* EMAN. MATTHEWS, *at the Bible in Pater-noster-Row; and* Jo. BUTTON, *in* NEWCASTLE UPON TINE. 1715.

8⁰. Pp. [4 unnumbered] + 1–444

Notes: Lee dates the first edition 31 March. The sheets, printed by Button in Newcastle, were brought to London to be published by Matthews. Matthews engaged a popular Dissenting minister to write a preface of recommendation; and although the Rev. Mr. Wright spoke highly of the book itself, he condemned the bad printing in "A Letter to the Publisher" (p. ii): "The Printer has been faulty to a Degree, that I am afraid will render the Reader very uneasy; and I wish the Author had thought fit to communicate his Papers to you before they had fallen into such Hands: . . . ."

Defoe's elaborate precaution of having his first considerable didactic work printed in Newcastle to prevent the discovery of his authorship did not succeed. When he brought out the second edition in London (17 September) he admitted that the secret was already known to some; but he still refused to disclose his name, in the hope that the author's imperfections would not serve as a stumbling block in the way of those who might otherwise benefit from it. Wright's preface was dropped after the first edition, but it had served its purpose. The book became one of the most popular moral treatises of the century. By 10 September 1720 it had reached its eighth edition, together with the second edition of a second volume. See No. 403.

Copy: BM. *Other copies:* BOD, NLS; BPL

310 A SHARP REBUKE FROM ONE OF THE PEOPLE CALLED QUAKERS. To Henry Sacheverell, The High-Priest of Andrew's Holbourn. *By the same Friend that wrote to Thomas Bradbury.* LONDON: *Printed and Sold by* S. KEIMER, *at the Printing Press in Pater-Noster-Row.* 1715. (*Price Six Pence.*)

8°. Pp. 3–35

Notes: Published on or before 26 March 1715.

Copy: BM. *Other copies:* BOD, DW, UL; BPL, Y

311 AN APOLOGY FOR THE ARMY. In A Short Essay On Fortitude, &c. *Written by an Officer.* Enimvero Militiam ipsam, gravem, infructuosam; denis in diem Assibus, Animam & Corpus aestimari. Tacitus. LONDON: *Printed for* J. ROBERTS, *near Oxford-Arms in Warwick-Lane.* 1715.

8°. Pp. 1–58

Notes: Published 5 April.

Copy: BM. *Other copies:* UL; BPL, C, H, IU, P, Y

312 THE SECOND-SIGHTED HIGHLANDER. Being Four Visions Of The Eclypse, And Something of what may follow. LONDON, *Printed for* J. BAKER, *at the Black-Boy in Pater-noster-Row.* 1715. (*Price Six-pence.*)

8°. Pp. 3–46

Notes: Published 20 April.

Copy: BM. *Other copies:* BOD; BPL, C, HEH, T, Y

313 SOME METHODS TO SUPPLY THE DEFECTS OF THE LATE PEACE Without entring into a New War. LONDON: *Printed*

for J. BAKER, *at the Black-Boy in Pater-noster-Row. Price 6d.* [1715]

8°. Pp. 3–40

Notes: Published 20 April.

Copy: CU. *Other copies:* IU, NYPL, T, Y

314 A REMONSTRANCE FROM SOME COUNTRY WHIGS To a Member of a Secret Committee. LONDON: *Printed for* J. MORPHEW *near Stationers-Hall,* MDCCXV. *Price 6d.*

8°. Pp. 3–40

Notes: Published 11 May.

Copy: BM. *Other copies:* BOD, CU, NLS; BPL, COR, F, HEH, I, IU, Y

*315 THE HAPPINESS OF THE HANOVER SUCCESSION, Illustrated from the Conduct Of The Late Administration, Wherein their Designs are farther Expos'd, and publick Justice demanded upon the Betrayers of our Constitution. LONDON: *Printed and Sold by* S. KEIMER, *at the Printing-Press in Pater-Noster-Row,* 1715. (*Price Six Pence.*)

8°. Pp. 3–34

Notes: Very probably, not certainly, Defoe's. Ostensibly an attack upon his own *Secret History of the White Staff,* upon the Earl of Oxford, and upon the Treaty of Utrecht. If it is Defoe's, it is an example of a tract written for the new Ministry, but slanted so as to do the Earl of Oxford no real harm.

Copy: BM. *Other copies:* BOD; BPL, HEH

316 AN ATTEMPT TOWARDS A COALITION OF ENGLISH PROTESTANTS, From the Weakness of the Pretensions of the several Parties, for being either Better Christians, or Better Subjects, upon any Principles wherein they differ. To which is added, Reasons for Restraining The Licentiousness Of The Pulpit and Press. LONDON *Printed, and Sold by* J. ROBERTS, *in Warwick-Lane.* 1715. (*Price Six-Pence.*)

8º. Pp. 3–40

Copy: Y. *Other copies:* BM; BPL, H, N

317 A SEASONABLE EXPOSTULATION WITH, AND FRIENDLY RE-
PROOF UNTO JAMES BUTLER, Who, by the Men of this
World, is Stil'd Duke of O[rmon]d, Relating to the Tu-
mults of the People. *By the same Friend that wrote to
Thomas Bradbury, the Dealer in many Words, and Henry
Sacheverell, the High-Priest of St. Andrew's Holbourn.*
LONDON: *Printed, and Sold by* S. KEIMER, *at the Printing-
Press in Pater-Noster-Row.* 1715. (*Price Six Pence.*)

8º. Pp. 5–31

Notes: Published 31 May.

Copy: BOD. *Other copies:* BM, UL; BPL, C, COR, HEH, N,
NYPL, P, T, Y

318 HIS MAJESTY'S OBLIGATIONS TO THE WHIGS Plainly Proved.
Shewing That He can neither with Safety, Reason, or Gratitude, depart from Them. That the Notion of a Tory Ministry is Ridiculous and Absurd; Contrary to His true Interest, and the security of His Person and Government; and
that His chief Support under Heaven, must, and do's, rely
on the Wisdome, Courage, Power, and Fidelity of the
Whigs. With some Comparison between the Characters of
both Parties. LONDON: *Printed for* J. BAKER, *at the Black-
Boy in Pater-Noster-Row,* 1715. *Price Six-pence.*

8º. Pp. 3–39

Notes: This rebuttal of Atterbury's *English Advice to the Free-
holders of Great Britain* cites (pp. 22–23) in a very complimentary fashion "an able Writer for the late Ministry," Defoe's
Secret History of the White-Staff (Nos. 280, 282, 298).

Copy: BM. *Other copies:* BOD, UL; HEH, IU, N

319 A BRIEF HISTORY OF THE PACIFICK CAMPAIGN In Flanders
Anno 1712. And of the Fatal Cessation of Arms. Shewing
The Traiterous Steps then taken; With plain Proof, That

the British General did regulate his Conduct according to the Instructions he received from the General of France. *By an Officer in the Army.* LONDON: *Printed for* J. BAKER, *at the Black-Boy in Pater-Noster-Row,* 1715. *Price 6d.*

8⁰. Pp. 1–40

Copy: IU. *Other copies:* BM, UL; BPL, HEH

320   SOME CONSIDERATIONS ON THE DANGER OF THE CHURCH From her own Clergy. Humbly Offer'd to the Lower-House of Convocation.

_____hunc Spargere Voces
In vulgum ambiguas._____

LONDON: *Printed, and Sold by* J. ROBERTS, *in Warwick-Lane.* J. HARRISON, *at the Royal Exchange, and* A. DOD, *near Temple-Bar.* 1715. (*Price Six-Pence.*)

8⁰. Pp. 5–40

Copy: BM. *Other copies:* BOD; BPL, C, HEH, IU, N, P, T, Y

321   AN HUMBLE ADDRESS TO OUR SOVEREIGN LORD THE PEOPLE. LONDON: *Printed for* J. BAKER *at the Black-boy in Pater-Noster-Row,* 1715. (*Price Sixpence.*)

8⁰. Pp. 1–36

Notes: Published sometime in the early summer of 1715, while the Duke of Ormond was still ostensibly loyal and before the Rebellion broke out in September.

Copy: BM. *Other copies:* BOD; BPL, C, COR, HEH, IU, T

322   THE HISTORY OF THE WARS, OF HIS PRESENT MAJESTY CHARLES XII. King of Sweden; From his First Landing in Denmark, To His Return from Turkey to Pomerania. *By a Scots Gentleman in the Sweedish Service.* LONDON: *Printed for* A. BELL *in Cornhil,* T. VARNAM *and* J. OSBORN *in Lombard-Street, and* W. TAYLOR *and* J. BAKER, *in Pater-Noster-Row.* 1715.

8⁰. Pp. [2 unnumbered] + 1–400

Notes: Published 6 July. See No. 372 for *A Short View of the Conduct of the King of Sweden* (1717) and No. 433 for an expanded edition of *The History of the Wars.*

Copy: BM. *Other copies:* BOD, NLS, UL; BPL, C, COR, F, H, HEH, I, IU, LC, N, NYPL, RPB, T, Y

323 AN ACCOUNT OF THE CONDUCT OF ROBERT EARL OF OXFORD. LONDON, *Printed in the Year* MDCCXV. *Price One Shilling.*

8°. Pp. 1–99

Notes: This defence of the Earl of Oxford was denounced by Oxford himself in the *London Gazette* (9 July 1715). The articles of impeachment against Oxford had been laid before the House of Commons 7 July. Perhaps the denunciation of Defoe's attempted defence was no more than Oxford's refusal to justify all the implications in Oxford's anticipated trial in the House of Lords. The tract was reissued, with cancels for the title-page and B[1], as *Memoirs Of Some Transactions During The Late Ministry of Robert E. of Oxford* (published 22 June 1717, before the abortive trial of Oxford in July of the same year). See No. 378. It would seem that in 1715 and in 1717 alike Defoe expected this tract to be of service to the defence of the Earl of Oxford.

Copy: CU. *Other copies:* BM, BOD; BPL, C, COR, F, H, HEH, I, IU, N, P, RPB, T, Y

324 A HYMN TO THE MOB. LONDON, *Printed, and Sold by S.* POPPING, *in Pater-noster-Row;* J. FOX, *in Westminster-Hall;* S. BOULTER, *at Charing-Cross;* A. BOULTER, *without Temple-Bar; and* J. HARRISON, *at the Royal Exchange in Cornhill.* 1715. *(Price 6d.)*

8°. Pp. [i]–vi + 1–40

Notes: Published 14 July. Five years earlier in the *Review* for 16 March 1710 (VI, 587) Defoe had written: "And I have some Thoughts of giving the World a short Tract I have had long by me, Entitled, *A History of the Mob*———" In the *Review* for 27 April 1710 (VII, 56) he listed as one of the forthcoming

items in a vast imaginary work called *City Politicks* "a long
and exact History of the Mob" to be concluded "With a Poeti-
cal Essay, call'd a Hymn to the Rabble, . . ." Apparently the
History and the *Hymn* were never published. However, certain
passages in *A Hymn to the Mob* (1715), such as pp. 38–39,
would have been more significant for readers in 1710; it is not
unlikely that they were written five years before their publication as part of *A Hymn to the Mob.*

Copy: BM. *Other copies:* BOD, NLS; BPL, H, HEH, IU, R, Y

325 AN ACCOUNT OF THE GREAT AND GENEROUS ACTIONS OF
JAMES BUTLER, (Late Duke of Ormond.) Dedicated to the
Famous University of Oxford. LONDON, *Printed for* J.
MOORE, *near St. Paul's, and sold by the Book-sellers. Price
Six-pence.* [1715]

8°. Pp. 3–48

Notes: No place, no date, but London 1715. Advertised by J.
Baker 8 October.

Copy: BM. *Other copies:* UL; BPL, HEH, Y

326 A VIEW OF THE SCOTS REBELLION: With Some Inquiry
What we have to fear from them? And What is the prop-
erest Method to take with them? LONDON: *Printed, and
Sold by* R. BURLEIGH *in Amen-Corner.* 1715. (*Price Six-
Pence.*)

8°. Pp. [3]–40

Notes: Published 15 October.

Copy: BM. *Other copies:* NLS, UL; BPL, H, HEH, IU, N, R, Y

327 THE TRAITEROUS AND FOOLISH MANIFESTO OF THE SCOTS
REBELS, Examin'd and Expos'd Paragraph by Paragraph.
LONDON: *Printed, and Sold by* R. BURLEIGH *in Amen-
Corner.* 1715. (*Price Six-Pence.*)

8°. Pp. [3]–32

Notes: Published 29 October by R. Burleigh. Advertised 10
November by S. Keimer: "This Day is Publish'd."

Copy: BM. *Other copies:* C, HEH

328 BOLD ADVICE: Or, Proposals For the entire Rooting out of
Jacobitism In Great Britain. Address'd to the present M[in-
istr]y. Redress our Grievances, or expect to be ruin'd by
them. LONDON: *Printed by* J. MOOR *near St. Pauls, and Sold
by the Booksellers of London and Westminster.* 1715.
(Price Six Pence.)

8⁰. Pp. 3–43

Notes: P. 16 refers to No. 189: "The *Doway Letter,* a Pamphlet,
which made a great Noise in its Time, which whether it was
Genuine or not, matters not much, yet, as it is written with a
true Judgment of things, is worth quoting; . . ."

Copy: BM. *Other copies:* BOD, CU, NLS; BPL, C, H, HEH,
IU, Y

329 AN ADDRESS TO THE PEOPLE OF ENGLAND: Shewing The
Unworthiness of their Behaviour to King George; The
Folly of the Pretended Reasons for the present Rebellion;
And the Strict Obligations we are all under for our Own
Sakes, as well as the King's, to Assist and Support Him.

Every Kingdom Divided against its self, is brought to Deso-
lation, Matt. xii. 25. They that Resist shall receive to themselves Damnation, Rom. xiii. 2
And They who say, Let us do Evil that Good may come of
it, Their Damnation is just, Rom. iii. 8.

LONDON: *Printed for* J. WYAT, *at the Rose in St. Paul's
Church-Yard.* M.DCC.XV. *Price Three Pence.*

4⁰. Pp. 3–24

Copy: HEH. *Other copies:* BOD; C

330 A TRUMPET BLOWN IN THE NORTH, And sounded in the
Ears of John Eriskine, Call'd by the Men of the World,
Duke of Mar. *By a Ministring Friend of the People call'd
Quakers.* With a Word of Advice and Direction to the said
John Eriskine, and his Followers[.] *Sold by* S. KEIMER, *at*

the Cheshire-Coffee-house in King's Arms-Court on Lud-gate-hill. *MDCCXVI* [for 1715]. *Price 6d.*

8°. Pp. 3–38

Notes: Published before 15 November. Lee dates it 10 November. IU has an Edinburgh edition (8°, pp. 3–31) with a similar title-page except for the bookseller's statement: "Printed for Henry Luke, and are to be found in his Shop, in the Salt-market. M.DCC.XV. The Price Three Pence." The second edition was published 24 November. An advertisement of the second edition claimed for the author "a full Prediction of their late Defeat, above a Month before it happen'd."

Copy: BOD. *Other copies:* UL; BPL, H, HEH, Y

331   A LETTER FROM ONE CLERGY-MAN TO ANOTHER, Upon The Subject Of The Rebellion. LONDON: *Printed for* JOHN BAKER *in Pater-noster-Row.* 1716 [for 1715]. *Price 3d.*

8°. Pp. 3–23

Notes: Published 11 November. The HEH copy has a very badly trimmed manuscript note: "published Octob. 20 [perhaps 28] 1716 [perhaps 1715]." 1716 is obviously too late, in view of the reference to immediately current events; and there is no sufficient reason to question the specific date given by the ad-vertisement in *The Evening Post* (10 November 1715): "To Morrow will be publish'd."

Defoe disguised his style to a large extent, to make this tract pass as the work of a clergyman of the Church of England; but there are several characteristic idioms and allusions, and there is one very complimentary reference (p. 19) to a recent tract of his own (No. 313): "If you please to procure that Sober Pamphlet, entitled, *The best Method of Supplying the De-fects of the late Peace;* or to that purpose; I believe it will satisfie you, that the Interests of the Church and King must of Necessity support the King, and the King the Church: And may this Interest and Union of the Church and Crown be in-separable, say I, in this sort for ever."

Copy: BOD. *Other copies:* BPL, HEH, T, Y

331a A CONFERENCE WITH A JACOBITE; Wherein the Clergy Of The Church of England Are vindicated from the Charge of Hypocrisy and Perjury, in Praying for the King, and taking the Oaths of Allegiance and Abjuration. LONDON: *Printed for* J. BAKER, *and* T. WARNER, *at the Black-Boy in Pater-Noster-Row.* 1716. *Price 3d.*

8°. Pp. [3]–23

Notes: Strikingly similar to No. 331 in argument. First attributed to Defoe in 1959 (Catalogue No. 69 of Peter Murray Hill Ltd.).

Copy: NLS. *Another copy:* Y

332 [LETTER FROM GENERAL FORSTER TO THE EARL OF MAR] [1715]

Notes: The original of this fictitious letter was dated 9 December 1715 and presumably was published in *The London Post* of approximately that date. Reprinted in Boyer's *Political State*, X, 346 (for 546)–551.

1 7 1 6

333 PROPER LESSONS FOR THE TORIES, To Be Read throughout the Year: But more particularly upon June 10. The Birth-Day of the Pretender, alias the Fugitive Hero. July 1. The Day on which the Battle of the Boyne (in Ireland) was fought; when K. James ran away from his Army, and left them to shift for themselves. August 1. The Crisis: Or, The Day of K. George's most happy Accession to the Crown. November 4. The Day on which K. William [of ever blessed Memory] was born; and upon which, He, and his Fleet arriv'd in Torbay, in the West of England. LONDON: Printed, and Sold by J. ROBERTS, *near the Oxford-Arms in Warwick-Lane.* 1716. (*Price Three-pence.*)

8°. Pp. 5–22

Notes: Probably, not certainly, Defoe's.

Copy: BM. *Other copies:* NLS; HEH

334 SOME ACCOUNT OF THE TWO NIGHTS COURT AT GREENWICH:
Wherein may be seen The Reason, Rise and Progress of the
late unnatural Rebellion, against His Sacred Majesty King
George, and his Government. LONDON: *Printed for* J.
BAKER *at the Black-boy in Pater-noster-Row,* 1716.

8º. Pp. 1–72

Copy: BM. *Other copies:* BOD (title supplied in manuscript),
CU, NLS, UL; BPL, C, COR, H, HEH, IU, N, T, Y

335 THE CASE OF THE PROTESTANT DISSENTERS IN ENGLAND,
Fairly Stated. Humbly inscrib'd to all true Lovers of Religion, Liberty, and their Country.

> "Be but of the Faction, you need not fear,
> You may blaspheme, Rebel, Whore, and Swear,
> And be as good a Church-man as they are.
>   Dr. O.

LONDON: *Printed for* R. FORD, *at the Angel in the Poultry;
and Sold by* J. ROBERTS *in Warwick-Lane, and* J. HARRISON
under the Royal Exchange. 1716. *Price Three Pence.*

8º. Pp. 3–24

Notes: Published 18 January 1716.

Copy: HEH. *Another copy:* NLS

336 THE ADDRESS OF THE EPISCOPAL CLERGY of the Diocese of
Aberdeen, to the Pretender, WITH REMARKS upon the said
address, [1716]

Fol. half-sheet. Pp. [2 unnumbered]

Notes: No place, no date, no publisher. Reprints the address
of the clergy of the Diocese of Aberdeen with anonymous remarks written in January 1716. The address (without the remarks) was reprinted by Defoe in No. 385 (pp. 65–66) as having
been presented to the Pretender at Feterosse 25 December 1715.

Copy: BM

337 THE ADDRESS OF THE MAGISTRATES AND TOWN COUNCIL OF
ABERDEEN, to the Pretender. WITH REMARKS upon the said
address, [1716]

Fol. half-sheet

Notes: No place, no date, no publisher. Reprints the address of
the magistrates and town council of Aberdeen, with anonymous
remarks. The address (without the remarks) was reprinted by
Defoe in No. 385 (p. 67) as having been presented to the Pretender at the same time as No. 336.

Copy: BM. *Another copy:* NLS

338 SOME THOUGHTS OF AN HONEST TORY IN THE COUNTRY,
Upon The Late Dispositions of some People to Revolt.
With Something of the Original and Consequences of their
present Disaffection to the Person and Government of the
King. *In a Letter to an Honest Tory in London.* LONDON:
Printed for R. BURLEIGH *in Amen-Corner.* 1716. (*Price
Six Pence.*)

8°. Pp. [3]–39

Notes: Published 28 January 1716. The Y title-page has been
altered in MS to read 1715, but 1716 is the correct date.

Copy: HEH. *Another copy:* Y

*339 THE DECLARATION OF THE FREE-HOLDERS OF GREAT BRIT-
AIN, In Answer to that of the Pretender. (1716)

Fol. half-sheet Pp. [1–2]

Notes: The tract concludes: "Dated January 19 in the Second
Year of our Publick Happiness." NLS copy has an old manuscript note at the end: "Feb. 2. 1716." The tract is probably, not
certainly, by Defoe.

Copy: NLS

340 THE CONDUCT OF SOME PEOPLE, ABOUT PLEADING GUILTY.
With some Reasons Why it was not thought proper to shew
Mercy to some who desir'd it. LONDON [.] *Printed: And*

Sold by J. BAKER, *at the Black-Boy in Pater-Noster-Row,* 1716. [*Price Six-Pence.*]

8°. Pp. 3–36

Notes: A justification of the King's refusal to pardon Lord Derwentwater.

Copy: BOD. *Other copies:* BPL, C, H, IU, Y

341   AN ACCOUNT OF THE PROCEEDINGS AGAINST THE REBELS, and other Prisoners, Tried before the Lord Chief Justice Jefferies, and other Judges, in the West of England, in 1685, for taking Arms under the Duke of Monmouth. With a compleat List of all the Persons that suffered, the Counties they suffer'd in, the Crimes they were tryed for, and the Punishments inflicted on them. Also an Account of what was done against those in Scotland, who took Arms there under the Earl of Argyle, &c. and against the Protestants in Ireland, by the late King James, and his Deputy Tyrconnel. *Published from an original Manuscript.* To which is prefix'd, the Duke of Monmouth's, the Earl of Argyle's, and the Pretender's Declarations; that the Reader may the better Judge of the Cause of the Several Rebellions. With what Measure you meet, it shall be measured to you again, Mat. 7. 2. LONDON: *Printed for* J. BAKER, *and* THO. WARNER, *at the Black Boy in Pater-noster-row,* 1716. *Price One Shilling.*

8°. Pp. iii–xxvi + 1–48

Notes: Published 21 February as a reply to the charge that the Government of George I had shown no mercy to the rebels. CU has a copy of the third edition in the same year.

Copy: BM. *Other copies:* CU; BPL, F, HEH, IU, N

342   THE PROCEEDINGS OF THE GOVERNMENT AGAINST THE REBELS, compared with the persecutions of the late Reigns. [1716]

Fol. half-sheet. Pp. [1–2]

Notes: No place, no date, but presumably London 1716. An abstract of No. 341, to which it refers explicitly. Apparently intended to carry the same argument to a much wider reading public. No printer's name and no price; probably the tract was given away.

Copy: BM

343 REMARKS ON THE SPEECH OF JAMES LATE EARL OF DER-WENTWATER, Beheaded on Tower-Hill for High-Treason, February 24, 1715/16. LONDON, *Printed for* R. BURLEIGH *in Amen-Corner.* 1716. (*Price 3d.*)

8°. Pp. 3–20

Notes: Very probably, not certainly, Defoe's.

Copy: BOD. *Other copies:* NLS; BPL, F, N

344 AN ESSAY UPON BUYING AND SELLING OF SPEECHES In A Letter To a Worshipfull Justice of the Peace, Being also A Member of a certain Worshipfull Society of Speech-Makers. LONDON: *Printed for* J. BAKER *and* T. WARNER, *in Pater-Noster-Row,* 1716. *Price Six-Pence.*

8°. Pp. 3–39

Notes: An attack on Steele for running into debt and then trying to raise money from the Government by joining the Opposition—as in his speech in the House of Commons (22 February 1716) favoring mercy to the rebels.

Copy: BM. *Other copies:* NLS; HEH, IU, N, Y

345 SOME CONSIDERATIONS ON A LAW FOR TRIENNIAL PARLIAMENTS. With an Enquiry, I. Whether there may not be a Time when it is necessary to suspend the Execution, even of such Laws as are most Essential to the Liberties of the People? II. Whether this is such a Time or no? LONDON: *Printed for* J. BAKER, *and* T. WARNER, *at the Black Boy in Pater-Noster-Row.* 1716. *Price 6d.*

8°. Pp. [3]–40

Notes: According to Lee, published in April. BM and BOD have a Dublin edition (pp. 32) dated 1716.

Copy: BM. *Other copies:* BOD, CU, NLS; BPL, C, COR, F, H, HEH, IU, N, NYPL, T, Y

346   THE ILL CONSEQUENCES OF REPEALING THE TRIENNIAL ACT: In A Letter To Mr. Sh[ippe]n. *Manibus Pedibusq;* LONDON: *Printed for* J. BAKER *and* T. WARNER *at the Black Boy in Pater-Noster-Row.* 1716. *Price Three Pence.*

8º. Pp. 1–12

Notes: Published 9 April 1716.

Copy: BPL. *Other copy:* BM

347   A DIALOGUE BETWEEN A WHIG AND A JACOBITE, Upon the Subject of the late Rebellion; And the Execution of the Rebel-Lords, &c. Occasion'd by The Phaenomenon in the Skie, March 6. 1715–16. O! Ye Hypocrites, ye can discern the Face of the Skie, but can ye not discern the Signs of the Times? Mat. xvi. 3. LONDON: *Printed for* J. ROBERTS, *in Warwick Lane: And Sold by the Booksellers of London and Westminster.* 1716. *Price Four-Pence.*

8º. Pp. 3–32

Notes: Advertised "This Day is published" on 10 May, but this seems rather late for the first edition. BOD has a copy of the third edition.

Copy: BM. *Other copies:* NLS; BPL, HEH

348   A TRUE ACCOUNT OF THE PROCEEDINGS AT PERTH; The Debates in the Secret Council there; with the Reasons and Causes of the suddain finishing and breaking up of the Rebellion. *Written by a Rebel.* LONDON: *Printed for* J. BAKER *at the Black-Boy in Pater-Noster-Row.* 1716.

8º. Pp. 1–76

Notes: BM has an old manuscript note on the title-page: "12 May." The tract is sometimes mistakenly attributed to the Master of Sinclair. On pp. 1–2 Defoe refers to his own forthcoming history of the rebellion (No. 351): ". . . it is not to be expected that I should enter here upon the particular Steps by which it was brought to such a Head, or of the posture of their Affairs in the Field at this Time; these Things are reserved for a fuller and larger Publication, which lies ready for the View of the World, as Times and Circumstances of Things shall allow."

Copy: BM. *Other copies:* NLS; BPL, C, P, Y

349 A JOURNAL OF THE EARL OF MARR'S PROCEEDINGS, From His First Arrival in Scotland, To His Embarkation for France. *Printed in France by Order of the Earl of Marr. Reprinted in* LONDON, *and Sold by* J. BAKER *in Pater-Noster-Row. Price 6d.* [1716]

8°. Pp. [iii]–xvi + [1]–32

Notes: Defoe wrote only the anti-Jacobite Introduction, pp. [iii]–xvi. The main body of the text (pp. [i]–32) was compiled by the Earl of Mar and others on the basis of a rough draft by Robert Leslie, and this was printed at Avignon. Defoe's reprint with his own Introduction was published in London about July. See *Huntington Library Quarterly*, XVII [1954], 209–228.

Copy: BM. *Other copies:* CU, NLS; BPL, HEH

350 REMARKS ON THE SPEECHES OF WILLIAM PAUL Clerk, AND JOHN HALL of Otterburn, Esq; Executed at Tyburn for Rebellion, the 13th of July, 1716. In which the Government and Administration both in Church and State, as founded upon the Revolution, are Vindicated from the Treasonable Reflections and false Aspersions thrown upon them in those Speeches, which were inserted at length, as they were deliver'd to the Sheriffs. LONDON, *Printed for* J. BAKER *and* T. WARNER *at the Black Boy in Pater-noster-Row.* M.DCC.XVI. (*Price 6d.*)

8°. Pp. 3–38

Copy: BM. *Other copies:* CU, DW, NLS, UL

351 THE ANNALS OF KING GEORGE, YEAR THE SECOND; Being a Faithful History of the Affairs of Great Britain, For the Year MDCCXVI. Containing also a full and compleat History of the Rebellion. LONDON, *Printed for* A. BELL, *at the Cross Keys and Bible in Cornhill;* W. TAYLOR, *at the*

Ship, and J. BAKER, *at the Black-Boy in Pater-Noster-Row,* 1717 [for 1716].

8º. Pp. iii–iv + [1]–352 + 1–99 + [8 unnumbered]

Notes: Advertised in *Mercurius Politicus* for September 1716 as published at 5*s.* by J. Baker and T. Warner at the Black-Boy in Pater-Noster-Row. A manuscript note on the title-page of the IU copy of the September issue of *Mercurius Politicus* dates the publication of that monthly "Oct: yᵉ 17ᵗʰ." Presumably *The Annals* appeared somewhat earlier in October.

For many years J. Baker had been one of Defoe's principal publishers. During 1716 and early 1717 he issued some of Defoe's works with his own imprint, some jointly with his new partner T. Warner. It is not clear that he issued anything for Defoe after 25 March 1717. On May 8 (No. 369, pp. 26–27) Defoe remarked that a certain explanation would be given "if Mr. Baker the Publisher were not just at the point of Death while this is in Press, . . ." By 26 April 1717 T. Warner was using the old address with his own name alone, and he was even issuing one of Defoe's books jointly with Eman. Matthews at the Bible in Pater-Noster-Row. From that time on, T. Warner continued to be one of Defoe's principal publishers until near the end of 1730 (shortly before Defoe's death on 24 April 1731), occupying J. Baker's old premises at the Black-Boy in Pater-Noster-Row.

Shortly before 20 May 1717 S. Baker (perhaps a relative of J. Baker) began to rival T. Warner by issuing many of Defoe's new works at the confusingly similar sign of the Black-Boy and Anchor in Pater-Noster-Row. S. Baker did not publish for Defoe after 1717.

The annual listed here and its sequel (No. 385) appeared as Volumes II and III in the six-volume series entitled *The Annals of King George.* The volume for *Year the Fourth* was prefaced by a declaration "that this Volume of the Annals is done by a different Hand from the former, and that considerable Alterations are made herein, both as to the Distribution of Materials, and manner of relation; . . ." Abel Boyer, who had been widely regarded as the first editor of the series, published an emphatic disclaimer at the end of *The Political State of Great-Britain* for 1716 (X, unpaged advertisement following the Index).

For Volumes II and III of the *Annals* Defoe wrote at least the account of the Jacobite rising and the military campaigns (singled out for special remark in the Preface to Volume II). This account is in Defoe's characteristic style, it overlaps many of his pamphlets on the subject, and it was borrowed from extensively by Defoe in his later work called *The History of the Reign of King George* (No. 407). In Volume III (pp. 286–289) Defoe gives characteristic expression to the disappointment of the Dissenters when their disabilities were not removed.

In No. 537 for June 1718 (pp. 262–263) Defoe defended his use of abstracts in the appendix: ". . . I borrow this Method from the Writers of the *Annals* of King GEORGE, as well as from the late excellent Bishop of *Sarum,* in his History of the Reformation, . . ."

Copy: BM. *Other copies:* NLS; C, IU, N

352 THE LAYMAN'S VINDICATION OF THE CHURCH OF ENGLAND, As well against Mr. Howell's Charge of Schism, As against Dr. Bennett's Pretended Answer to it. LONDON, *Printed for A. and* W. BELL, *at the Cross-Keys in Cornhill: And sold by* J. BAKER, *at the Black-Boy in Pater-noster-Row,* 1716.

8°. Pp. 1–79

Notes: Published 22 October.

Copy: BM. *Other copies:* BOD, DW; BPL, C, HEH

353 SECRET MEMOIRS OF THE NEW TREATY OF ALLIANCE WITH FRANCE: In which some of the First Steps in that remarkable Affair are discovered; with some Characters of Persons. LONDON, *Printed and Sold by* J. ROBERTS, *at the Oxford-Arms in Warwick-Lane,* 1716.

8°. Pp. 1–36

Notes: Published 10 November. BM and BOD have a Dublin reprint dated 1716. Ostensibly written by someone at the French Court.

Copy: BM. *Other copies:* BOD, CU; BPL, C, F, H, HEH, I, IU, N, P, Y

1 7 1 7

354   SECRET MEMOIRS OF A TREASONABLE CONFERENCE AT S[OM-
ERSET] HOUSE, For Deposing The Present Ministry, and
making a new Turn at Court. LONDON, *Printed for* J.
MORE, *near St. Paul's,* 1717. *Price One Shilling.*

8°. Pp. 1–78

Notes: Second edition published 16 January.

Copy: BM. *Other copies:* BOD (defective), CU, NLS; BPL, C,
COR, F, H, HEH, IU, P, Y

355   THE DANGER OF COURT DIFFERENCES: Or, The Unhappy
Effects Of A Motley Ministry: Occasion'd by the Report of
Changes at Court. LONDON, *Printed and Sold by* J. BAKER,
and T. WARNER, *at the Black-Boy in Pater-noster-Row.*
1717. *Price 6d.*

8°. Pp. 3–47

Notes: Published 17 January.

Copy: BM. *Other copies:* C, F, HEH, IU, Y

356   THE QUARREL OF THE SCHOOL-BOYS AT ATHENS, As lately
Acted at a School Near Westminster. LONDON, *Printed for*
J. ROBERTS, *at the Oxford Arms in Warwick-Lane,* 1717.
Price 6d.

8°. Pp. 3–38

Notes: Published 26 January. Quoted in No. 533 for January
1717 (pp. 40–42).

Copy: C. *Other copies:* BM, BOD; BPL, F, I, IU, P, T

357   FACTION IN POWER: Or, The Mischiefs And Dangers Of A
High-Church Magistracy, Shewing, I. That the Nation can
never have a settled Peace, nor the Constitution be safe,
while Persons Disaffected to the Protestant Government are
possest of any Part of its Authority. II. The many Hardships

His Majesty King George's best Subjects lie under from their Insolence and Oppression.

Iram atque animos a crimine sumunt.

LONDON: *Printed for R. Burleigh in Amen-Corner, 1717.* (*Price One Shilling.*)

8°. Pp. 1–59

Notes: Published 31 January.

Copy: BM. *Other copies:* BOD; BPL, H, HEH

358 AN IMPARTIAL ENQUIRY INTO THE CONDUCT Of the Right Honourable Charles Lord Viscount T[ownshend] [.]
————Remember Milo's End,
Wedg'd in that Timber which he strove to rend.

LONDON, *Printed for A.* DODD, *at the Peacock without Temple-Bar.* 1717.

8°. Pp. 1–76

Notes: Published 5 February.

Copy: BM. *Other copies:* BOD, CU; C, COR, F, H, HEH, IU, Y

359 AN ARGUMENT PROVING THAT THE DESIGN OF EMPLOYING AND ENOBLING FOREIGNERS, Is a Treasonable Conspiracy against the Constitution, dangerous to the Kingdom, an Affront to the Nobility of Scotland in particular, and Dishonourable to the Peerage of Britain in general. With an Appendix; Wherein an insolent Pamphlet, Entituled, The Anatomy of Great Britain, is Anatomiz'd; and its Design and Authors detected and exposed. LONDON; *Printed for the Booksellers of London and Westminster.* 1717. *Price One Shilling.*

8°. Pp. 1–102

Notes: Published 11 February; the third edition published 9 March. The tract contains a reference (p. 3) to *The Quarrel Of*

the School-Boys At Athens (No. 356), which was published 26
January. See also No. 369. The issue of No. 533 for February
1717 (dated February 6 by a manuscript note on the title-page
of the IU copy) quotes this tract at length (pp. 80–87).

Copy: BM. *Other copies:* BOD, CU, NLS, UL; BPL, C, COR,
F, H, HEH, I, IU, N, NYPL, P, R, Y

360 AN ACCOUNT OF THE SWEDISH AND JACOBITE PLOT. With A
Vindication of our Government from the horrid Aspersions
of its Enemies. And A Postscript, relating to the Post-Boy
of Saturday, Feb. 25. In a Letter to a Person of Quality,
occasion'd by the Publishing of Count Gyllenborg's Letters.
LONDON; *Printed for* S. POPPING *at the Black Raven in
Pater-Noster-Row,* J. HARRISON *at the Royal-Exchange, and*
A. DODD *at the Peacock without Temple-Bar.* M.DCC.XVII.
(*Price Six-Pence.*)

8°. Pp. 5–40

Notes: BPL has two copies which differ only in the retention or
omission of eight words on the title-page: "occasion'd by the
publishing of Count Gyllenborg's Letters." I do not know which
of the BPL copies represents the earlier issue.

Copy: BOD. *Other copies:* BPL (two copies), F (lacks pp. 34–38)

361 A CURIOUS LITTLE ORATION, DELIVER'D BY FATHER ANDREW.
1717

Notes: I have been unable to locate a copy of the first edition.
The second edition was published 16 March (8°, pp. iii–iv +
5–19 + [20]). BM and DW have copies. The title-page of the
BM copy reads: "*A Curious Little Oration, Deliver'd by Father
Andrew, Concerning the Present Great Quarrels That divide
the Clergy of France.* The Second Edition. Translated from the
Fourth Edition of the French, by Dan. De F[o]e. London,
Printed: And sold by J. Roberts in Warwick-Lane; and A[.]
Dodd, at the Peacock without Temple-Bar; and M. Baldwin, in
Stories-Passage, St. James's Park, MDCCXVII. [*Price Three
Pence.*]"

362 AN EXPOSTULATORY LETTER, TO THE B[ISHOP] OF B[ANGOR]
Concerning A Book lately publish'd by his Lordship, En-

titul'd, A Preservative Against the Principles and Practices
of The Nonjurors, &c. LONDON: *Printed for* E. SMITH, *in
Cornhill. Price 6d.* [1717].

8°. Pp. [1]–30

Copy: BM. *Other copies:* NLS; BPL, C, HEH, IU

363   FAIR PAYMENT NO SPUNGE: Or, Some Considerations On
The Unreasonableness of Refusing to Receive back Money
Lent on Publick Securities. And The Necessity of Setting
the Nation Free from the Insupportable Burthen of Debt
and Taxes. With a View of the Great Advantage and Benefit which will arise to Trade and to the Landed Interest, as
well as to the Poor, by having these Heavy Grievances taken
off. LONDON, *Printed: And sold by* J. BROTHERTON *and* W.
MEDDOWS *at the Black Bull in Cornhill, and* J. ROBERTS *in
Warwick-Lane.* 1717. *Price One Shilling.*

8°. Pp. [6 unnumbered] + 1–79

Notes: Published before 19 March. Cited on p. 144 of No. 533
for March 1717.

Copy: BOD. *Other copies:* DW, UL; BPL, COR, F, Y

364   WHAT IF THE SWEDES SHOULD COME? With Some Thoughts
About Keeping The Army on Foot, Whether they Come or
Not. LONDON: *Printed for* J. ROBERTS, *near the Oxford-
Arms in Warwick-Lane.* MDCCXVII. Price Six-Pence.

8°. Pp. 3–38

Notes: Published 20 March.

Copy: BM. *Other copies:* NLS; BPL, C, H, R, T, Y

365   THE QUESTION FAIRLY STATED, Whether Now is not the
Time to do Justice to the Friends of the Government, as
well as to its Enemies? And Whether the old Excuse of its,
Not being a proper Season, will serve any longer. Stand by
your Friends, do Justice to your Enemies, and fear no Body.
LONDON, *Printed for* J. ROBERTS *in Warwick-lane;* J. HAR-

RISON *under the Royal Exchange; and* A. DODD *without Temple-Bar.* 1717.

8°. Pp. [3]–33

Notes: Published 22 March. See No. 335. Much of this tract (pp. 14–16 and parts of 17, 18) was reprinted almost verbatim in No. 389 (pp. 26–28).

Copy: BM. *Other copies:* DW; C, H, IU, N, P, T, Y

366 THE DANGER AND CONSEQUENCE OF DISOBLIGING THE CLERGY consider'd, As it Relates To making a Law for Regulating the Universities, and Repealing some Laws Which Concern The Dissenters, In a Letter to a Noble Lord in Oxfordshire. LONDON: *Printed for* J. BAKER, *at the Black-Boy in Pater-noster-row,* 1716–17. *Price 6d.*

8°. Pp. 3–38

Notes: Published before 25 March. Advertised at least as early as 8 April.

Copy: BM. *Other copies:* C, IU, T, Y

367 REASONS FOR A ROYAL VISITATION; Occasion'd by the Present Great Defection Of The Clergy From The Government. Shewing The Absolute Necessity of Purging the Universities, and Restoring Discipline to the Church. Make the Tree good, and the Fruit will be good.

> Of all the Plagues with which Mankind are curst,
> Ecclesiastick Tyranny's the worst.

LONDON, *Printed for* J. ROBERTS, *near the Oxford Arms in Warwick Lane.* 1717.

8°. Pp. [1]–64

Notes: Published 11 April.

Copy: BM. *Other copies:* UL; C, HEH, IU, Y

368 MEMOIRS OF THE CHURCH OF SCOTLAND, In Four Periods. I. The Church in her Infant-State, from the Reformation to

the Queen Mary's Abdication. II. The Church in its grow-
ing State, from the Abdication to the Restoration. III. The
Church in its persecuted State, from the Restoration to the
Revolution. IV. The Church in its present State, from the
Revolution to the Union. With An Appendix, of some
Transactions since the Union. LONDON, *Printed for* EMAN.
MATTHEWS *at the Bible, and* T. WARNER *at the Black-Boy,
both in Pater-Noster-Row,* 1717.

8°. Pp. [2 unnumbered] + 1–232 + 137–333 (for 233–429) +
Appendix of 9 unnumbered pages

Notes: Lee dates this 26 April. Except for the Appendix, the
manuscript had been written about nine years earlier; and the
book was published at this time to support the representations
of the delegates sent to London by the Scottish General Assembly. In 1719 it was advertised as printed for and sold by W.
Taylor at the Sign of the Ship in Pater-Noster-Row (see the advertisements appended to No. 417, *The Farther Adventures of
Robinson Crusoe*).

Copy: BM. *Other copies:* BOD, CU, NLS, UL; BPL, C, F, H,
HEH, I, IU, N, NYPL, R, RPB, T, Y

369 A FARTHER ARGUMENT AGAINST ENNOBLING FOREIGNERS, In
Answer To the Two Parts of the State Anatomy: With a
Short Account of the Anatomizer.

> T–l–nd Blasphemes the Holy-Ghost,
> The Bribed of Bribes Accuses;
> Of Foreign Rogues the Traytor Boasts,
> The King, who was Your Lord of Hosts,
> That Ra——l How Abuses.

> A Letter to a Member of Parliament.

LONDON: *Printed for* E. MOORE *near St. Paul's,* 1717. *Price
6d. Where may be had the first Part, Price 1s.*

8°. Pp. 1–43

Notes: Published 8 May. The title-page quotes a political ballad
which Defoe had published sixteen years earlier (No. 36). See
also No. 359.

Copy: BM. *Other copies:* BPL, C, H, IU, P, T, Y

370   THE CONDUCT OF ROBERT WALPOLE, ESQ; From The Beginning of the Reign of her late Majesty Queen Anne, to
the present Time.

> When I behold the Man whose long try'd Faith,
> Whose prudent Conduct, and superiour Merit,
> Has rais'd his Country's Glory to the Sky,
> And made her Name a Terror to the Nations;
> This Man, in spite of Faction, I will Praise,
> Will hold him Dear, and bind him to my Heart.
>   Tragedy of Sir Walter Raleigh, Ms.

LONDON: *Printed for* T. WARNER, *at the Black Boy in Pater-*
Noster-Row. 1717. *Price One Shilling. Where may be had,*
The Conduct of the Lord Townshend. Price One Shilling.

8°. Pp. [1]–66

Notes: Published 16 May. *An Impartial Enquiry Into the Con-*
duct Of the Right Honourable Charles Lord Viscount T[own-
shend] had been published 5 February.

Copy: BM. *Other copies:* CU; BPL, C, COR, F, H, HEH, I, N,
P, Y

371   THE REPORT REPORTED: Or, The Weakness and Injustice
Of The Proceedings Of The Convocation In Their Cen-
sure Of The Ld. Bp. of Bangor, Examin'd and Expos'd.
Judge Righteous Judgment. LONDON, *Printed for* S. BAKER,
at the Black-Boy and Anchor, in Pater-noster-Row, 1717.
Price Six-pence.

8°. Pp. 3–39

Notes: Published sometime before 20 May; second edition 22
May.

Copy: BM. *Other copies:* BOD, DW, NLS; BPL, C, F, IU, Y

372   A SHORT VIEW OF THE CONDUCT OF THE KING OF SWEDEN.

LONDON, *Printed, and Sold by* A. DODD, *at the Peacock without Temple-Bar.* (*Price 6d.*) [1717].

8°. Pp. [3]-40

Notes: No date, but 1717. Published 24 May. Professedly written from an ultra-royalist point of view, and largely a condensation and reworking of No. 322.

Copy: BM. *Other copies:* HEH, Y

373 A GENERAL PARDON CONSIDER'D, In Its Circumstances and Consequences: Particularly relating to The Exceptions said to be now in Debate; And To The Reason why it came out no sooner. LONDON, *Printed for* S. BAKER, *at the Black-Boy and Anchor in Pater-noster-Row,* 1717. *Price Six-pence.*

8°. Pp. 3-37

Notes: Published 24 May.

Copy: BOD. *Other copies:* NLS, UL; BPL, C, H, Y

374 OBSERVATIONS ON THE BISHOP'S ANSWER TO DR. SNAPE. By a Lover of Truth. LONDON: *Printed for* S. BAKER, *at the Black-Boy and Anchor in Pater-noster-Row,* 1717. *Price Six-pence.*

8°. Pp. 3-34

Copy: BM. *Other copies:* DW; C, Y

375 A VINDICATION OF DR. SNAPE, In Answer To Several Libels lately publish'd against him. With Some further Remarks on the Bishop of Bangor's Sermon: By which it will plainly appear who is the truest Friend to the Church, the Bishop or the Doctor.—*O Tempora! O Mores!* LONDON: *Printed for* A. DODD *at the Peacock without Temple-Bar. Price Six Pence.* [1717]

8°. Pp. 3-32

Notes: Published on or before 30 May.

Copy: BM. *Other copies:* CU; BPL, C, IU, Y

376 A REPLY TO THE REMARKS Upon The Lord Bishop of Bangor's Treatment Of The Clergy And Convocation. Said to be Written by Dr. Sherlock. Turno Tempus erit cum magno optaverit Emptum Intactum Pallanta. Title of the Remarks. LONDON: *Printed for S.* BAKER, *at the Black-Boy and Anchor in Pater-noster-Row,* 1717. *Price Six Pence.*

8°. Pp 3–39

Copy: BM. *Another copy:* BPL

377 MINUTES OF THE NEGOTIATIONS OF MONSR. MESNAGER At the Court of England, Towards the close of the last Reign. Wherein Some of the most Secret Transactions of that Time, relating to the Interest of the Pretender, and a Clandestine separate Peace, are detected and laid open. *Written by Himself. Done out of French.* LONDON: *Printed for S.* BAKER, *at the Black-Boy and Anchor in Pater-noster-Row,* 1717.

8°. Pp. 3–326

Notes: Published 17 June. To support the claim that the book was a genuine translation from the French of Mesnager, an alternative title-page was printed: *"Minutes Of The Negotiation* [sic] *of Monsr. Mesnager At The Court of England, Written by Himself. Done out of French.* Antwerp, printed for Jean van Borscelen. 1717."

In 1956 I secured from Pickering & Chatto Ltd. a perhaps unique copy containing both title-pages, that of Baker followed by that attributed to van Borscelen. The explanation given in Pickering & Chatto's Catalogue No. 358 is as follows: "The Antwerp title is cancelled in the majority of copies and the stub of the leaf is visible. It is presumably a title for sale in the Low Countries and a joint undertaking of the two booksellers, Baker and van Borscelen." However, van Borscelen seems to have been a fictitious name. The Antwerp title-page (like Defoe's occasional use of ostensible imprints from The Hague and Dantzic and his allusion to a French original published at Cologne) was meant to obscure the actual details of publication in London. One title or the other was meant to be cancelled; in this copy the two were retained by oversight.

In *The Political State of Great-Britain* for June 1717 (XIII, 627–639), published sometime after mid-July, Abel Boyer made a savage attack on the *Minutes* as a forgery by Defoe, declaring (p. 628) that "no such Book has yet been publish'd either in *France* or *Holland;* or, indeed, in any Country in *Europe.*" Apparently Boyer believed that Antwerp was in Holland. To counteract this attack, an advertisement was inserted in *The Post-Boy* for 27 July, supplying the name of the supposed translator (who in turn was to vouch for the genuineness of the original manuscript): "In a few days will be publish'd, The Second Edition of Minutes of the Negotiations of Mr. Mesnager at the Court of England, towards the Close of the last Reign. Wherein some of the most secret Transactions of that Time, relating to the Interest of the Pretender, and a Clandestine separate Peace, are detected and laid open. Written by himself. Done out of French. By Rowland Wynche Gent. To which is added, by way of Preface, A Vindication of the said Book from the Misrepresentations of Mr. A. Boyer; wherein its Genuineness is made very clear by the Translator's Testimony. Printed for S. Baker at the Black-Boy and Anchor in Pater-noster-Row."

In 1736 a different publisher, J. Roberts, published an edition (without Defoe's preface to the second edition), and he called this the "second edition." Roberts' title-page reads: *"Minutes Of The Negotiation* [*sic*] *of Monsr. Mesnager At The Court of England, During the Four last Years of the Reign of her late Majesty Q. Anne. Containing many Curious Particulars of those Times. Written by Himself. Done out of French.* The Second Edition. London: Printed for J. Roberts, near the Oxford-Arms in Warwick-Lane. MDCCXXXVI." Roberts' edition is completely reset, although it seems to follow the first edition closely, with pp. [3]–326 in octavo. The odd recurrence of the singular number (in *Negotiation*) suggests that Roberts' printer perhaps used a copy with the Antwerp title.

Copy: BM. *Other copies:* BOD, CU, NLS, UL; BPL, C, CH, COR, F, H, HEH, IU, LC, N, NYPL, P, R, RPB, T, Y

378 MEMOIRS OF SOME TRANSACTIONS DURING THE LATE MINISTRY Of Robert E. of Oxford. LONDON: *Printed for* T. WARNER, *at the Black-Boy in Pater-noster-Row.* 1717. *Price One Shilling.*

8°. Pp. 1–99

Notes: Published 22 June. Except for the new title-page, this is identical with *An Account Of The Conduct Of Robert Earl of Oxford* (No. 323).

Copy: BM. *Other copies:* F, IU

379   A DECLARATION OF TRUTH TO BENJAMIN HOADLY, One of the High Priests of the Land, And Of the Degree whom Men call Bishops. *By a Ministring Friend, who writ to Tho. Bradbury, A Dealer in many Words.* LONDON: *Printed for* E. MORE *near St. Paul's, and Sold by the Booksellers of London and Westminster,* 1717. *Price Six Pence.*

8°. Pp. 3–31

Notes: Attributed to a Quaker. Published 29 June.

Copy: BM. *Other copies:* BOD, CU, DW, NLS, UL; C, COR, H, HEH, IU, NYPL, P, RPB, T, Y

380   A HISTORY OF THE CLEMENCY OF OUR ENGLISH MONARCHS, From the Reformation, down to the Present Time. With some Comparisons. LONDON: *Printed for* N. MIST, *and sold by* T. WARNER, *at the Black Boy in Pater-Noster-Row. 1717. Price 6d.*

8°. Pp. 1–30

Notes: P. 24 refers to Defoe's previous refusal to expect a king to exercise Godlike mercy, but states that George—unlike God himself—has not required repentance before forgiveness. Published sometime after 15 July, when the Act of Grace received the royal assent; for it is a reply to a Jacobite tract by Matthias Earbery, in which the author had referred to "the Act lately promulgated." In the title of Earbery's tract nine of the first ten words are identical with Defoe's: *The History Of The Clemency Of Our English Monarchs. The Usage Prisoners, who Surrender'd at Discretion, have met with from their Hands. Compar'd with several Matters of Fact which have lately occur'd in this Kingdom. With an Account of the Manner of issuing forth*

Acts of Grace and Pardon in former Reigns. Written for the Information of the present Age, and of Posterity. . . .

The similarity of titles leads to frequent confusion between Earbery's tract and Defoe's far more scarce reply. For instance, H reports a copy of Defoe's reply, but I have not yet been able to check this for verification. Defoe summarized both tracts in No. 533 for September 1717 (pp. 561–578 and 578–593).

Copy: CU. *Another copy:* NLS

381 THE CONDUCT OF CHRISTIANS MADE THE SPORT OF INFIDELS. *In a Letter From a Turkish Merchant at Amsterdam To the Grand Mufti at Constantinople:* On Occasion of some of our National Follies, but especially the late scandalous Quarrel among the Clergy. LONDON: *Printed for* S. BAKER *at the Black Boy and Anchor in Pater-Noster-Row.* 1717. [*Price Six-Pence.*]

8°. Pp. 3–38

Notes: Published 30 July. Quoted at length in No. 537 for August 1717 (pp. 477–488).

Copy: BM. *Other copies:* BPL, C, Y

382 THE OLD WHIG AND MODERN WHIG REVIVED, In The Present Divisions at Court: Or, The Difference betwixt Acting upon Principle and Interest exemplified by some of our present Patriots. LONDON: *Printed for* S. BAKER, *at the Black-Boy and Anchor, in Pater-noster-Row,* 1717. *Price Six-pence.*

8°. Pp. 3–48

Notes: Published 1 August.

Copy: BM. *Other copies:* NLS; BPL, Y

383 A LETTER TO ANDREW SNAPE, Occasion'd by the Strife that lately appeared among the People call'd, Clergy-men. *By the Author of the Declaration of Truth.* LONDON: *Printed for* T. WARNER, *at the Black-Boy in Paternoster-Row,* 1717. (*Price 6d.*)

8°. Pp. 1–30

Notes: Attributed to a Quaker. Published 24 August.

Copy: BM. *Other copies:* DW; BPL, F

384   THE CASE OF THE WAR IN ITALY STATED: Being a Serious
Enquiry How Far Great-Britain Is Engaged to Concern it
Self in the Quarrel between the Emperor and the King of
Spain. Pax Quaeritur Bello. LONDON: *Printed for* T. WAR-
NER, *at the Black-Boy in Pater-noster-Row*, 1718 [for 1717].
Price 6d.

8°. Pp. 1–34

Notes: Published 18 December.

Copy: BM. *Other copies:* BOD; BPL, C, H, HEH, IU

385   THE ANNALS OF KING GEORGE, YEAR THE THIRD: Contain-
ing not only the Affairs of Great Britain, But the General
History of Europe during that Time. LONDON: *Printed for*
A. BELL, *at the Cross-Keys and Bible in Cornhill;* T.
VERNON, *and* J. OSBOURN, *at the Oxford-Arms in Lombard-
Street; and* W. TAYLOR, *in Pater-Noster-Row.* 1718 [for
1717].

8°. Pp. [1]–376 + 1–129

Notes: Published on or before 30 December. For Defoe's share
in this compilation, see No. 351. P. 262 restates Defoe's reply to
Earbery's tract in No. 380.

Copy: BM. *Other copies:* C, HEH, IU, N

1 7 1 8

386   CONSIDERATIONS ON THE PRESENT STATE OF AFFAIRS In
Great-Britain. LONDON: *Printed for* J. ROBERTS *near the
Oxford Arms in Warwick-Lane.* MDCCXVIII.

4°. Pp. [1]–40

Notes: Published 10 January. The running title is "Considerations on His Majesty's speech." BM has a copy with a variant

title-page: *"The Juncture: Or Considerations On His Majesty's Speech At the Opening of the Present Session of Parliament, November 21, 1717. [5 lines of quotation.] London: Printed for J. Roberts near the Oxford Arms in Warwick-Lane. MDCCXVIIII [sic]."* I have had no opportunity to determine which tract represents the earlier version; but Mr. A. F. Allison of the British Museum informs me that the slight variations are apparently those of the author and not merely literal and typographical.

Copy: BM. *Other copies:* BOD; C, HEH, IU

387 THE DEFECTION FARTHER CONSIDER'D, Wherein The Resigners, As some would have them stil'd, Are really Deserters. But when the Righteous turneth away from his Righteousness, and committeth Iniquity, and doth according to all the Abominations that the wicked Man doth, Shall he live? All his Righteousness that he hath done, shall not be mentioned: In his Trespass that he hath trespassed, and in his Sin that he hath sinned, in them shall he die, Ezek. 18. 24. LONDON: *Printed, and Sold by* WILLIAM BOREHAM, *at the Angel in Pater-Noster-Row.* 1718. (*Price 6d.*) [Qui Jupiter Vult Perdere hos dementat.]

8°. Pp. 3–38

Notes: Published 16 January; second edition 8 February.

Copy: BM. *Other copies:* BOD, CU; BPL, C, COR, F, IU, Y

388 SOME PERSONS VINDICATED AGAINST THE AUTHOR OF THE DEFECTION, &c. And that Writer Convicted of Malice and Falshood. R[obert] W[alpole], Esq; Much Malice mingled with but little Wit. Dryd. LONDON: *Printed for* WILLIAM BOREHAM, *at the Angel in Pater-Noster-Row.* 1718. (*Price 6d.*)

8°. Pp. 3–40

Notes: Published 28 January.

Copy: BM. *Other copies:* BOD (lacks all after D₄), DW, NLS, UL; BPL, F, HEH, I, IU, P, Y

389   MEMOIRS OF THE LIFE And Eminent Conduct Of that Learned and Reverend Divine, DANIEL WILLIAMS, D. D. With Some Account of his Scheme for the vigorous Propagation of Religion, as well in England as in Scotland and several other Parts of the World. Address'd to Mr. Peirce. LONDON: *Printed for* E. CURLL, *at the Dial and Bible against St. Dunstan's Church in Fleet-street,* M.DCC.XVIII. *Price 2s. 6d. Bound.*

8°. Pp. 1–[86]

Notes: Published 25 February. Advertised on that date in *The Post Boy,* in an obvious appeal to the Dissenters: "Printed for E. Curll against St. Dunstan's Church in Fleetstreet; and sold by J. Matthews in Pater-noster-row, R. Robertson in S. Paul's Church-yard, T. Cox in Cheapside, J. Clark and R. Ford in the Poultry, and A. Bell in Cornhill, price 2s. stich'd, 2s. 6d. bound. Where may be had, A Collection of all the Inscriptions on the Tombs and Grave-Stones in the Dissenters' Burying-Ground in Bunhill-Fields; price 1s. 6d." See No. 365.

Copy: BM. *Other copies:* BOD, CU, DW; H, I, T

390   MR. DE LA PILLONNIERE'S VINDICATION: Being An Answer To The Two Schoolmasters, And Their Boys Tittle Tattle, Wherein The Dispute between Dr. Snape and Mr. Pillonniere is set in a True Light. *By the Author of the Lay-Man's Vindication.* LONDON: *Printed for* T. WARNER, *at the Black-Boy in Paternoster-Row,* 1718. *(Price 6d.)*

8°. Pp. 1–34

Copy: BM. *Other copies:* BOD; HEH, IU

391   A BRIEF ANSWER TO A LONG LIBEL: Being An Examination Of A Heap of Scandal, Published by the Author of the Scourge, Entituled, The Danger of the Church's Establishment, From the Insolence of Protestant Dissenters. Tantum Religio potuit suadere Malorum. LONDON: *Printed, and Sold by* WILLIAM BOREHAM, *at the Angel in Pater-Noster-Row.* 1718. *(Price 6d.)*

8°. Pp. 3–40

Copy: BM. *Another copy:* CU

392 A LETTER FROM THE JESUITS TO FATHER DE LA PILLONNIERE. In Answer to The Letter sent to Them by that Father, and published by Dr. Snape, in his Vindication, &c. LONDON: *Printed for* T. WARNER, *at the Black Boy in Pater-noster-Row.* 1718. *Price Six Pence.*

8°. Pp. [3]–43

Notes: Signed by "The Fathers of the Society of Jesus." A defence of Bishop Hoadly and La Pillonniere against Dr. Snape, under the pretence of rebuking La Pillonniere for disloyalty to the Jesuits.

Copy: IU. *Other copies:* BOD, DW, NLS; BPL, HEH

393 A GOLDEN MINE OF TREASURE OPEN'D FOR THE DUTCH. *By a Lover of Britain.* LONDON: *Printed in the Year,* 1718.

8°. Pp. 1–55

Notes: Ostensibly by two authors—pp. 1–32 by a foreigner, presumably a Swede; the "Application" which follows by an Englishman. Probably, not certainly, by Defoe. The style is much like his, but the defence of Sweden against the attempted expansion of Hanover places the author in opposition to the Ministry of the day. Perhaps written in support of Walpole against Stanhope and Sunderland.

Copy: IU. *Other copies:* BOD, CU; BPL, HEH

394 MISERERE CLERI: Or, The Factions of the Church. Being a Short View Of The Pernicious Consequences Of The Clergy's Intermedling with Affairs of State. In Nomine Domini incipit omne malum. LONDON: *Printed for* W. BOREHAM, *at the Angel in Pater-noster-row.* [*Price Six Pence.*] [1718]

8°. Pp. 3–35

Notes: Published 17 March; second edition 25 March.

Copy: BM. *Other copies:* BOD, NLS; C, HEH, N

395   SOME REASONS WHY IT COULD NOT BE EXPECTED the Government Wou'd Permit the Speech or Paper Of James Shepheard, Which he Delivered at the Place of Execution, to be Printed. With some Account of the Paper it self. LONDON: *Printed for W.* BOREHAM *at the Angel in Pater-noster-row.* 1718. (*Price Six Pence.*)

8°. Pp. 3–30

Notes: Published 27 March. Defoe summarized this tract in No. 537 for March 1718 (pp. 107–115). His preliminary remarks refer to "this Author, *let him be who he will,*" and they conclude: "It is reported, that this Piece has been Published by Order or Direction of some Persons too high to name, and that the Government it self has thought it highly necessary to have the Eyes of the abused People opened in a thing of such Consequence; but this I do not assert: . . ."

Copy: BM. *Other copies:* BOD; BPL

*396   THE JACOBITES DETECTED; In The Methods They Made Use of To draw young Men into an Association against His Majesty King George. Discite Justitiam moniti, & non temnere Divos. Virg. LONDON: *Printed for J.* ROBERTS, *near the Oxford-Arms in Warwick-lane,* 1718.

8°. Pp. 5–35

Notes: Published 9 April. Very probably, not certainly, by Defoe.

Copy: BOD. *Other copies:* NLS; BPL

397   DR. SHERLOCK'S VINDICATION OF THE TEST ACT EXAMIN'D, And The False Foundations Of It Exposed. In Answer to so much of his Book against the Bishop of Bangor, As Relates to the Protestant Dissenters. LONDON: *Printed for S.* POPPING *at the Black-Raven in Pater-noster-row,* J. HARRISON *at the Royal-Exchange, and A.* DODD, *without Temple-Bar,* 1718. (*Price Six-Pence.*)

8°. Pp. [3]–40

Copy: BM. *Other copies:* DW, NLS; BPL, F

398   A Brief Comment upon His Majesty's Speech: Being Reasons for strengthening the Church of England, by taking off the Penal Laws against Dissenters. *By one called a Low-Church-Man.* London: *Printed for* T. Warner, *at the Black Boy in Paternoster-Row,* 1718. (*Price Sixpence.*)

8°. Pp. 1–38

Notes: Published 10 April. Fictitious attribution to a Low Churchman.

Copy: BM. *Another copy:* Y

399   A Vindication of the Press: Or, An Essay On The Usefulness of Writing, On Criticism, And The Qualification of Authors. Wherein is shewn, That 'tis for the Advantage of all Governments to encourage Writing, otherwise a Nation would never be secure from the Attempts of its most secret Enemies; Barbarous and prejudic'd Criticisms on Writings are detected, and Criticism is justly stated. With an Examination into what Genius's and Learning are necessary for an Author in all manner of performances. London: *Printed for* T. Warner, *at the Black-Boy in Pater-Noster-Row.* MDCCXVIII. [*Price Sixpence.*]

8°. Pp. [3]–36

Notes: Published 21 April.

Copy: IU. *Another copy:* NYPL

400   A Letter from Some Protestant Dissenting Laymen, In the Behalf of that whole Body, To their Friends of the British Parliament, Concerning Their Treatment under the Present Administration. Occasion'd by their Disappointment from the late Session. London: *Printed, and Sold by* W. Graves, *at the Black Spread Eagle in Pater-Noster-Row.* 1718. (*Price Six-pence.*)

8°. Pp. [3]–36

Notes: Published 1 May.

Copy: BM. *Other copies:* NLS; C

401   MEMOIRS OF PUBLICK TRANSACTIONS IN THE LIFE AND MIN-
      ISTRY OF his GRACE THE D. OF SHREWSBURY. In which will
      be found much of the History of Parties, and especially of
      Court-Divisions, during the last Four Reigns; which no
      History has yet given an Account of. Plus valet occultatis
      Testis quam Auriti Decem. LONDON: *Printed for* THO.
      WARNER, *at the Black-Boy, in Pater-Noster-Row,* 1718.
      Price Two Shillings.

      8º. Pp. i–ii + 1–139

      Notes: Date of publication uncertain. Advertised 18 February:
      "Next Week will be publish'd" (i. e., between 24 February and
      1 March). But on 5 May it was advertised: "This Day is pub-
      lished." Possibly published by 1 March; perhaps held back
      more than two months for fear of censorship. A manuscript
      note on p. 64 of the BM copy of the edition of 1733 confuses
      this book with a much earlier and very different one, *Memoirs
      of Secret Service:* "Ld Peterborough was charged to have written
      this book with the aid of Dr Davenant. It was burnt by the
      hangman pursuant to the Order of the H. of Lords." Refers (p.
      119) to No. 377, and quotes (pp. 127–131) a passage from No.
      334 (pp. 68–72).

      Copy: BM. *Other copies:* BOD, CU, UL; BPL, C, COR, F, IU,
      NYPL, P, T, Y

402   A LETTER FROM PARIS, Giving An Account Of The Death
      Of the Late Queen Dowager, And of Her Disowning The
      Pretender To be Her Son, With some Observations. LON-
      DON: *Printed, and Sold by* WILLIAM BOREHAM, *at the Angel
      in Pater-Noster-Row,* 1718. *Price Six Pence.*

      8º. Pp. [3]–40

      Notes: Published 10 May. Ostensibly a letter from St. Germains
      giving an account of the Queen Dowager's death (April 30,
      O. S.), followed by "Observations" written by someone in Eng-
      land. No. 537 for May 1718 (pp. 209–226) reprints the entire
      "Letter" from the tract (pp. [3]–28). It omits the "Observations"
      (pp. 29–40) with the following apology (p. 226): "There are
      some very pertinent Observations in the Tract above-mentioned,

relating to the Consequences of such a Disowning her Son; but as I have not Room for them here, and also because a farther Account is promised to be given by the same Author, as well of the Fact as of the Observations also, I purposely omit them." If Defoe ever published the proposed sequel, I have not seen it.

Copy: IU. *Other copies:* NLS; Y

403 THE FAMILY INSTRUCTOR, In Two Parts. I. Relating to Family Breaches, and their obstructing Religious Duties. II. To the great Mistake of mixing the Passions in the Managing and Correcting of Children. With a great Variety of Cases, relating to setting Ill Examples to Children and Servants. VOL. II. LONDON: *Printed for* EMMAN. MAT-THEWS, *at the Bible in Pater-Noster-Row.* MDCCXVIII.

12°. Pp. [i]–vi + 1–404

Notes: 3d edition published 4 June 1728. See No. 309.

Copy: BM. *Other copies:* BPL, R

404 A HISTORY OF THE LAST SESSION OF THE PRESENT PARLIA-MENT. With a Correct List of Both Houses. LONDON: *Printed, and Sold by* W. BOREHAM, *at the Angel in Pater-Noster-Row.* 1718. *Price 1s. 6d.*

8°. Pp. 3–4 + 5–136

Notes: Published 12 June.

Copy: BM. *Other copies:* BOD; BPL, H, Y

405 A LETTER TO THE AUTHOR OF THE FLYING-POST; In Answer To a most malicious false Story of His from Edinburgh; and to a celebrated Deistical Letter of His from the Grecian Coffee-House. Wherein, The grave Misrepresentations and Blunders of that Libeller are expos'd; His unjust Charges against the Church proved false and groundless; The Reverend Clergy vindicated from His Calumnies; His unsufferable Ill-breeding and Ignorance lash'd; and His own Arguments retorted upon Himself. The whole being both Merry and Serious.

——— Ridentem dicere verum
Quid vetat?———

LONDON: *Printed for, and Sold by* A. MOORE *near St. Paul's,* 1718. (*Price Six-pence.*)

8°. Pp. [1 unnumbered] + [i]–40

Notes: A bantering quasi-Tory tract in which Defoe ridicules George Ridpath and defends Mist's *Weekly-Journal* (in which he then had the principal hand). The tract is in the form of a letter dated "London, 1. August, 1718."

Copy: HEH. *Another copy:* BOD

406　A CONTINUATION OF LETTERS WRITTEN BY A TURKISH SPY At Paris. Giving an impartial Account to the Divan at Constantinople of the most Remarkable Transactions of Europe, and discovering several Intrigues and Secrets of the Christian Courts, especially that of France; continued from the Year 1687, to the Year 1693. *Written originally in Arabick, Translated into Italian, and from thence into English.* LONDON, *Printed for* W. TAYLOR, *at the Sign of the Ship in Pater-Noster-Row,* 1718.

12°. Pp. [18 unnumbered] + 1–304

Notes: The frontispiece gives a picture of the supposed author, Mahomet the Turkish Spy. Published 20 August, and advertised as Volume the First; but the series was not carried on. Copies are sometimes numbered 9 on the spine; but sets of the well-known *Letters Written by a Turkish Spy* are always found with no more than the original eight volumes.

Copy: BOD. *Other copies:* BPL, C, IU

407　THE HISTORY OF THE REIGN OF KING GEORGE, From the Death of her late Majesty Queen Anne, to the First of August, 1718. Collected from the most authentick Vouchers; supported by Evidence of Fact, and entirely Unconcern'd in the separate Interest of Persons or Parties. To be continued Yearly. Oculatae nostrae sunt Manus, Credunt

quod Vivent. LONDON: *Printed for N. Mist in Carter-Lane,*
1719 [for 1718].

8º. Pp. [1]–252 + [12 unnumbered] + 1–232 + [8 unnumbered]

Notes: Published 29 November 1718. On 9 April 1719 Mist still
advertised it: "This day is published." Apparently no attempt
was made to continue the proposed series. To a large extent
this book is a rearrangement and a reprint of Nos. 351 and 385.
It condenses the material Defoe had used earlier; and like some
of Defoe's other writings for Mist, it implies a sympathy for the
Tories and the unfortunate Jacobites, whose cause he represents
as hopeless. Like *Mercurius Politicus,* this serves as subtle propaganda for the Government.

Copy: BM. *Another copy:* BOD

408 THE MEMOIRS OF MAJR. ALEXANDER RAMKINS, A High-
land-Officer, Now in Prison at Avignon. Being An Account
of several remarkable Adventures during about Twenty
Eight Years Service in Scotland, Germany, Italy, Flanders
and Ireland; exhibiting a very agreeable and instructive
Lesson of Human Life, both in a Publick and a Private
Capacity, in several pleasant Instances of his Amours, Gal-
lantry, Oeconomy, &c. LONDON: *Printed for* R. KING *at the
Queen's-head, and* W. BOREHAM *at the Angel in Pater-
noster-row,* 1719 [for 1718]. *Price 1s. 6d. Stitch'd, and 2s.
Bound.*

12º. Pp. [2 unnumbered] + 1–182

Notes: Published 9 December, 1718. Major Ramkins' "Twenty
Eight Years Service" anticipated Robinson Crusoe's "Eight and
Twenty Years" on the desert island (25 April 1719). On 3 December 1719 Boreham alone reissued the unsold sheets at a
lower price, omitting the publishers' preface and the leaf giving
the half-title, but substituting a new title undoubtedly suggested
by the recent success of *The Life and Strange Surprizing Adventures of Robinson Crusoe:* (BM) *The Life And strange Surprising Adventures of Majr. Alexander Ramkins, A Highland-
Officer, Now in Prison At Avignon.* The remainder of the title

was repeated from the first edition, and the edition was post-dated 1720.

Copy: BM. *Another copy:* BOD

1 7 1 9

409   A FRIENDLY REBUKE TO ONE PARSON BENJAMIN; Particularly relating to his Quarreling with his Own Church, and Vindicating the Dissenters. *By One of the People called Quakers.* LONDON: *Printed for E.* MOORE *near St. Paul's.* 1719. *Price 6d.*

8⁰. Pp. 3–32

Notes: Published 6 January. Fictitious attribution to a Quaker.

Copy: BM. *Other copies:* BOD, CU, DW, UL; BPL, C, F, H, HEH, IU, T

410   OBSERVATIONS AND REMARKS UPON THE DECLARATION OF WAR against Spain, And upon the Manifesto Publish'd in the Name of the King of France, explaining the said Declaration. From whence the Reason and Justice of the said War is confirm'd as well on the Part of Great Britain, as on the Part of France. LONDON: *Printed for W.* BOREHAM, *at the Angel in Pater-noster-row,* 1719. *Price 6d.*

8⁰. Pp. 3–44

Notes: The French Declaration of War and the King's Manifesto explaining that Declaration had both been published on 31 December 1718 (O. S.). Defoe's tract is largely made up by quotations from and elaborations on the Manifesto.

Copy: IU. *Another copy:* HEH

411   MERRY ANDREW'S EPISTLE TO HIS OLD MASTER BENJAMIN, A Mountebank at Bangor-Bridge, On the River Dee, near Wales. Pestifero vomuit Colubar Sermone Britannus. Prosp. de vit. Pelag. LONDON: *Printed for E.* SMITH *in Corn-hill.* 1719[.] *Price 6d.*

8º. Pp. 3–32

Notes: Fictitious attributions to a Merry-Andrew. Published 31 January. Defoe summarized this tract in No. 533 for March 1719 (pp. 161–171).

Copy: BM. *Other copies:* BOD; BPL

412 THE LIFE AND STRANGE SURPRIZING ADVENTURES OF ROBINSON CRUSOE, Of York, Mariner: Who lived Eight and Twenty Years, all alone in an un-inhabited Island on the Coast of America, near the Mouth of the Great River Oroonoque; Having been cast on Shore by Shipwreck, wherein all the Men perished but himself. With An Account how he was at last as strangely deliver'd by Pyrates. *Written by Himself.* LONDON: *Printed for* W. TAYLOR *at the Ship in Pater-Noster-Row.* MDCCXIX.

8º. Pp. [2 unnumbered] + [1]–364. Frontispiece (portrait)

Notes: Published 25 April; second edition 9 May; third edition 4 June; fourth edition 7 August, with a map of the world showing Crusoe's travels. The title-page named W. Taylor as the publisher, but the sharers in his venture were named in the first advertisement of the first edition: "Printed for W. Taylor at the Ship in Pater-Noster-Row, J. Graves in St. James's street, T. Harbin at the New Exchange, J. Brotherton and W. Meadows at the Black-Bull in Cornhill." The legend that the book was refused by almost every bookseller before Taylor published it is disproved by the fact that it was undertaken jointly by five considerable booksellers. T. Cox's pirated and abridged edition was published 6 August. For various states of Taylor's first edition see H. C. Hutchins, *Robinson Crusoe and its Printing* (New York, 1925).

Copy: BM. *Other copies:* BOD, CU, UL; BPL, C, CH, COR, H, HEH, IU, NYPL, P, PML, R

413 A LETTER TO THE DISSENTERS. LONDON: *Printed for* J. ROBERTS *in Warwick-Lane.* 1719. (*Price Six-pence.*)

8º. Pp. 3–27

Notes: Lee dates this in May. Defoe had published a different tract with the same title in 1713.

Copy: BOD. *Other copies:* DW; BPL

414   THE ANATOMY OF EXCHANGE-ALLEY: Or, A System of Stock-Jobbing. Proving that Scandalous Trade, as it is now carry'd on, to be Knavish in its Private Practice, and Treason in its Publick; Being a clear Detection I. Of the Private Cheats used to Deceive one another. II. Of their Arts to draw Innocent Families into their Snares, understood by their New Term of Art (viz.) (being let into the Secret.) III. Of their Raising and Spreading False News to Ground the Rise or Fall of Stocks upon. IV. Of their Joyning with Traytors in Raising and Propagating Treasonable Rumours to Terrify and Discourage the People with Apprehensions of the Enemies to the Government. V. Of their Improving those Rumours, to make a Run upon the Bank, and Ruin publick Credit. VI. Of the dangerous Consequences of their Practices to the Government, and the Necessity there is to Regulate or Suppress them. To which is added, Some Characters of the most Eminent Persons concern'd now, and for some Years past, in Carrying on this Pernicious Trade. *By a Jobber.* LONDON: *Printed for* E. SMITH *near Exchange-Alley.* 1719. *Price One Shilling.*

8°. Pp. 1–64. Pp. 17–24 are misnumbered 9–16.

Notes: Fictitious attribution to a Jobber. Published 1 July; second edition 10 September.

Copy: BM. *Other copies:* BOD; BPL, C, CH, COR, H, HEH, LC, NYPL, RPB, T, Y

415   SOME ACCOUNT OF THE LIFE, And Most Remarkable Actions, OF George Henry BARON DE GOERTZ, Privy-Counsellor And Chief Minister of State, To The Late King of Sweden. LONDON: *Printed for* T. BICKERTON, *at the Crown, in Pater-Noster-Row.* MDCCXIX.

8°. Pp. [1]–46. Frontispiece portrait of Goertz

Notes: Goertz was executed 2 March 1719. Lee dates the tract about May 1719, but it was advertised in *The Daily Courant* on 13 July 1719: "This Day is Published."

Copy: BM. *Other copies:* BOD, UL; BPL, C, IU, LC, T

416   THE JUST COMPLAINT OF THE POOR WEAVERS Truly Represented, with as much Answer As it deserves, to a Pamphlet
Lately written against them Entitled The Weavers Pretences examin'd, &c. LONDON: *Printed for* W. BOREHAM *at
the Angel in Pater-Noster-Row.* MDCCXIX.

8°. Pp. 3–[44]

Notes: Published 11 August.
Copy: BM. *Other copies:* BOD, UL; H, Y

417   THE FARTHER ADVENTURES OF ROBINSON CRUSOE; Being the
Second and Last Part Of His Life, And of the Strange
Surprizing Accounts of his Travels Round three Parts of
the Globe. *Written by Himself.* To which is added a Map
of the World, in which is Delineated the Voyages of Robinson Crusoe. LONDON: *Printed for* W. TAYLOR *at the Ship in
Pater-Noster-Row.* MDCCXIX.

8°. Pp. [5 unnumbered] + [1]–373. Folding map of the world as
frontispiece

Notes: Published 20 August.

Copy: BM. *Other copies:* BOD, UL; BPL, C, COR, H, HEH, I,
IU, JCB, NYPL, PML, R, RPB, T

418   THE GAMESTER. A Benefit-Ticket For all that are concern'd
in the Lotteries; Or The Best Way how to get the 20000 l.
Prize. Together with Some necessary and seasonable Re-
marks on the Schemes of Insurance relating to the present
Lotteries. LONDON: *Printed for* J. ROBERTS *in Warwick-
Lane.* 1719. *Price* [illegible]

4°. Pp. [3]–14

Notes: Published in the month following 5 September. Cited
with high approval by Defoe in *Mercurius Politicus* (Septem-

ber 1719, p. 554) and abstracted at length in the same issue (pp. 556–563). In *The Gamester* Defoe proposes a weekly periodical explaining the evils of gambling, and especially the mathematical odds involved.

Copy: H. *Another copy:* MPRL

419   THE GAMESTER. NO. II. Demonstrating What was laid down in No. I. as to the Schemes of Insurance upon Lottery Tickets, &c. With some Observations, how those evil and pernicious Practices, affect the sensible Decay of our Trade. As Also A Scheme, by which any one may easily calculate the true Grounds of his Hope and Expectation, or their just and real Value, as to the gaining of Prizes in 1, 2, 3, 4, 5, &c. Number of Tickets; founded upon mathematical Principles, concerning the Doctrine of Chances. LONDON: *Printed for* J. ROBERTS *in Warwick-Lane.* 1719. (*Price Four-Pence.*)

4°. Unnumbered page of explanation of mathematical terms on verso of title-page + pp. [3]–12 + a large folding sheet (Table No. I, giving a calculation of the chances of lottery tickets while the chance of one to five obtains)

Notes: Published presumably one week later than the preceding tract, with increased attention to the importance of the mathematics of chance in such legitimate business undertakings as insurance. No sequel is known, although the tract concludes with a promise to continue the discussion of Table No. I: "But the further Uses of this Table, which are many, and great, shall be the Subject of several of the following Papers."

Copy: BPL. *Another copy:* MPRL

420   A BRIEF STATE OF THE QUESTION, Between the Printed and Painted Callicoes And the Woollen and Silk Manufacture, As far as it relates to the Wearing and Using of Printed and Painted Callicoes in Great-Britain. LONDON: *Printed for* W. BOREHAM *at the Angel in Pater-noster-Row.* 1719.

8°. Pp. [6 unnumbered] + [1]–48

Notes: Published 1 September. Apparently this tract was not completed in time for inclusion in No. 533 for August 1719; on pp. 524–528 Defoe reprints only the introduction and he gives an erroneous title: *The True State of the Question, between the Woollen and Silk Manufacture, and the printed and painted Callicoes, &c.* In the next issue of No. 533 (September 1719, pp. 564–587) he quotes the title correctly and quotes or summarizes the tract at great length. On p. 564 he states that the tract had been widely disseminated to influence legislation: "This Book has been Industriously handed about all over the Kingdom, great Numbers having been given away to the Ministers of State and Members of Parliament all over *England,* to apprize them of the Thing, and Interest them in its favour: As also to the Manufacturers, Clothiers, &c. in every part, to animate them in the Cause; we shall, *so far,* tho' without any Design or Interest on one side or other, joyn in spreading it, by giving an Abstract of this Work also, that against the time it becomes Popular, and may be the Subject of common Discourse, our Readers, if they please, may be Masters of the Story."

UL has a copy of the second edition of the same year, identical in pagination but obviously reset throughout, with an old manuscript note on the title-page: "Novemb."

Copy: BM. *Other copies:* BOD, UL; BPL, F, H, HEH, I, IU, P, T, Y

421 CHARITY STILL A CHRISTIAN VIRTUE: Or, An Impartial Account Of The Tryal And Conviction Of the Reverend Mr. Hendley, For Preaching A Charity-Sermon at Chisselhurst. And of Mr. Campman, Mr. Prat, and Mr. Harding, for Collecting at the same Time the Alms of the Congregation. At the Assizes held at Rochester, on Wednesday, July 15. 1719. Humbly offer'd to the Consideration of the Clergy of the Church of England. Let us oppress the poor Righteous Man; let us not spare the Widow, nor Reverence the Grey Hairs of the Aged. Let our Strength be the Law of Justice; for that which is feeble, is found to be nothing worth, Wisd. Solom. 2. 10, 11. LONDON: *Printed for* T. BICKERTON, *at the Crown in Pater-Noster-Row,* 1719. (*Price One Shilling.*)

8°. Pp. [2 unnumbered] + 1–72. Frontispiece showing charity collection in the church at Chisselhurst [Chislehurst]

Notes: Published 10 October. One of the very few tracts in which Defoe seems to have been a collaborator rather than sole author. As editor of the Tory journal *Mercurius Politicus,* he seems to have been called on to prepare for the press an account of local Whig tyranny which had been sketched out by a High-Churchman. Part of the tract is certainly his, part seems certainly by another hand. For this tract the supposed author, the Rev. Mr. Hendley (Handley), was taken into custody with his printer (Burton) and his publisher (Bickerton) on 23 October (or 25 October by another account) and later released on bail. If Hendley was not the principal author, he was at least willing to receive credit for it and to be prosecuted accordingly. Read's *Original Weekly Journal* (31 October) reported that the tract aroused great interest: "we hear, hundreds have been sold in Town, in a very short time."

Copy: BM. *Other copies:* BOD, CU, UL; BPL, C, F, H, HEH, IU, P, Y

422   THE DUMB PHILOSOPHER; or Great Britain's Wonder, Containing I. A Faithful and very Surprizing Account how Dickory Cronke, A Tinner's Son in the County of Cornwal, was born Dumb, and continued so for 58 years; and how some Days before he died, he came to his Speech: With Memoirs of his Life, and the Manner of his Death. II. A Declaration of his Faith and Principles in Religion: With a Collection of Select Meditations, Composed in his Retirement. III. His Prophetical Observations upon the Affairs of Europe, more particularly of Great-Britain, from 1720, to 1729. *The whole extracted from his Original Papers,* and confirmed by unquestionable Authority. To which is annexed. His Elegy, written by a young Cornish Gentleman, of Exeter Coll. in Oxford; with an Epitaph by another Hand. Non quis, sed quid. LONDON: *Printed for* THO. BICKERTON, *at the Crown in Pater-Noster-Row.* 1719. *(Price 1s.)*

8°. Pp. v–viii + 9–64

Notes: Published 13 October; second edition 27 May 1720. Supposedly based on the hero's original papers. The elegy (ostensibly written by a student of Exeter College, Oxford) is dated 25 August 1719. The tract, professedly an account of the life and reflections of an obscure Cornishman, is actually related to Defoe's other political prophecies (see Nos. 195 and 234). For the tract's political implications, see *The Huntington Library Quarterly,* IV [1940], 107–117.

Copy: BM. *Other copies:* BOD, CU; BPL, C, CH, COR, H, HEH, I, IU, P, T, Y

423 THE PETITION OF DOROTHY DISTAFF, ETC., TO MRS. REBECCA WOOLLPACK. [1719?]

Notes: Reprinted by Defoe in *Mercurius Politicus* for December 1719, pp. 794–803. See "Additional Titles," 424a.

424 THE KING OF PIRATES: Being An Account Of The Famous Enterprises of Captain Avery, The Mock King of Madagascar. With His Rambles and Piracies; wherein all the Sham Accounts formerly publish'd of him, are detected. *In Two Letters from himself;* one during his Stay at Madagascar, and one since his Escape from thence. LONDON, *Printed for* A. BETTESWORTH *in Pater-noster Row,* C. KING *in Westminster-Hall,* J. BROTHERTON *and* W. MEADOWS *in Cornhill,* W. CHETWOOD *in Covent-Garden, and sold by* W. BOREHAM *in Pater-noster Row.* 1720 [for 1719]. (*Price 1s. 6d.*)

8°. Pp. iii–vi + 1–93

Notes: Published 10 December; second edition in 1720.

Copy: IU. *Other copies:* BM; BPL, C, CH, HEH, T

1720

425 AN HISTORICAL ACCOUNT OF THE VOYAGES AND ADVENTURES OF SIR WALTER RALEIGH. With the Discoveries and Conquests he made for the Crown of England. Also a particular Account of his several Attempts for the Discovery of the

Gold Mines in Guiana, and the Reason of the Miscarriage, shewing, that it was not from any Defect in the Scheme which he laid, or in the Reality of the Thing it self, but in a treacherous Discovery of his Design and of the Strength he had with him, to the Spaniards. To which is added, An Account how that rich Country might now be with Ease, Possess'd, Planted and Secur'd to the British Nation, and what Immense Wealth and Encrease of Commerce might be rais'd from thence. Humbly Proposed to the South-Sea-Company. LONDON: *Printed, and sold by* W. BOREHAM, *at the Angel in Pater-noster-row.* MDCCXIX [for 1720]. *Price 1s.*

8º. Pp. 3–55

Notes: Dottin dates this in January 1720. But as late as 26 August 1720 it was advertised in *The Daily Post:* "This Day is publish'd, Humbly proposed to the South-Sea Company." If the tract had actually appeared in January 1720, this late advertisement might have been no more than the publisher's effort to arouse interest in it at a time when the South Sea Bubble was nearing its collapse.

Copy: BM. *Other copies:* UL; HEH, N

426   THE CHIMERA: Or, The French Way Of Paying National Debts, Laid open. Being An Impartial Account of the Proceedings in France, for Raising a Paper Credit, and Settling the Mississippi Stock. *Printed for* T. WARNER, *at the Black-Boy in Pater-Noster-Row.* 1720. (*Price One Shilling.*)

8º. Pp. 1–32 + 41–76

Notes: Published 5 January. There are at least two variant settings. BM, three UL copies, HEH, IU, and the Lilly Collection of IU have pp. 1–32 and 41–76. JRM and one UL copy are identical in text (although carefully reset) with pp. 1–48 + 57–76. In all copies Defoe refers on p. 57 to a proclamation on p. 49, although no page is numbered 49 in JRM. No part of the text is omitted in any of the copies, and the signatures appear in regular order; but the pages are incorrectly numbered, so that each copy appears to have a gap of eight pages.

The BM copy has an old manuscript note: "By Mr Laws." The attribution is impossible, for the tract is a savage attack on John Law.

Copy: BM. *Other copies:* BOD, NLS, UL; BPL, C, CH, COR, F, H, HEH, I, IU, JRM, LC, NYPL, P, Y

427   THE CASE OF THE FAIR TRADERS, humbly represented to the Honourable the House of Commons: Being a clear View and State of Clandestine Trade, as now carry'd on in Great Britain. [1720]

Fol. half-sheet

Notes: No place, no publisher, no date, but London 1720 and given away gratis. The short title is printed horizontally on the verso. It was intended for distribution at the door of St. Stephen's Chapel, and it was printed to permit easy folding. Published sometime before 13 February 1720, when Defoe cited it with approval. On p. 20 of *The Trade To India Critically and Calmly Consider'd* (No. 428) he quoted one paragraph from this "printed Paper, handed about at the Door of the House of Commons."

Copy: H

428   THE TRADE TO INDIA CRITICALLY AND CALMLY CONSIDER'D, And prov'd to be destructive to the general Trade of Great Britain, as well as to the Woollen and Silk Manufactures in Particular. LONDON: *Printed for* W. BOREHAM *at the Angel in Pater-noster Row.* 1720. *Price 6d.*

8°. Pp. 3–45 + [1]

Notes: Published 13 February. On pp. 5–6 No. 420 is quoted as an authoritative statement of the opposition of English manufacturers of woolen and linen goods to the use of printed or painted calicoes.

Copy: BM. *Other copies:* BOD, CU, UL; BPL, C, COR, F, H, HEH, IU, NYPL, P, Y

429   THE CASE FAIRLY STATED between the Turky Company And The Italian Merchants. *By A Merchant.* LONDON: *Printed for* J. ROBERTS *in Warwick-Lane.* 1720.

8°. Pp. 3–44

Notes: Fictitious attribution to a merchant. Published 13 February. At least three editions appeared in 1720. The IU copy and the 44-page UL copy are somewhat differently set, so that "House of Commons" appears on p. 25 in the first and on p. 24 in the second. I do not know whether IU or UL is earlier.

The third, and probably the last, variant has pp. 3–48, with the title-page concluding: "London: Printed in the Year 1720." This variant is also to be found in UL as well as in BM. Mr. J. H. P. Pafford, Goldsmiths' Librarian of the University of London, has given me the following judgment regarding the UL 48-page copy: it appears to be an expanded version of the 44-page edition, the text throughout has been slightly enlarged, pp. 44–48 contain "the Heads of some few restrictive Orders" which do not appear in the 44-page edition, and references in the 44-page copy to the House of Commons (p. 24) and to the pending Bill indicate that this is the earlier edition and that the Bill became an Act before the 48-page edition was printed.

Copy: IU. *Other copies:* BM, BOD, UL; BPL, C, F, H, HEH, N, NYPL, P, Y

430   THE COMPLEAT ART OF PAINTING. *A Poem Translated from the French of M. du Fresnoy. By D. F. Gent.* LON-DON: *Printed for* T. WARNER, *at the Black-Boy in Pater-Noster-Row,* 1720. (*Price One Shilling.*)

8°. Pp. 1–53

Notes: Published 25 March. The last of Defoe's writings to which he laid claim publicly.

Copy: BOD. *Other copies:* BPL, C, RPB, Y

431   A LETTER TO THE AUTHOR OF THE INDEPENDENT WHIG. Wherein The Merits of the Clergy are consider'd; the Good vindicated, and the Bad expos'd. With Some Account of the late Controversy in the Church. *By one who has no Dependance on Church, State, or Exchange-Alley.*

Those that plead a special Call to the Ministry, shou'd

prove it by Miracle, or irresistable Reason; without them, their Pretences are Hypocrisy and Schism.

Religion is not only a good, but a necessary Thing; but the Use that Knaves and Fools make of it almost beats Men of Sense and Honesty out of it.

Maxims of the late Marquis of Hallifax.

LONDON: *Printed and Sold by* A. MOORE, *near St. Paul's* 1720. (*Price Sixpence.*)

8°. Pp. [3]–32

Copy: BPL. *Other copies:* C, F

432 THE HISTORY OF THE LIFE AND ADVENTURES OF MR. DUN-CAN CAMPBELL, A Gentleman, who, tho' Deaf and Dumb, writes down any Stranger's Name at first Sight; with their future Contingencies of Fortune. Now Living in Exeter Court over-against the Savoy in the Strand. Gentem quidem nullam video neque tam humanam atque doctam; neque tam immanem tamque barbaram, quae non significari futura & quibisdam intelligi praedicque posse causeat. Cicero de Divinatione, lib. x. LONDON: *Printed for* E. CURLL: *And sold by* W. MEARS *and* T. JAUNCY *without Temple Bar,* W. MEADOWS *in Cornhill,* A. BETTESWORTH *in Pater-Noster-Row,* W. LEWIS *in Covent Garden, and* W. GRAVES *in St. James's Street.* M.DCC.XX. (*Price 5s.*)

8°. Pp. iii–[xxiv] + [1]–320. Frontispiece (portrait). 3 plates (facing pp. 11, 39, and 71)

Notes: Lee dates the first edition 30 April. The second edition was published 7 July. The complicated history of this work can be traced in considerable detail, and it is clear that Defoe had no further hand in it after he had written the original version (perhaps as early as 1717). On 8 March 1717 an announcement was made that it was shortly to be published, and that it was written by J. B. (*i.e.,* Defoe). On 3 September 1719 proposals were being circulated for publishing it by subscription. On 26 December 1719 it had been delayed by waiting for new subscriptions, but it was announced as very speedily to be published. On 3 May 1720 it had appeared in two forms —in a subscription edition on fine paper, to be had only from Campbell himself, and in the ordinary edition for the trade.

On 18 June 1720 a rival publisher brought out *Mr. Campbell's Pacquet,* an attempt to take advantage of the notoriety of the book, with at least one contribution by William Bond (*alias* Capt. Stanhope or H. Stanhope). On 7 July it was announced that the second edition of the *History* had been delayed; but this appeared on 4 August, with the same material as the first edition but completely reset, and with a new picture of Campbell which obviously represents a different man. The JRM copy of the second edition has no plate facing p. 39 but adds another (facing p. 129) which gives a third and still different likeness of Campbell.

On 20 June 1728 Curll combined unsold sheets of the first edition with sheets from *Mr. Campbell's Pacquet* to patch together a third edition, now called *The Supernatural Philosopher,* prefaced by glowing praise from Sir Richard Steele and announced as the work of "William Bond, Esq; of Bury St. Edmonds, Suffolk." Possibly Bond had nothing to do with this last compilation except as the author of one or more of the poems in *Mr. Campbell's Pacquet. The Supernatural Philosopher* went into a second edition on 23 July 1728.

Probably Defoe wrote the original *History* for pay. But he seems to have found the fortune-teller Campbell an amusing charlatan—as so many eminent contemporaries did; and he had a genuine interest in two of the principal topics discussed in the book—second sight and the possibility of instructing deaf mutes. There is no evidence that he collaborated with William Bond or Mrs. Eliza Haywood in later revision.

Like *The Memoirs of Ramkins* (1718), *The History of Duncan Campbell* was apparently written earlier than *Robinson Crusoe;* but, unlike *The Memoirs of Ramkins,* its title-page was never changed to imitate that of *Robinson Crusoe.* However, after the phenomenal success of *Robinson Crusoe,* it was (both in 1719 and 1720) usually advertised as *The History of the Life and surprising Adventures of the Celebrated Mr. Duncan Campbell.* It is not unlikely that the life of Campbell, which must have been virtually completed by March 1717, was published more than three years later in the hope of sharing the popularity of *Robinson Crusoe.*

Copy: BM. *Other copies:* BOD, CU, NLS, UL; BPL, C, CH, COR, F, H, HEH, I, IU, N, NYPL, P, R, RPB, T, Y

433 THE HISTORY OF THE WARS, OF HIS LATE MAJESTY CHARLES XII. KING OF SWEDEN, From his First Landing in Denmark, To His Return from Turkey to Pomerania. The Second Edition. With a Continuation to the Time of his Death. *By a Scots Gentleman in the Swedish Service.* LONDON: *Printed by H. P. for A.* BELL *at the Cross Keys and Bible in Cornhil, W.* TAYLOR *at the Ship in Pater-Noster-Row, and J.* OSBORN *at the Oxford Arms in Lombard-Street,* MD.CC.XX.

8°. Pp. [2 unnumbered] + [1]–402. Frontispiece (portrait)

Notes: Lee dates this 21 May; but as Dr. Fritz Wölcken has pointed out to me, there is no known advertisement earlier than that in *The Post-Boy* for 24 May, where this book is advertised together with No. 434. Attributed to a Scots Gentleman in the Swedish Service, and internal evidence indicates some special source of information. Pp. [1]–248 represent the original edition of 1715 (completely reset, with a few corrections); pp. [249]–402 give the continuation.

Copy: BM. *Other copies:* CU; BPL, C, COR, H, T

434 MEMOIRS OF A CAVALIER: Or A Military Journal Of The Wars in Germany, And the Wars in England; From the Year 1632, to the Year 1648. *Written Threescore Years ago by an English Gentleman,* who served first in the Army of Gustavus Adolphus, the glorious King of Sweden, till his Death; and after that, in the Royal Army of King Charles the First, from the Beginning of the Rebellion, to the End of that War. LONDON: *Printed for A.* BELL *at the Cross Keys in Cornhill, J.* OSBORN *at the Oxford Arms in Lombard-Street, W.* TAYLOR *at the Ship and Swan, and* T. WARNER *at the Black Boy in Pater-noster-Row.* [1720].

8°. Pp. [5 unnumbered] + [1]–338

Notes: No date, but 1720. Lee dates this 21 May; but as Dr. Fritz Wölcken has pointed out to me, there is no known ad-

vertisement earlier than that in *The Post-Boy* for 24 May, where
this book is advertised together with No. 433. Fictitious attribution to the hero, whose manuscript was supposedly secured
as plunder at (or after) the battle of Worcester (1651) by the
father of the owner who signed his initials I. K. Later in the
eighteenth century a serious attempt was made to identify the
author-hero as the Honourable Col. Andrew Newport (who was
only eight years old at the time when the Cavalier was supposed to be viewing the siege of Magdeburg in Germany).

Copy: BM. *Other copies:* BOD, CU, UL; BPL, C, CH, COR,
F, H, HEH, I, IU, N, NYPL, P, R, RPB, T, Y

435   THE LIFE, ADVENTURES, AND PYRACIES, OF THE FAMOUS
CAPTAIN SINGLETON: Containing An Account of his being
set on Shore in the Island of Madagascar, his Settlement
there, with a Description of the Place and Inhabitants: Of
his Passage from thence, in a Paraguay, to the main Land
of Africa, with an Account of the Customs and Manners of
the People: His great Deliverance from the barbarous Natives and wild Beasts: Of his meeting with an Englishman, a
Citizen of London, among the Indians, the great Riches he
acquired, and his Voyage Home to England: As also Captain Singleton's Return to Sea, with an Account of his
many Adventures and Pyracies with the famous Captain
Avery and others. LONDON: *Printed for* J. BROTHERTON, *at
the Black Bull in Cornhill,* J. GRAVES *in St. James's Street,*
A. DODD, *at the Peacock without Temple bar, and* T. WAR-
NER, *at the Black Boy in Pater-Noster-Row.* 1720.

8°. Pp. 1–344

Notes: Attributed to Captain Singleton himself. Published 4
June. On 19 August 1721 and later Mist was advertising his
own edition. Although the original title-page states that the
Englishman in Africa was a citizen of London, nothing is said
of that in the text. This episode is an echo of the story on
which Defoe based much of the book, the narrative of Mr.
Freeman which he retold eight years later in his *Atlas Maritimus & Commercialis* (No. 501, pp. 252–253).

Copy: BM. *Other copies:* BOD, NLS, UL; BPL, C, CH, COR, H, HEH, I, IU, LC, N, NYPL, R, T, Y

436 SERIOUS REFLECTIONS During The Life And Surprising Adventures OF ROBINSON CRUSOE, With His Vision Of The Angelick World. *Written by Himself.* LONDON: *Printed for* W. TAYLOR, *at the Ship and Black-Swan in Pater-Noster-Row.* 1720.

8°. Pp. [14 unnumbered] + [1]–270 + [1]–84. Frontispiece (folding map of Crusoe's island)

Notes: Published 6 August. P. 270 concludes with "Finis." The later section of 84 pages is separately paged, with independent signatures, except that the catchword "A" appears at the bottom of p. 270.

Copy: BM. *Other copies:* NLS, UL; BPL, C, COR, H, HEH, I, IU, N, NYPL, R, T, Y

437 THE SOUTH-SEA SCHEME EXAMIN'D; And The Reasonableness thereof Demonstrated. *By a hearty Well-Wisher to Publick Credit.* LONDON. *Printed for* J. ROBERTS, *near the Oxford-Arms in Warwick-Lane.* MDCCXX.

8°. Pp. [2 unnumbered] + 1–39

Notes: Published 8 October or perhaps earlier. The tract itself concludes with the entry: "March 8. 1719–20. South-Sea Stock 182 to 184." CU has a copy of the third edition, reset, with no date and no price of the stock.

Copy: BOD. *Other copies:* F, N

1 7 2 1

438 A TRUE STATE OF THE CONTRACTS Relating to the Third Money-Subscription Taken by the South-Sea Company. LONDON, *Printed for* J. ROBERTS, *near the Oxford-Arms in Warwick-Lane.* M.DCC.XXI. (*Price Four-Pence.*)

8°. Pp. 3–24

Copy: IU. *Other copies:* BOD, UL; BPL

439 A VINDICATION OF THE HONOUR AND JUSTICE OF PARLIA-
MENT Against a most Scandalous Libel, Entituled, The
Speech of John A[islabie], Esq; LONDON: *Printed for A.
MORE, near St. Paul's; and Sold by the Booksellers of Lon-
don and Westminster.* [*Price Six-pence.*] [1721]

8°. Pp. [i–ii] + 1–36

Notes: Lee mistakenly dates this in February (probably on the
assumption that it followed closely after Aislabie's dismissal
from office on 22 or 23 January). But the tract which Defoe
was answering (*The Speech of the Right Honourable John
Aislabie, Esq;*) bore on its title-page the date of Aislabie's
speech: "Wednesday the 19th of July 1721." On 31 August
Defoe's tract was advertised: "This Day is publish'd."

Copy: BM. *Other copies:* BPL, C, H, HEH, NYPL, N, P, Y

440 THE GENUINE WORKS OF MR. DANIEL D'FOE. [1721]

Notes: On 4 October 1721, in *The St. James's Post*, T. Warner
at the Black-Boy in Pater-Noster-Row advertised among the
books which he sold the following: "The Genuine Works of
Mr. Dan D'Foe, in 2 Vol. in 8vo. to which is now added by
the Author, a Compleat Key to the whole Work, pr. 12s."
Presumably this was another offering of the unsold sheets
from 1705 with a new title-page and a key. The new title-page
and the key are often assigned to 1710; but in the various advertisements of reissues of Defoe's collected works, I have seen
no evidence that these appeared before 1721. See Nos. 58, 91,
197, and 258.

441 BRIEF OBSERVATIONS ON TRADE AND MANUFACTURES; And
particularly of our Mines and Metals, And The Hard-
Ware Works, Of which the said Mines and Metals are the
Foundations. LONDON: *Printed in the Year* 1721.

8°. Pp. [3]–16

Copy: UL

442 SOME ACCOUNT OF THE LIFE OF SIR CHARLES SEDLEY. [Pre-
fixed to *The Works Of the Honourable Sir Charles Sedley,*

Bart. In Two Volumes. Containing his Poems, Plays, &c.
With Memoirs of the Author's Life, by an Eminent Hand.
. . . London, Printed for S. Briscoe, at the Bell-Savage on
Ludgate-hill, and sold by T. Bickerton, in Pater-noster
Row. MDCCXXII (for 1721).]

12°. Defoe's biographical introduction is pp. [3]–11 in Vol. I.

Notes: The publication was unaccountably delayed. As early
as 12 August the set was announced to be delivered to subscribers in a few days. On 11 November it was actually published. On 9 December Bickerton was warning subscribers that
he was jointly concerned with Briscoe, and that notes or sums
of money paid on account must be signed by himself as well as
by Briscoe.

Copy: BM. *Other copies:* BOD, NLS, UL; BPL, HEH, I, N,
NYPL, T, Y

443 THE CASE OF MR. LAW, TRULY STATED. In Answer to a
Pamphlet, entitul'd, A Letter to Mr. Law. LONDON: *Printed*
for A. MOORE, *near St. Paul's, and sold by the Booksellers*
of London and Westminster. 1721. *(Price Six-pence.)*

8°. Pp. [3]–38

Notes: The pamphlet to which this is a reply concluded with
the date "Nov. 11, 1721."

Copy: UL. *Other copies:* BPL, I, IU

1 7 2 2

444 A COLLECTION OF MISCELLANY LETTERS, Selected out of
Mist's Weekly Journal. THE FIRST VOLUME. LONDON:
Printed by N. MIST, *in Great Carter-Lane,* MDCCXXII.

12°. Pp. [28 unnumbered] + 1–310

Notes: The preface and dedication of this first volume were
signed by N. Mist; but the collection was apparently made by
Defoe, who contributed to this and the three subsequent volumes. The miscellany, planned to give financial relief to Mist

during his difficulties with the Government, was being offered
for subscription by the late spring of 1721. On 19 August it was
announced as ready to be delivered to subscribers by the middle of September. The Dedication was dated by Mist: "King's-
Bench Prison, Sep. 29. 1721." But the first and second volumes
were not actually published until 6 January 1722; the octavo
impression was announced to come out a few days later. For
Volume II see No. 445; for Volumes III and IV see Nos. 491
and 492.

Copy: BM. *Other copies:* BOD, CU, NLS; BPL, COR, I, IU,
T, Y

445   A COLLECTION OF MISCELLANY LETTERS. Selected out of
Mist's Weekly Journal. THE SECOND VOLUME. LONDON:
Printed by N. MIST, *in Great Carter-Lane*, MDCCXXII.

12°. Pp. [17 unnumbered] + 1–332

Notes: See previous entry. Both the dedication and the preface
are signed by N. Mist: "King's-Bench Prison, Nov. 10, 1721."
See Nos. 444, 491, and 492. In the IU copy the table of contents is misplaced at the end.

Copy: BM. *Other copies:* BOD, CU, NLS; BPL, COR, I, IU

446   THE FORTUNES AND MISFORTUNES OF THE FAMOUS MOLL
FLANDERS, &c. Who was Born in Newgate, and during a
Life of continu'd Variety for Threescore Years, besides her
Childhood, was Twelve Year a Whore, five times a Wife
(whereof once to her own Brother) Twelve Year a Thief,
Eight Year a Transported Felon in Virginia, at last grew
Rich, liv'd Honest, and died a Penitent, Written from her
own Memorandums. LONDON: *Printed for, and Sold by* W.
CHETWOOD, *at Cato's-Head, in Russel-street, Covent-Gar-
den; and* T. EDLING, *at the Prince's-Arms, over-against
Exerter-Change* [sic] *in the Strand.* MDDCXXI [sic] [for
1722].

8°. Pp. [iii]–xiii + [1]–424

Notes: Supposedly edited from the heroine's manuscripts. The
book concludes: "Written in the Year 1683." Published 27

January 1722; second edition by Brotherton 23 July; third edition by Chetwood 21 December. It is not clear what relation existed between the editions of Chetwood and Brotherton; both men served at times as Defoe's authorized publishers. A piratical abridged edition was published by J. Read, which Lee dates as early as July 1723.

Copy: BM. *Other copies:* C, CH, H, HEH, IU, NYPL, P, R, Y

447 DUE PREPARATIONS FOR THE PLAGUE As well for Soul as Body. Being some seasonable Thoughts upon the Visible Approach of the present dreadful Contagion in France; the properest Measures to prevent it, and the great Work of submitting to it. Psal. XCI. 10. There shall no Evil befal thee, neither shall the Plague come nigh thy Dwelling. LONDON: *Printed for* E. MATTHEWS, *at the Bible,* and J. BATTEY *at the Dove in Pater-Noster-Row.* MDCCXXII.

12º. Pp. [iii]–xi + 1–272

Notes: Published 8 February. The preface refers approvingly to the recent effort of the Ministry to enforce an unpopular quarantine; both *Due Preparations* and *A Journal of the Plague Year* were intended partly as propaganda to support the administration of Sir Robert Walpole.

Copy: BM. *Another copy:* T

448 RELIGIOUS COURTSHIP: Being Historical Discourses, On The Necessity of Marrying Religious Husbands and Wives only. As Also Of Husbands and Wives being of the same Opinions in Religion with one another. With an Appendix Of the Necessity of taking none but Religious Servants, and a Proposal for the better managing of Servants. LONDON: *Printed for* E. MATTHEWS, *at the Bible,* and A. BETTESWORTH, *at the Red-Lyon in Pater-noster-Row;* J. BROTHERTON, *and* W. MEADOWS, *in Cornhil.* MDCCXXII.

8º. Pp. [6 unnumbered] + [1]–358

Notes: Published 20 February. The second edition of 1729 makes two corrections of names which were called for in the

Errata (p. 358) of the first edition, and on the title-page it sub-stitutes "J. Brotherton, at the Bible" for "J. Brotherton, and W. Meadows."

Copy: BM. *Other copies:* UL; BPL, C, CH, COR, H, HEH, I, N, R, Y

449 A JOURNAL OF THE PLAGUE YEAR: Being Observations or Memorials, Of the most Remarkable Occurrences, As well Publick as Private, Which happened in London During the last Great Visitation In 1665. *Written by a Citizen who continued all the while in London.* Never made publick before [.] LONDON: *Printed for* E. NUTT *at the Royal-Exchange;* J. ROBERTS *in Warwick-Lane;* A. DODD *without Temple-Bar; and* J. GRAVES *in St. James's-street.* 1722.

8°. Pp. [1]–287

Notes: Published 17 March. Attributed to a citizen who con-tinued all the while in London. Signed H. F., the initials of Defoe's uncle Henry Foe, a saddler in the parish of St. Botolph Aldgate. *Due Preparations For the Plague Year* was a miserably printed little book advertised as "very proper to be given away," and it is now one of the scarcest of Defoe items. *The Journal* was well printed in octavo and published by four well-estab-lished booksellers, with no preface to apologize for its publica-tion and no advertisements to lower its dignified appearance.

Copy: BM. *Other copies:* BOD, UL; BPL, C, CH, COR, H, HEH, IU, NYPL, P, PML, R, T, Y

450 A BRIEF DEBATE UPON THE DISSOLVING THE LATE PARLIA-MENT, And Whether we ought not to Chuse the same Gen-tlemen Again. LONDON: *Printed for* J. ROBERTS, *near the Oxford-Arms in Warwick-Lane,* 1722. *(Price 6d.)*

8°. Pp. [1]–38

Notes: Lee dates this in April, but it probably appeared during the electioneering in March. On 10 March Parliament was dissolved, and on 13 March a proclamation was signed and published calling a new Parliament. Until sometime in April elections were being held, although by a series of prorogations the new Parliament did not convene until 9 October. The pamphlet was probably written and published while there was still time to influence the elections.

Copy: CU. *Other copies:* UL; HEH, IU, N

451 AN IMPARTIAL HISTORY OF THE LIFE AND ACTIONS OF PETER ALEXOWITZ, The Present Czar of Muscovy: From his Birth down to this present Time. Giving an Account of his Travels and Transactions in the several Courts of Europe; with his Attempts and Successes in the Northern and Eastern Parts of the World: In which is intermix'd the History of Muscovy. *Written by a British Officer in the Service of the Czar.* LONDON: *Printed for* W. CHETWOOD, *at Cato's-Head in Russel-Street, Covent-Garden;* J. STAGG, *in Westminster-Hall;* J. BROTHERTON, *at the Bible, near the Royal-Exchange, and* T. EDLIN, *at the Prince's Arms over-against Exeter-Exchange in the Strand.* MDCCXXIII [for 1722]. [*Price Bound 5d.*]

8°. Pp. 1–420

Notes: Published 22 November 1722; second edition in April 1724. The I copy has "An Impartial Account" instead of "An Impartial History." Fictitious attribution to a British Officer in the Service of the Czar; actually based in large part on the notes previously used for *The History of the Wars, Of his late Majesty Charles XII. King of Sweden* (1720).

Copy: BM. *Other copies:* BOD, CU, DW, NLS; BPL, C, CH, COR, F, HEH, I, IU, N, T, Y

452 THE HISTORY AND REMARKABLE LIFE OF the truly Honourable COL. JACQUE, Commonly Call'd Col. Jack, Who was Born a Gentleman, put 'Prentice to a Pick-Pocket, was Six and Twenty Years a Thief, and then Kidnapp'd to Virginia. Came back a Merchant, married four Wives, and five of them prov'd Whores; went into the Wars, behav'd bravely, got Preferment, was made Colonel of a Regiment, came over, and fled with the Chevalier, and is now abroad compleating a Life of Wonders, and resolves to dye a General.

LONDON: *Printed, and Sold by* J. BROTHERTON, *at the Royal-Exchange;* T. PAYNE, *near Stationers-Hall;* W. MEARS, *at the Lamb, and* A. DODD, *at the Peacock without Temple-Bar;* W. CHETWOOD, *in Covent Garden;* J. GRAVES, *in St. James's-Street;* S. CHAPMAN, *in Pall-Mall, and* J. STAGG, *at Westminster Hall.* MDCCXXIII [for 1722]. *Price Six Shillings.*

8°. Pp. iii–vii + 1–399

Notes: Ostensibly written by Col. Jacque. The Preface is signed "The Editor." Published 20 December 1722; second edition 19 January 1723; third edition 13 September 1723. The discrepancy between the title-page, in which the hero is represented as a successful rebel, and the actual narrative, in which he becomes a humble and grateful suppliant for King George's mercy, is explained by the fact that the book was planned before Bishop Atterbury's conspiracy was discovered, but published while Atterbury was a prisoner in the Tower awaiting trial for treason. In December 1722 Defoe would not have represented a successful Jacobite as a hero.

Copy: Y. *Other copies:* BPL, C, CH, HEH

1723

453   A MEMORIAL TO THE CLERGY OF THE CHURCH OF ENGLAND, Relating to Their Conduct since the Revolution. Together With some Advice to them upon the present State of Affairs. *By a Clergyman.* I Cor. xiv. 20. Brethren, be not Children in Understanding: Howbeit in Malice be ye Children, but in Understanding be Men. LONDON: *Printed for* J. ROBERTS, *near the Oxford-Arms in Warwick-Lane.* M.DCC.XXIII. (*Price One Shilling.*)

8°. Pp. 3–61

Notes: Fictitious attribution to a clergyman.

Copy: CU. *Other copies:* BOD; IU

*454   THE WICKEDNESS OF A DISREGARD TO OATHS; And The Pernicious Consequences Of It To Religion and Government. In which Is Particularly Consider'd a Paper, Taken at the Lord North and Grey's, Printed in the Appendix to the Report of the Committee of the House of Lords. *Printed in the Year* 1723.

8°. Pp. [3]–38

Notes: No place, no publisher, but certainly London. Published 18 June. Very probably, not certainly, by Defoe.

Copy: BM. *Other copies:* BOD, CU; HEH

1 7 2 4

*455 CONSIDERATIONS ON PUBLICK CREDIT. In a Letter To A Member of Parliament. LONDON: *Printed for* J. ROBERTS, *near the Oxford-Arms, in Warwick-Lane.* MDCCXXIV. (*Price Four-Pence.*)

8°. Pp. 3–23

Notes: Published 10 January. Probably, not certainly, by Defoe.

Copy: BM. *Other copies:* NLS, UL; C, F, HEH

456 THE FORTUNATE MISTRESS: Or, A History Of The Life And Vast Variety of Fortunes Of Mademoiselle de Beleau, Afterwards Call'd The Countess de Wintselsheim, in Germany. Being the Person known by the Name of the Lady ROXANA, in the Time of King Charles II. LONDON: *Printed for* T. WARNER *at the Black-Boy in Pater-Noster-Row;* W. MEADOWS *at the Angel in Cornhil;* W. PEPPER *at the Crown in Maiden-Lane, Covent-Garden;* S. HARDING *at the Post-House in St. Martin's-Lane; and* T. EDLIN *at the Prince's-Arms against Exeter-Exchange in the Strand.* [1724]

8°. Pp. [4 unnumbered] + [1]–407

Notes: Published 29 February. Ostensibly written by the heroine, whose title the BM *Catalogue* misprints as "The Countess of Wintselsheim." The spurious continuation in modern editions was added in the 1740's (Aitken dates it 1745). Frontispiece portrait of "The Famous Roxana."

Copy: BM. *Other copies:* UL; BPL, C, CH, H, HEH, I, IU, NYPL, R, Y

457   THE GREAT LAW OF SUBORDINATION CONSIDER'D; Or, The Insolence and Unsufferable Behaviour of Servants in England duly enquir'd into. Illustrated With a great Variety of Examples, Historical Cases, and Remarkable Stories of the Behaviour of some particular Servants, suited to all the several Arguments made use of, as they go on. In Ten Familiar Letters. Together with a Conclusion, being an earnest and moving Remonstrance to the House-keepers and Heads of Families in Great-Britain, pressing them not to cease using their utmost Interest (especially at this Juncture) to obtain sufficient Laws for the effectual Regulation of the Manners and Behaviour of their Servants. As Also A Proposal, containing such Heads or Constitutions, as wou'd effectually answer this great End, and bring Servants of every Class to a just (and yet not a grievous) Regulation. LONDON: *Sold by* S. HARDING, *at the Post-House, in St. Martin's-Lane;* W. LEWIS, *in Covent-Garden;* T. WORRALL, *at the Judge's-Head, against St. Dunstan's-Church, Fleet-Street;* A. BETTESWORTH, *in Pater-Noster-Row;* W. MEAD-OWS, *in Cornhill; and* T. EDLIN, *at the Prince's-Arms, against Exeter Exchange, in the Strand, 1724. Three Shillings Sixpence.*

8°. Pp. i–ii + 1–302

Notes: Published 2 April. Ostensibly written by a Frenchman naturalized in England to his brother in France. The IU copy has a frontispiece engraving of Defoe tipped in. About 1726 the unsold sheets were offered for sale by a different bookseller, with no preface and with a new title-page: (BM) *"The Behaviour Of Servants In England Inquired into. With a Proposal Containing Such Heads or Constitutions as would effectually Answer this Great End, and bring Servants of every Class to a just Regulation.* London: Printed for H. Whittridge under the Royal-Exchange. Price 2s. stitcht, or 3 s. bound."

Copy: BM. *Other copies:* BOD, CU, NLS, UL; BPL, C, CH, COR, F, H, HEH, I, IU, N, R, RPB, T, Y

458 A GENERAL HISTORY OF THE Robberies and Murders Of
the most notorious PYRATES, And also Their Policies, Discipline and Government, From their first Rise and Settlement in the Island of Providence, in 1717, to the present
Year 1724. With The remarkable Actions and Adventures
of the Female Pyrates, Mary Read and Anne Bonny. To
which is prefix'd An Account of the famous Captain Avery
and his Companions; with the Manner of his Death in
England. The Whole digested into the following Chapters;

Chap. I. Of Captain Avery.   VIII. Of Captain England.
    II. The Rise of Pyrates.   IX. Of Captain Davis.
    III. Of Captain Martel.   X. Of Captain Roberts.
    IV. Of Captain Bonnet.   XI. Of Captain Worley.
    V. Of Captain Thatch.   XII. Of Captain Lowther.
    VI. Of Captain Vane.   XIII. Of Captain Low.
    VII. Of Captain Rackam.   XIV. Of Captain Evans.
    And their several Crews.

To which is added, A short Abstract of the Statute and
Civil Law, in Relation to Pyracy. *By Captain Charles
Johnson.* LONDON: *Printed for* CH. RIVINGTON *at the Bible
and Crown in St. Paul's Church-Yard,* J. LACY *at the Ship
near the Temple-Gate, and* J. STONE *next the Crown Coffee-house the back of Greys-Inn,* 1724.

8°. Pp. [20 unnumbered] + 17–320. Plates facing pp. 86 and 117.
BM lacks plate facing p. 202 in JRM copy.

Notes: The first edition of the first volume was published 14
May 1724. The second edition (T. Warner, with some additions and rearrangement) was published 27 August; the third
edition (T. Warner, with further additions and changes) 12
June 1726; the fourth edition sometime in 1726. The *History*
is unique among Defoe's writings in having been elaborately
reviewed by Defoe himself (Mist's *Weekly-Journal,* 23 May, 6
June, and 29 August 1724). Of the extremely numerous reprints or adaptations of all or part of its contents, none has
any authority except Dr. Philip Gosse's reprint of the third
edition (Kensington, 1925–1927) and Mr. Arthur Hayward's
arbitrarily edited but very useful reprint of the fourth edition

(London, 1926 and 1955). Even in the 1955 reprint the *History* is still mistakenly attributed to the fictitious Captain Charles Johnson. For a discussion of Defoe's authorship see my *Defoe in the Pillory and Other Studies* (Bloomington, Indiana, 1939), pp. 126–188, and the review by Geoffrey Callender in *Mariner's Mirror* XXVI (1940), 97–99.

The second volume, devoted particularly to the pirates of Madagascar and to a long narrative of a sailor's captivity in Magadoxa (taken almost verbatim from a manuscript in the Sloane Collection of the British Museum), was not published until 25 July 1728. Its title-page reads:

The History of the Pyrates, Containing the Lives of

Captain Misson.	Captain Fly.
Captain Bowen.	Captain Howard.
Captain Kidd.	Captain Lewis.
Captain Tew.	Captain Cornelius.
Captain Halsey.	Captain Williams.
Captain White.	Captain Burgess.
Captain Condent.	Captain North.
Captain Bellamy.	

And their several Crews. Intermix'd with a Description of Magadoxa in Ethiopia; the natural Hatred and Cruelty of the Inhabitants to all Whites; their Laws, Manners, Customs, Government and Religion: With a particular Account of the beautiful Tombs, and their Ceremony of guarding them, taken from Captain Beavis's Journal; and that of a Molotto, who belong'd to the said Captain, was taken by, and lived several Years with the Magadoxians. To the whole is added An Appendix, which compleats the Lives of the first Volume, corrects some Mistakes, and contains the Tryal and Execution of the Pyrates at Providence, under Governor Rogers; with some other necessary Insertions, which did not come to Hand till after the Publication of the first Volume, and which makes up what was defective. Collected from Journals of Pyrates, brought away by a Person who was taken by, and forc'd to live with them 12 Years; and from those of Commanders, who had fallen into their Hands, some of whom have permitted their Names to be made use of, as a Proof of the Veracity of what we have published. The Whole instructive and entertaining. Vol. II. *By Capt. Charles*

Johnson, Author of Vol. I. *Omne tulit punctus, qui miscuit utile dulci. Hor.* London: *Printed for, and Sold by.* T. Woodward, *at the Half-moon, over-against St. Dunstan's Church, Fleet-street.*

8º. Pp. [12 unnumbered] + 1–413. Folding map (the Middle Part of America, with inset of the Isles of Cape Verd)

Notes: The 1726 edition of Vol. I and the 1728 edition of Vol. II are usually regarded as the complete fourth edition of the *History,* but they are often mistakenly assigned to the same year (1726). A second edition of the second volume (which I have not seen) was advertised as published on 1 January 1729. All these editions (except the last) are in BM. The first volume was pirated by Edward Midwinter 31 July 1725. Excerpts and condensations from the same volume (chiefly concerning Teach and to a less extent Stede Bonnet and Edward England) were being reprinted (without acknowledgment) in Brice's *Weekly Journal* in Exon in December 1725.

Copy: BM. *Other copies:* HEH, N

459   A Tour Thro' the Whole Island of Great Britain, Divided into Circuits or Journies. Giving A Particular and Diverting Account of Whatever is Curious and worth Observation, Viz. I. A Description of the Principal Cities and Towns, their Situations, Magnitude, Government, and Commerce. II. The Customs, Manners, Speech, as also the Exercises, Diversions, and Employments of the People. III. The Produce and Improvement of the Lands, the Trade, and Manufactures. IV. The Sea Ports and Fortifications, the Course of Rivers, and the Inland Navigation. V. The Publick Edifices, Seats, and Palaces of the Nobility and Gentry. With Useful Observations upon the Whole. Particularly fitted for the Reading of such as desire to Travel over the Island. *By a Gentleman.* London: *Printed, and Sold by* G. Strahan, *in Cornhil.* W. Mears, *at the Lamb without Temple-Bar.* R. Francklin, *under Tom's Coffee-house, Covent-Garden.* S. Chapman, *at the Angel in Pall-Mall.* R. Stagg, *in Westminster-Hall, and* J. Graves, *in St. James's-street.* MDCCXXIV.

8°. Pp. [iii]–viii + 1–144 + 1–121 + [1]–127 + 1 page of Errata + [i]–xvi. Folding map of the siege of Colchester facing p. 21; the index first appeared in Vol. II. In the BM copy the index is in Vol. I, and there is a frontispiece map of England and Wales; but the map of the siege of Colchester is misplaced in Vol. II.

Notes: Published 21 May. Attributed to a Gentleman (later said to be a member of the Church of England). The index was issued a year later together with the index to Vol. II (*The Daily Courant,* 8 June 1725). For Vols. II and III see Nos. 460 and 461.

Copy: IU. *Other copies:* BM, BOD, CU, UL; BPL, C, CH, COR, F, H, HEH, I, N, NYPL, P, R, T, Y

460   A TOUR THRO' THE WHOLE ISLAND OF GREAT BRITAIN . . . VOL. II. 1725. [Title identical with the preceding, as far as: "such as desire to Travel over the Island."] With a Map of England and Wales, by Mr. Moll. VOL. II. *By a Gentleman.* LONDON: *Printed: And sold by* G. STRAHAN, *in Cornhill.* W. MEARS, *at the Lamb without Temple-Bar.* R. FRANCK- LIN, *under Tom's Coffee-house, Covent-Garden.* S. CHAP- MAN, *and* J. JACKSON, *in Pall-Mall. And* J. STAGG, *in West- minster-Hall.* MDCCXXV.

8°.   Pp.   [iii]–viii + [1]–192 + [1]–200 + i–xvi + [xvii]–xxxvi. Folding map of England and Wales. In the BM copy the folding map of England and Wales is transferred to Vol. I and the map of the siege of Colchester is misplaced here.

Notes: Attributed to a Gentleman (a member of the Church of England). Published 8 June 1725.

Copy: IU. *Other copies:* BM, BOD, CU, UL; BPL, C, CH, H, HEH, I, N, NYPL, P, R, T, Y

461   A TOUR THRO' THE WHOLE ISLAND OF GREAT BRITAIN . . . VOL. III. 1727 (for 1726). [Title identical with the two pre- ceding, as far as: "such as desire to Travel over the Island."] VOL. III. Which completes this Work, and contains a Tour thro' Scotland, &c. With a Map of Scotland, by Mr. Moll. *By a Gentleman.* LONDON, *Printed: And Sold by* G. STRA-

HAN, *In Cornhill.* W. MEARS, *at the Lamb without Temple-Bar. And* J. STAGG, *in Westminster-Hall.* MDCCXXVII.

8°. Pp. [iii]–viii + [1]–239 + 1–230 + 21 pages of Index (unpaged). Folding map of Scotland

Notes: Attributed to a Gentleman (a member of the Church of England). Published 9 August 1726.

Copy: IU. *Other copies:* BM, BOD, CU, UL; BPL, C, CH, H, HEH, I, N, NYPL, P, R, T, Y

462   THE ROYAL PROGRESS: Or, A Historical View Of The Journeys, or Progresses, which several Great Princes have made to visit their Dominions, And Acquaint themselves with their People.

> Like Eden Fruitful, like Arabia Gay,
> So blest, they scarcely know for what to pray;
> England in native Glory ever springs;
> A Country fitted for the View of Kings.
>
> Mutato nomine, de te narratur.

LONDON: *Printed by* JOHN DARBY *in Bartholomew-Close; and Sold by* J. ROBERTS *in Warwick-Lane,* J. BROTHERTON *in* CORNHILL, *and* A. DODD *without Temple-Bar.* 1724. *Price One Shilling.*

8°. Pp. v–viii + 1–71

Notes: Published 1 June. Urges that George I become popular by progresses among his people.

Copy: IU

463   [LETTER ABOUT THE KING'S INTENDED PROGRESS.] 1724

Notes: I have not seen the original, ostensibly dated from Nottingham 8 June 1724 and reprinted in Boyer's *Political State of Great-Britain* for June 1724 (XXVII, 615–618). The letter, in a style very characteristic of Defoe, is supposed to recount a dream which had come to the writer after reading *The Royal Progress* (a tract which Defoe had published one week earlier). The letter, wherever it was first published, is certainly by Defoe. There are numerous analogues in the *Tour* and in *Memoirs of a Cavalier.*

464   TWO LETTERS TO THE AUTHOR OF THE FLYING-POST. 1724

Notes: The originals were presumably published in *The Flying-Post*, but I know only the reprints in Boyer's *Political State of Great-Britain* for August 1724 (XXVIII, 203–212). The first letter begins with a jocular personal allusion to Defoe, and it continues with a reply to Mist's *Weekly Journal* (with which Defoe was still connected). The second concludes with a gratuitous defence of Wood's patent for copper coinage, which Defoe was to defend very shortly afterward in *Some Farther Account Of The Original Disputes In Ireland* (1724). Both letters are signed Publius, but they are almost certainly by Defoe.

465   A NARRATIVE OF THE PROCEEDINGS IN FRANCE, For Discovering and Detecting the Murderers of the English Gentlemen, September 21. 1723, near Calais. With an Account of the Condemnation and Sentence of Joseph Bizeau and Peter Le Febre, Two notorious Robbers, who were the principal Actors in the said Murder; particularly in the killing Mr. Lock. Together with their Discovery, and Manner of perpetrating that execrable Murder; and also large Memoirs of their Behaviour during their Torture, and upon the Scaffold, their impeaching several other Criminals, and a brief History of their past Crimes, as well in Company with their former Captain, the famous Cartouche, as since his Execution. In which Is a great Variety of Remarkable Incidents, and Surprizing Circumstances, never yet made Publick. *Translated from the French.* LONDON: *Printed for* J. ROBERTS, *in Warwick-Lane.* M.DCC.XXIV. (*Price 2s.*)

8°. Pp. [1]–108

Notes: Apparently based on French originals; but the introductory matter, the comments, the explanations, and all the expanded passages are highly characteristic of Defoe. Announced 27 July as "In the Press and speedily will be published." Published 14 August; second edition later in 1724.

Copy: BM. *Other copies:* BPL, C, H, HEH, I, P, RPB, T, Y

466 A NARRATIVE OF ALL THE ROBBERIES, ESCAPES, &c. OF JOHN
SHEPPARD: Giving an Exact Description of the manner of
his wonderful Escape from the Castle in Newgate, and of
the Methods he took afterward for his Security. Written by
himself during his Confinement in the Middle Stone-Room,
after his being retaken in Drury-Lane. To which is added,
A true Representation of his Escape from the Condemn'd
Hold, curiously engraven on a Copper Plate. The whole
Publish'd at the particular Request of the Prisoner. LON-
DON: *Printed and Sold by* JOHN APPLEBEE, *a little below
Bridewell-Bridge, in Black-Fryers.* 1724. (*Price Six Pence.*)

8°. Pp. 3–31. 3 plates, of which the first and third (showing Sheppard's career in seven compartments and "Jack Shepherd in the
Stone Room in Newgate") have been added, according to a note
in the HEH copy by Robert Hoe, the former owner.

Notes: The first edition (HEH), the second edition (BM), the
third edition (BM), the seventh edition (Y), and the eighth edition (IU) seem to be identical in text except for slight differences
in the title-pages. The eighth edition (BM) has an extra engraving entitled "Jack Shepherd, drawn from the life." Published
15 August; second edition 17 November; fourth edition 19 November; fifth edition 20 November; sixth edition 23 November;
seventh edition 2 December; eighth edition sometime in December.

Copy: HEH. *Another copy:* T

467 SOME FARTHER ACCOUNT OF THE ORIGINAL DISPUTES IN IRE-
LAND, About Farthings and Halfpence. *In a Discourse With
a Quaker of Dublin.* Quaerenda Pecunia primum. *Printed
in the Year* 1724.

8°. Pp. 3–47

Notes: No place or publisher, but London. Fictitious discussion
with a Dublin Quaker.

Copy: BM. *Other copies:* UL; BPL, T, Y

468   THE HISTORY OF THE REMARKABLE LIFE OF JOHN SHEP-
PARD, Containing A particular Account of his many Robberies and Escapes, Viz. His robbing the Shop of Mr. Bains
in White-Horse-Yard of 24 Yards of Fustian. Of his breaking
and entering the House of the said Mr. Bains, and stealing
in Goods and Money to the Value of 20 l. Of his robbing
the House of Mr. Charles in May Fair of Money, Rings,
Plate, &c. to the Value of 30 l. Of his robbing the House
of Mrs Cook in Clare-Market, along with his pretended
Wife, and his Brother, to the Value of between 50 and 60 l.
Of his breaking the Shop of Mr. Phillips in Drury-Lane,
with the same Persons, and stealing Goods of small Value.
Of his entring the House of Mr. Carter, a Mathematical
Instrument Maker in Wytch–street, along with Anthony
Lamb and Charles Grace, and robbing of Mr. Barton, a
Master Taylor who belonged therein, of Goods and Bonds
to the Value of near 300 l. Of his breaking and entering
the House of Mr. Kneebone, a Woolen-Draper, near the
New Church in the Strand, in Company of Joseph Blake
alias Blewskin and William Field, and stealing Goods to the
Value of near 50 l. Of his robbing of Mr. Pargiter on the
Highway near the Turnpike, on the Road to Hampstead,
along with the said Blewskin. Of his robbing a Lady's
Woman in her Mistress's Coach on the same Road. Of his
robbing also a Stage Coach, with the said Blewskin, on the
Hampstead Road. Likewise of his breaking the Shop of
Mr. Martin in Fleet-street, and stealing 3 silver Watches of
15l. Value.

Also A particular Account of his rescuing his pretended
Wife from St. Giles's Round House. Of the wonderful Escape himself made from the said Round–House. Of the
miraculous Escape he and his said pretended Wife made
together from New-Prison, on the 25th of May last. Of his
surprizing Escape from the Condemn'd Hold of Newgate
on the 31st of August: Together with the true manner of
his being retaken; and of his Behaviour in Newgate, till the
most astonishing and never to be forgotten Escape he made

from thence, in the Night of the 15th of October. *The Whole taken from the most authentick Accounts,* as the Information of divers Justices of the Peace, the several Shop-keepers above-mentioned, the principal Officers of Newgate and New Prison, and from the Confession of Sheppard made to the Rev. Mr. Wagstaff, who officiated for the Ordinary of Newgate. LONDON: *Printed and Sold by* JOHN APPLEBEE *in Black-Fryers,* J. ISTED, *at the Golden-Ball near Chancery-Lane in Fleet Street, and the Book-sellers of London and Westminster. (Price One Shilling.)* [1724]

8º. Pp. [3 unnumbered] + [1]–56

Notes: IU has a copy (undated) with the same title-page except for the conclusion: "London: Printed for the Booksellers of London and Westminster. Price Four Pence." This is in 8º, with pp. [3]–28, and with a plate showing two views of Sheppard in chains in his prison cell.

Copy: Y. *Another copy:* BPL

469   A NEW VOYAGE ROUND THE WORLD, By A Course never sailed before. Being A Voyage undertaken by some Merchants, who afterwards proposed the Setting up an East-India Company in Flanders. Illustrated with Copper Plates. LONDON: *Printed for* A. BETTESWORTH, *at the Red-Lyon, in Pater-Noster-Row; and* W. MEARS, *at the Lamb, without Temple-Bar.* M.DCC.XXV [for 1724].

8º. Pp. [1]–208 + [1]–205. Frontispiece (map of the globe), 3 plates (facing p. 40 in Part I and pp. 59 and 93 in Part II)

Notes: Published 7 November. The attribution of authorship is more involved than usual for Defoe. The reader is told (p. 6) that the narrator speaks for the Captain, and that the Captain's name will be given although the name of the actual author remains concealed: ". . . I shall for the present conceal my Name, and that of the Ship also; . . . the Captain in whose Name I write this, gives me leave to make use of his Name, and conceal my own." But the Captain's name is never mentioned, and the supposed narrator is forgotten so completely that the Captain seems to speak throughout in his own person.

Copy: BM. *Other copies:* BOD, CU, NLS, UL; BPL, C, CH, COR, F, H, HEH, I, IU, JCB, N, NYPL, P, R, RPB, T, Y

1725

*470 An Epistle from Jack Sheppard to the late L[or]d C[hance]ll[o]r of E[nglan]d, who when Sheppard was try'd, sent for him to the Chancery Bar. [1725]

Fol. half-sheet

Notes: The colophon reads "Printed in the Year, 1725." 11 stanzas of three lines each, with the refrain "Which no Body can deny." Macclesfield had been convicted on 27 May by the House of Lords. Defoe was presumably the only man living who had waged a lifelong campaign against the misappropriation of the funds of orphans in London by legal authority, who had become the outstanding expert on the lives of Sheppard, Blueskin, and Jonathan Wild, who had a deep personal grievance against the Earl of Macclesfield, and who wrote satirical street ballads. However, the spellings "Jail" and "Jonathan Wilde" are unusual for him, and some other details are not characteristic. However, "jail" is not unknown elsewhere, and "Jonathan Wilde" occurs in No. 481 (p. 17). Perhaps, not certainly, Defoe's.

Copy: IU. *Another copy:* BM

471 The Life of Jonathan Wild, From His Birth to his Death. Containing His Rise and Progress in Roguery; his first Acquaintance with Thieves; by what Arts he made himself their Head, or Governor; his Discipline over them; his Policy and great Cunning in governing them; and the several Classes of Thieves under his Command. In which all his Intrigues, Plots and Artifices are accounted for, and laid open. Intermix'd with Variety of diverting Stories. *By H. D. late Clerk to Justice R——* London: *Printed for* T. Warner, *at the Black Boy in Pater-noster-Row.* 1725. [*Price One Shilling.*]

8°. Pp. iii–vii + 1–71

Notes: Published 29 May. Second edition 6 July. Attributed to H. D., late Clerk to Justice R——. It was Lord Chief Justice Raymond (later Lord Raymond) who sentenced Wild to execution.

Copy: BM. *Other copies:* BPL, F, RPB, T, Y

472   EVERY-BODY'S BUSINESS, IS NO-BODY'S BUSINESS; Or, Private Abuses, Publick Grievances; Exemplified In the Pride, Insolence, and Exorbitant Wages of our Women-Servants, Footmen, &c. With a Proposal for amendment of the same; as also for clearing the Streets of those Vermin call'd Shoe-Cleaners, and substituting in their stead many Thousands of Industrious Poor, now ready to starve. With divers other Hints, of great Use to the Publick. Humbly submitted to the Consideration of our Legislature, and the careful perusal of all Masters and Mistresses of Families. *By Andrew Moreton, Esq;* LONDON: *Sold by* T. WARNER, *at the Black Boy in Pater-Noster-Row;* A. DODD, *without Temple-Bar; and* E. NUTT, *at the Royal-Exchange.* 1725. *Price Six Pence.*

8°. Pp. [3]–34

Notes: Defoe's first use of his favorite pseudonym, Andrew Moreton, Esq; Published 3 June; second edition 8 June; third edition 12 June; fourth edition 19 June; fifth edition, with the addition of a Preface, 22 July.

Copy: BM. *Other copies:* NLS, UL; H, HEH, Y

473   THE TRUE AND GENUINE ACCOUNT Of The Life and Actions OF THE LATE JONATHAN WILD; Not made up of Fiction and Fable, but taken from his Own Mouth, and collected from Papers of his Own Writing. LONDON: *Printed and Sold by* JOHN APPLEBEE, *in Black-Fryers;* J. ISTED, *at the Golden-Ball near Chancery-Lane in Fleet-street; and the Book-sellers of London and Westminster,* 1725. (*Price Six-Pence.*)

8°. Pp. [iii]–viii + [1]–40. Frontispiece (portrait)

Notes: Professedly based on Wild's conversation and papers. Published 8 June. Lee dates the second edition 10 June. Third edition 12 June.

Copy: BM. *Other copies:* BPL, F, Y

A Tour Thro' the Whole Island of Great Britain . . . Vol. II. 1725. [See No. 460.]

474   An Account of The Conduct and Proceedings Of The late John Gow alias Smith, Captain of the late Pirates, Executed for Murther and Piracy Committed on Board the George Gally, afterwards call'd the Revenge; With A Relation of all the horrid Murthers they committed in cold Blood; As Also Of their being taken at the Islands of Orkney, and sent up Prisoners to London. London: *Printed and Sold by* John Applebee, *in Black-Fryers.* [*Price One Shilling.*] [1725]

8°. Pp. iii–viii + 1–62

Notes: No date, but 1725. There is some confusion about the date of publication, perhaps because the tract was unexpectedly delayed in the press. On 31 May Applebee announced in *The Daily Post* that it "is now actually in the Press, and will be publish'd in a few Days." In an advertisement at the end of *The True and Genuine Account . . . Of the Late Jonathan Wild* (published 8 June) it was said to be forthcoming: "Speedily will be publish'd, (of which Notice will be given in the *Daily-Post* and *Post-Boy*)." Lee dates the publication 11 June, which seems to be three weeks too early. In *The Post-Boy* for 1 July it was announced with the unusually explicit statement: "This Day about Noon will be publish'd." And in *The Daily Post,* the other newspaper in which Applebee had promised to announce the tract, a disclaimer was published on 7 July by James Fea, one of the principals in the story, denouncing the narrative of Gow——, which he said had appeared on Thursday, 1 July. Defoe's tract was intended for publication about 11 June, but it was apparently delayed until 1 July.

Copy: BM. *Another copy:* BPL

475   The Complete English Tradesman. 1726 [for 1725]

Notes: This manual was spoiled by revisions made not long after Defoe's death. But even in his lifetime it went through a bewildering series of modifications, which can best be stated in general terms. The newspaper advertisements of the day are extremely confusing, for they often describe three different stages of the book at virtually the same time.

On 7 September 1725 Rivington published the first volume, with ten numbered sections addressed specifically to young beginners in trade; and this was dated 1726. On 11 September he was advertising an expansion of the work with twelve sections (the form in which it is usually found). On 20 November this expanded version was advertised as "Lately published." The so-called second edition (actually the third) was published 10 September 1726 (dated 1727), with a separately paged supplement (which in turn was offered for sale separately to those who already owned an earlier edition). H has a copy of this separate supplement (1727). On 17 May 1727 a second volume was published (dated 1727), and this was divided into two parts with independent pagination. Volume II was directed primarily to the more experienced tradesmen. On 12 July 1728 the two volumes were offered together as a so-called second edition (actually the fourth edition of the first volume). Beginning in 1727, the spelling of "Complete" was changed to "Compleat."

BM has copies of the second issue of the first edition, the second edition, and the first edition of the second volume. All have the following imprint: "London: Printed for Charles Rivington at the Bible and Crown in St. Paul's Church-Yard." All are in octavo and all are anonymous. The pagination is as follows: second issue of first edition, iii–[xviii] + 1–447; second edition, iii–[xx] + 1–368 + [1]–148; first edition of Vol. II, [v]–xvi + [1]–298 + 1–176. I has a copy of the Dublin edition of 1726.

476 A GENERAL HISTORY OF DISCOVERIES AND IMPROVEMENTS, In useful Arts, Particularly in the great Branches of Commerce, Navigation, and Plantation, in all Parts of the known World. A Work which may entertain the Curious with the view of their present State; prompt the Indolent to retrieve those Inventions that are neglected, and animate the diligent to advance and perfect what may be thought wanting. To be continued Monthly. *Numb. I for October.*

LONDON: *Printed for* J. ROBERTS, *at the Oxford-Arms, in Warwick-Lane. Price One-Shilling.* 1725–1727 [for 1726].

8°. Pp. iii–viii + 1–72

Notes: The next two monthly numbers had identical title-pages, except for the changed numbers and dates. *Numb. II for November* had pp. 73–152. *Numb. III for December* had pp. 152–232. The fourth part had pp. 233–307 besides an unpaged index of five pages, and it had a new title-page: "*The Fourth and Last Part, with a compleat Index to the Whole.* London: Printed for W. Mears, F. Clay, and D. Brown, without Temple-Bar, and sold by J. Roberts, at the Oxford-Arms, in Warwick-Lane. Price One-Shilling. Where may be had the three former Parts. Price One-Shilling each."

The monthly issues had been falling behind their scheduled dates of publication. The October number had appeared on 12 October 1725; the November number on 27 November 1725; the December number on 1 February 1726; and the January number on 27 May 1726. On 13 December 1726 the four numbers were published together as a single book with a new title-page: (BM, NLS) *The History Of the Principal Discoveries and Improvements, In the Several Arts and Sciences: Particularly the great Branches of Commerce, Navigation, and Plantation, In all Parts of the known World.* London: Printed for W. Mears, at the Lamb, F. Clay, at the Bible, and D. Browne at the Black-Swan, without Temple-Bar. MDCCXXVII." 8°. Pp. iii–viii + 1–307 + 5-page index (unpaged). This volume was made up by binding the monthly parts together, by adding a conclusion and an index, and by substituting one new general title-page for the four separate title-pages.

Copy: BM. *Other copies:* BOD, NLS, UL; BPL, C, F, I, IU, LC, Y

1726

477 A BRIEF CASE OF THE DISTILLERS, And of the Distilling Trade in England, Shewing How far it is the Interest of England to encourage the said Trade, as it is so considerable an Advantage To the Landed Interest, to the Trade and Navigation, To the Public Revenue, and To the Employ-

ment of the Poor. Humbly recommended to the Lords and Commons of Great Britain, in the present Parliament assembled. LONDON, *Printed for* T. WARNER *at the Black-Boy in Pater-noster-row.* M.DCC.XXVI. *Price One Shilling.*

8º. Pp. iii–viii + 1–52

Notes: Published 10 March.

Copy: UL. *Other copies:* BM; BPL, F, HEH, IU, Y

478 A BRIEF HISTORICAL ACCOUNT OF THE LIVES OF THE SIX NOTORIOUS STREET-ROBBERS, Executed at Kingston, Viz. William Blewet, Edward Bunworth, Emanuel Dickenson, Thomas Berry, John Higges, and John Legee. With a particular Relation of their early Introduction into the desperate Trade of Street-Robbing, and especially of Murther, and of several Robberies which they, and others of their Gang, have been concern'd in. LONDON: *Printed for* A. MOORE *near St. Paul's.* 1726. (*Price Six Pence.*)

8º. Pp. [3]–40

Notes: Published 6 April (the day of the execution). J. Roberts had brought out a rival publication the day before. The second edition was published before 11 April.

Copy: BPL

479 AN ESSAY UPON LITERATURE: Or, An Enquiry into the Antiquity and Original of Letters; Proving That the two Tables, written by the Finger of God in Mount Sinai, was the first Writing in the World; and that all other Alphabets derive from the Hebrew. With a short View of the Methods made use of by the Antients, to supply the want of Letters before, and improve the use of them, after they were known. LONDON; *Printed for* THO. BOWLES, *Printseller, next to the Chapter-House, St. Paul's Church-Yard;* JOHN CLARK, *Bookseller, under the Piazzas, Royal-Exchange; and* JOHN BOWLES, *Printseller, over-against Stocks Market,* M.DCC.XXVI.

8°. Pp. 1–127

Copy: BM. *Other copies:* UL; BPL, C, COR, H, HEH, IU, N, T, Y

480   THE POLITICAL HISTORY OF THE DEVIL, As Well Ancient as Modern: In Two Parts. Part I. Containing a State of the Devil's Circumstances, and the various Turns of his Affairs, from his Expulsion out of Heaven, to the Creation of Man; with Remarks on the several Mistakes concerning the Reason and Manner of his Fall. Also his Proceedings with Mankind ever since Adam, to the first planting of the Christian Religion in the World. Part II. Containing his more private Conduct, down to the present Times: His Government, his Appearances, his Manner of Working, and the Tools he works with.

> Bad as he is, the Devil may be abus'd,
> Be falsely charg'd, and causelessly accus'd,
> When Men, unwilling to be blam'd alone,
> Shift off those Crimes on Him which are their Own.

LONDON: *Printed for* T. WARNER *at the Black Boy in Paternoster Row,* 1726.

8°. Pp. [6 unnumbered] + [1]–408. Frontispiece (Satan enthroned)

Notes: Published 7 May. In the second edition (which Lee dates 20 April 1727) the title was changed from *The Political History* to *The History,* and the original preface was replaced by one telling of the great success of the first edition.

Copy: BM. *Other copies:* BOD, CU, UL; BPL, C, CH, COR, F, H, HEH, I, IU, LC, N, NYPL, P, PML, R, RPB, T, Y

481   UNPARALLEL'D CRUELTY: Or, The Tryal of Captain Jeane of Bristol. Who was convicted at the Old Bailey for the Murder of his Cabbin-Boy, who he put to Death in the most horrid and barbarous Manner that ever was heard of. To which is added, An account of his Life and Conversation, both before and after his Condemnation; with his Dying

Speech, and Behaviour at the Place of Execution. LONDON: *Printed for* T. WARNER, *at the Black-Boy in Pater-Noster-Row.* M.DCC.XXVI. (*Price 6d.*)

8°. Pp. [1]–33

Notes: The dates are even more difficult than usual for a criminal life. Jeane was hanged on 13 May; but the first edition was published on 7 May, the second on 22 May. IU has a copy with an old manuscript note dating the tract 17 May. The pamphlet itself says that the narrative was published in *Applebee's Journal* on the previous Saturday (14 May). Perhaps the pamphlet was rapidly revised to include the latest events, like the different editions of a modern evening newspaper. It is clear that dying speeches were by this time often available some days before the executions, and that accounts of behavior at the scaffold were sometimes written in advance. Apparently this was Defoe's last tract dealing with the trial of a criminal.

Copy: BM. *Other copies:* BPL, HEH, IU, T

482   THE FRIENDLY DAEMON, Or The Generous Apparition; Being A True Narrative of a miraculous Cure, newly perform'd upon that famous Deaf and Dumb Gentleman, Dr. Duncan Campbell, By a familiar Spirit that appear'd to him in a white Surplice, like a Cathedral singing Boy.

> If by our Senses Spirits we perceive,
> Or from the Strength of Fancy, so believe,
> No Fault we do commit that merits blame,
> If to the Publick we report the same;
> For whether by our Eyes we Spectres see
> Or by a special Sight, we must agree,
> Things are to us as they appear to be.

LONDON *Printed; and Sold by* J. ROBERTS *in Warwick-Lane* MDCCXXVI.

8°. Pp. 3–39

Notes: Published 7 June. In an advertisement of 3 September Campbell seemed to claim the authorship for himself.

Copy: UL. *Other copies:* BPL, H, R

483 THE FOUR YEARS VOYAGES OF CAPT. GEORGE ROBERTS; Being a Series of Uncommon Events, Which befell him In a Voyage to the Islands of the Canaries, Cape de Verde, and Barbadoes, from whence he was bound to the Coast of Guiney. The Manner of his being taken by Three Pyrate Ships, commanded by Low, Russell, and Spriggs, who, after having plundered him, and detained him 10 Days, put him aboard his own Sloop, without Provisions, Water, &c. and with only two Boys, one of eighteen, and the other of Eight Years of Age. The Hardships he endur'd for above 20 Days, 'till he arriv'd at the Island of St. Nicholas, from whence he was blown off to Sea (before he could get any Sustenance) without his Boat and biggest Boy, whom he had sent ashore; and after Four Days of Difficulty and Distress, was Shipwreck'd on the Unfrequented Island of St. John, where, after he had remained near Two years, he built a Vessel to bring himself off. With a particular and curious Description, and Draught of the Cape de Verd Islands; their Roads, Anchoring Places, Nature and Production of the Soils; The Kindness and Hospitality of the Natives to Strangers, their Religion, Manners, Customs, and Superstitions, &c. Together with Observations on the Minerals, Mineral Waters, Metals, and Salts, and of the Nitre with which some of these Islands abound. *Written by Himself,* And interspers'd with many Pleasant and Profitable Remarks, very instructive for all those who use this Trade, or who may have the Misfortune to meet with any of the like Distresses either by Pyracy or Shipwreck. Adorn'd with several Copper Plates. LONDON: *Printed for* A. BETTESWORTH, *at the Red Lyon, in Pater-Noster-Row, and* J. OSBORN, *at the Ship, at St. Saviour's Dock-Head, near Horsely-Down.* 1726.

8°. Pp. [4 unnumbered] + 1–458. Folding map of the Cape de Verde Islands. 4 plates (facing pp. 166, 422, 423, 438)

Notes: Published 15 July. Attributed to Captain George Roberts.

Copy: IU. *Other copies:* BM, BOD, CU, NLS, UL; BPL, C, COR, H, HEH, I, N, NYPL, P, R, T, Y

484 MERE NATURE DELINEATED: Or, A Body without a Soul.
Being Observations Upon The Young Forester Lately
brought to Town from Germany. With Suitable Applica-
tions. Also, A Brief Dissertation upon the Usefulness and
Necessity of Fools, whether Political or Natural. LONDON:
Printed for T. WARNER, *at the Black Boy, in Pater-Noster-
Row.* 1726. (*Price 1s. 6d.*)

8°. Pp. iii–iv + [1]–123

Notes: Published 23 July.

Copy: IU. *Other copies:* BPL, HEH, R

A TOUR THRO' THE WHOLE ISLAND OF GREAT BRITAIN . . .
VOL. III. 1727 (for 1726). [See No. 461.]

485 SOME CONSIDERATIONS UPON STREET-WALKERS. With A Proposal for lessening the present Number of them. In Two
Letters to a Member of Parliament. To which is added, *A
Letter from One of those Unhappy Persons,* when in Newgate, and who was afterwards executed, for picking a Gentleman's Pocket, to Mrs. ——— in Great P[ult]ney Street.

> Keep thy Eyes from wand'ring, Man of Frailty;
> Beware the dang'rous Beauty of the Wanton;
> Fly their Inticements, Ruin like a Vulture
> Waits on their Steps.   Otway's Orphan.

LONDON: *Printed for* A. MOORE, *near St. Paul's. Price 6d.*
[1726]

4°. Pp. [1]–18

Notes: Includes letter ostensibly written by a street-walker. Published 14 October. Lee dates the second edition in January 1727.

Copy: BM. *Other copies:* BOD; IU

486 THE PROTESTANT MONASTERY: Or, A Complaint Against
The Brutality of the present Age. Particularly The Pertness
and Insolence of our Youth to Aged Persons. With A Cau-

tion to People in Years, how they give the Staff out of their own Hands, and leave themselves at the Mercy of others. Concluding With a Proposal for erecting a Protestant Monastery, where Persons of small Fortunes may end their Days in Plenty, Ease, and Credit, without burthening their Relations, or accepting Publick Charities. *By Andrew Moreton, Esq; Author of Every-Body's Business is No-Body's Business.* LONDON: *Printed for* W. MEADOWS, *at the Angel in* Cornhill; *and sold by* J. ROBERTS, *in Warwick-Lane;* E. NUTT, *under the Royal Exchange;* A. DODD, *without Temple-Bar; and* N. BLANFORD, *at Charing-Cross.* 1727 [for 1726].

8°. Pp. [iii]–viii + [1]–31

Notes: Published 19 November. Attributed to Andrew Moreton, Esq. See *Chickens Feed Capons* (No. 513).

Copy: BM. *Other copies:* NLS, UL; BPL, IU, N, P, R, T, Y

487   A SYSTEM OF MAGICK; Or, A History Of The Black Art. Being An Historical Account of Mankind's most early Dealing with the Devil; and how the Acquaintance on both Sides first began.

> Our Magick, Now, commands the Troops of Hell,
> The Devil himself submits to Charm and Spell.
> The Conj'rer in his Circles and his Rounds
> Just whistles up his Spirits, as Men do Hounds.
> Th' obsequious Devil, obeys the Sorcerer's Skill,
> The Mill turns round the Horse, that first turns
> round the Mill.

LONDON, *Printed: And Sold by* J. ROBERTS *in Warwick-Lane.* MDCCXXVII [for 1726].

8°. [8 unnumbered] + [1]–403. Frontispiece (magician in his study)

Notes: Published 24 November. In advertisements for some later editions (e. g., that of 21 January 1730) the book was attributed to Andrew Moreton, Esq; (Defoe's favorite pseudonym).

Copy: IU. *Other copies:* BM, BOD, NLS, UL; BPL, C, CH, COR, H, HEH, I, LC, N, NYPL, P, R, RPB, T, Y

1727

488 THE EVIDENT APPROACH OF A WAR; And Something of The Necessity of It, In Order to Establish Peace, and Preserve Trade. Pax Quaeritur Bello. To which is added, An Exact Plan and Description of the Bay and City of Gibraltar. LONDON: *Printed, and Sold by* J. ROBERTS *in Warwick-Lane; and* A. DODD *in the Strand.* 1727. [*Price 1s. 6d.*]

8°. Pp. [2 unnumbered] + 1–59. Folding map of Gibraltar (facing p. 53)

Notes: Published 10 January; second edition 2 February. Pp. 40–46 cite No. 233 very approvingly and quote it at length.

Copy: BM. *Other copies:* BOD, CU, DW, NLS; BPL, COR, F, H, IU, JCB, P, RPB, T, Y

489 CONJUGAL LEWDNESS: Or, Matrimonial Whoredom.

> Loose Thoughts, at first, like subterranean Fires,
> Burn inward, smothering, with unchast Desires;
> But getting Vent, to Rage and Fury turn,
> Burst in Volcano's, and like Ætna burn;
>> The Heat increases as the Flames aspire,
>> And turns the solid Hills to liquid Fire.
> So sensual Flames, when raging in the Soul,
> First vitiate all the Parts, then fire the Whole;
>> Burn up the Bright, the beauteous, the Sublime,
>> And turn our lawful Pleasures into Crime.

LONDON: *Printed for* T. WARNER, *at the Black Boy in Pater-Noster-Row.* MDCCXXVII.

8°. Pp. iii–[viii] + [1]–406

Notes: Published 30 January. Later in the same year (on 10 June according to Lee) this was reissued by Warner with no change except the substitution of a long title beginning *A Treatise Concerning The Use And Abuse Of The Marriage Bed.* In this reissue p. 1 (with its heading "Conjugal Lewdness, &c.") was not reset.

Copy: BM. *Other copies:* UL; IU, Y

490   THE EVIDENT ADVANTAGES To Great Britain and its Allies FROM THE APPROACHING WAR: Especially in Matters of Trade. To which is Added Two Curious Plans, One of the Port and Bay of Havana; the other of Porto-Belo. LONDON: *Printed: And Sold by* J. ROBERTS *in Warwick-Lane; and* A. DODD *in the Strand.* 1727. [*Price 1s.*]

8°. Pp. [2 unnumbered] + 1–44. Maps of Havana and Porto-Bello (facing pp. 32, 38)

Notes: Published 2 February.

Copy: BM. *Other copies:* BOD, DW, NLS; BPL, F, H, HEH, IU, JCB, LC, N, P, RPB, T, Y

491   A COLLECTION OF MISCELLANY LETTERS, Selected out of Mist's Weekly Journal. The Third Volume. LONDON: *Printed for* T. WARNER, *in Pater-Noster-Row,* MDCCXXVII.

12°. Pp. [10 unnumbered] + 1–312

Notes: On 4 February 1727 announced for publication on the next Monday (6 February). On 11 February advertised: "This Day is publish'd, in 12 mo." See Nos. 444, 445, and 492.

Copy: BM. *Other copies:* BOD; IU, Y

492   A COLLECTION OF MISCELLANY LETTERS, Selected out of Mist's Weekly Journal. THE FOURTH VOLUME. LONDON: *Printed for* T. WARNER, *in Pater-Noster-Row,* MDCCXXVII.

12°. Pp. [2 unnumbered] + 1–312

Notes: On 4 February 1727 announced for publication on the next Monday (6 February). On 11 February advertised: "The Day is publish'd, in 12 mo." See Nos. 444, 445, and 491.

Copy: BM. *Other copies:* BOD; IU, Y

493   A Brief Deduction of the Original, Progress, And Im-
mense Greatness of the British Woollen Manufacture:
With An Enquiry whether it be not at present in a very
Declining Condition: The Reasons of its Decay; and the
Only Means of its Recovery. London, *Printed; And Sold by*
J. Roberts *in Warwick-Lane, and* A. Dodd *at the Peacock
without Temple-Bar.* 1727 [*Price One Shilling.*]

8°. Pp. [2 unnumbered] + 1–52

Notes: Published 15 March.

Copy: BM. *Other copies:* UL; IU, Y

494   An Essay on the History and Reality of Apparitions.
Being An Account of what they are, and what they are not;
whence they come, and whence they come not. As Also How
we may distinguish between the Apparitions of Good and
Evil Spirits, and how we ought to behave to them. With a
great Variety of Surprizing and Diverting Examples, never
Publish'd before.

> By Death transported to th' Eternal Shore,
> Souls so remov'd revisit us no more:
> Engross'd with Joys of a Superior Kind,
> They leave the trifling Thoughts of Life behind.

London, *Printed: And Sold by* J. Roberts *in Warwick-
Lane.* MDCCXXVII.

8°. Pp. [9 unnumbered] + [1]–395

Notes: Frontispiece (Caesar's ghost appearing in Brutus' tent).
5 plates (facing pp. 101, 139, 237, 295, 370). Published 21 March
1727. The same sheets were reissued with a new title-page as
*The Secrets of the Invisible World Disclos'd: Or, An Universal
History of Apparitions Sacred and Prophane, Under all De-
nominations.* This was advertised 23 November 1728 as printed
for J. Peele, and on 13 February and 2 March 1729 as printed
for J. Clarke, A. Millar, and J. Green.

Copy: IU. *Other copies:* BM, BOD, CU, UL; BPL, C, CH, COR,
F, H, HEH, I, LC, N, NYPL, RPB, T, Y

THE COMPLEAT ENGLISH TRADESMAN. VOL. II. 1727. [See No. 475.]

A TREATISE CONCERNING THE USE AND ABUSE OF THE MARRIAGE BED. 1727. [See No. 489.]

495   A NEW FAMILY INSTRUCTOR: In Familiar Discourses Between A Father and his Children, On the most Essential Points of the Christian Religion. In Two Parts. Part I. Containing a Father's Instructions to his Son upon his going to Travel into Popish Countries; And to the rest of his Children, on his Son's turning Papist; confirming them in the Protestant Religion, against the Absurdities of Popery. Part II. Instructions against the Three Grand Errors of the Times; Viz. 1. Asserting the Divine Authority of the Scripture; against the Deists. 2. Proofs, that the Messias is already come, &c.; against the Atheists and Jews. 3. Asserting, the Divinity of Jesus Christ, that he was really the same with the Messias, and that the Messias was to be really God; against our Modern Hereticks. With a Poem upon the Divine Nature of Jesus Christ, in Blank Verse. *By the Author of the Family Instructor.* LONDON: *Printed for* T. WARNER, *at the Black-Boy in Pater-Noster-Row.* M.DCC.XXVII.

8⁰. Pp. iii–xv + [1]–384

Notes: Published 6 September. Attributed to *the Author of The Family Instructor.* As only a few readers were supposed to know that Defoe had written *The Family Instructor,* this sequel must have been expected to pass as an anonymous work.

Copy: IU. *Other copies:* BPL, COR, H, R, Y

496   PAROCHIAL TYRANNY: Or, The House-Keeper's Complaint Against The insupportable Exactions, and partial Assessments of Select Vestries, &c. With a Plain Detection of many Abuses committed in the Distribution of Publick Charities: Together With a Practicable Proposal for Amendment of the same; which will not only take off great Part of the

Parish Taxes now subsisting, but ease Parishioners from serving troublesome Offices, or paying exorbitant Fines. *By Andrew Moreton, Esq;* LONDON: *Printed; and sold by* J. ROBERTS *in Warwick Lane.* [*Price Six Pence.*] [1727]

8°. Pp. [1]-36

Notes: Published 9 December 1727. Attributed to Andrew Moreton, Esq;

Copy: BM. *Other copies:* UL; BPL, H, IU, R, Y

1 7 2 8

497   SOME CONSIDERATIONS ON The Reasonableness and Necessity Of Encreasing and ENCOURAGING THE SEAMEN. Founded on the Gracious Expressions, in their Favour, contained in His Majesty's Speech from the Throne. With some Proposed Schemes for the Effectual Performing it, without Prejudice either to the Navy, or the Commerce. Never made Publick before. LONDON: *Printed: And Sold by* J. ROBERTS *in Warwick-Lane.* MDCCXXVIII. [*Price One Shilling.*]

8°. Pp. [2 unnumbered] + 1-51

Notes: Published 23 February. The original proposal (to which Defoe refers on pp. 35-38) was presented by Defoe to the Select Committee of the House of Lords about 30 January 1704/5 and later printed in *Manuscripts of the House of Lords 1704-1706* (1912). See *Letters*, ed. Healey, pp. 73-77.

Copy: BM. *Other copies:* NLS, UL; C, H, IU, NYPL, Y

498   AUGUSTA TRIUMPHANS: Or, The Way To Make London The most flourishing City in the Universe. First, By establishing an University where Gentlemen may have Academical Education under the Eye of their Friends. II. To prevent Murder, &c. by an Hospital for Foundlings. III. By suppressing pretended Mad-Houses, where many of the fair Sex are unjustly confin'd, while their Husbands keep Mistresses, &c. and many Widows are lock'd up for the Sake of

their Jointure. IV. To save our Youth from Destruction, by clearing the Streets of impudent Strumpets, Suppressing Gaming-Tables, and Sunday Debauches. V. To avoid the expensive Importation of Foreign Musicians, by forming an Academy of our own. VI. To save our lower Class of People from utter Ruin, and to render them useful, by preventing the immoderate Use of Geneva: With a frank Explosion of many other common Abuses, and incontestable Rules for Amendment. Concluding with An Effectual Method to prevent Street Robberies, And A Letter to Coll. Robinson, on account of the Orphan's Tax. LONDON: *Printed for* J. ROBERTS *in Warwick-Lane, and Sold by* E. NUTT *at the Royal-Exchange,* A. DODD *without Temple-Bar,* N. BLAND-FORD *at Charing-Cross, and* A. STAGG *in Westminster-Hall.* 1728. [*Price One Shilling.*]

8°. Pp. [3]–63

Notes: Published 16 March. The concluding letter to Col. Robinson is dated 28 February 1727–8. In the second edition (published 26 September) the same concluding letter is dated 23 September 1728. See *The Generous Projector* (No. 514).

Copy: BM. *Other copies:* BOD; BPL, C, F, H, IU, N, T, Y

499 A PLAN OF THE ENGLISH COMMERCE. Being a Compleat Prospect Of The Trade of this Nation, as well the Home Trade as the Foreign. In Three Parts. Part I. Containing a View of the present Magnitude of the English Trade, as it respects, 1. The Exportation of our Own Growth and Manufacture. 2. The Importation of Merchants Goods from Abroad. 3. The prodigious Consumption of both at Home. Part II. Containing an Answer to that great and important Question now depending, Whether our Trade, and Especially our Manufactures, are in a declining Condition, or no? Part III. Containing several Proposals entirely New, for Extending and Improving our Trade, and Promoting the Consumption of our Manufactures, in Countries wherewith we have Hitherto had no Commerce. Humbly offered

to the Consideration of the King and Parliament. LONDON: *Printed for* CHARLES RIVINGTON, *at the Bible and Crown in St. Paul's Church-Yard.* M.DCC.XXVIII.

8º. Pp. [22 unnumbered] + [1]–368

Notes: Published 23 March. A second edition, dated 1730, used unsold sheets, but added a separately paged 40-page appendix and substituted a new title: (BM) "*A Plan Of The English Commerce. Being A Compleat Prospect Of The Trade of this Nation, as well the Home Trade as the Foreign. Humbly offered to the Consideration of the King and Parliament. The Second Edition. To which is added, An Appendix, Containing A View of the Increase of Commerce, not only of England, but of all the Trading Nations of Europe since the Peace with Spain. The whole containing Several Proposals, entirely New, for Extending and Improving our Trade, and Promoting the Consumption of our Manufactures, in Countries wherewith we have Hitherto had no Commerce.* London: Printed for Charles Rivington, at the Bible and Crown in St. Paul's Church-Yard. 1730." This second edition was advertised for sale on 13 January 1731. No. 507, largely based on No. 499, concludes with a full-page advertisement of *A Plan of the English Commerce.*

Copy: BM. *Other copies:* BOD, NLS, UL; BPL, C, CH, COR, F, H, HEH, I, IU, LC, N, NYPL, P, R, RPB, T, Y

500 THE MEMOIRS OF AN ENGLISH OFFICER, Who serv'd in the Dutch War in 1672. to the Peace of Utrecht, in 1713. Containing Several Remarkable Transactions both by Sea and Land, and in divers Countries, but chiefly those wherein the Author was personally concern'd. Together with a Description of many Cities, Towns, and Countries, in which he resided; their Manners and Customs, as well Religious as Civil, interspers'd with many curious Observations on their Monasteries and Nunneries, more particularly of the famous one at Montserat. On the Bull-Feasts, and other publick Diversions; as also on the Genius of the Spanish People, amongst whom he continued several Years a Prisoner of War. No Part of which has before been made Pub-

lick. *By Capt. George Carleton.* LONDON, *Printed for* E. SYMON, *over against the Royal* Exchange, Cornhill. MDCCXXVIII.

8°. Pp. [6 unnumbered] + [1]–352

Notes: Attributed to Capt. George Carleton. From contemporary manuscript notes in the copy in the possession of Sir Harold Williams, it is clear that Carleton was a real man, that he hung around the press while the book was being printed, and that he was responsible for some "ffoists" of his own, including the utterly irrelevant conclusion of the book. This only strengthens the certainty that Defoe was the author, using the name of Carleton for his own purpose. The book was a defence of the Spanish campaign of the Earl of Peterborough; and according to the notes in Sir Harold Williams' copy, the manuscript had met with Peterborough's approval.

Published 16 May. Shortly afterward the book was reissued with two cancellations. On the first page of the dedication (A₂) the impossible title "Spencer Lord Compton, Baron of Wilmington" was replaced by the correct title which had been given Sir Spencer Compton on 11 January 1728: "Spencer Lord Wilmington." And the prefatory leaf "To The Reader" was reset so as to omit the postscript which had read: "Some few Paragraphs in this Work being, through mistake, inserted in wrong Places, the Author desires his Readers to excuse it, especially as they were not discovered, till it was too late to alter their Position without considerable Charge."

On 27 May the book was reissued in a third state, with the two cancellations as above and with a new title-page: (BM) *"The Military Memoirs Of Capt. George Carleton. From the Dutch War, 1672. In which he Serv'd, to the Conclusion of the Peace at Utrecht, 1713. Illustrating Some of the most Remarkable Transactions, both by Sea and Land, during the Reigns of King Charles and King James II. hitherto unobserv'd by all the Writers of those Times. Together with An exact Series of the War in Spain; and a particular Description of the several Places of the Author's Residence in many Cities, Towns, and Countries; their Customs, Manners, &c. Also Observations on the Genius of the Spaniards (among whom he continued some Years a Prisoner) their Monasteries and Nunneries (especially that*

*fine one at Montserat) and on their publick Diversions; more
particularly their famous Bull-Feasts.* London, Printed for
E. Symon, over against the Royal Exchange, Cornhill,
MDCCXXVIII." Copies of the first issue are found in BM, C,
and HW; copies of the second in C, IU, and JRM; copies of the
third in BM, C, and IU.

In 1740 the same publisher reissued unsold sheets without
dedication or preface, cancelling the first leaf so as to print the
new half-title and supplying a new title-page beginning: (JRM)
*"A True and Genuine History (Containing Abundance of curi-
ous Circumstances) Of The Two Last Wars against France and
Spain."* In 1741 this was reissued by Francis Gosling with minor
changes (BM). In 1743 the original unsold sheets were still being
offered to the public, this time by Tho. Astley with a new title-
page beginning *"The Memoirs of Cap. George Carleton, An
English Officer, . . ."* JRM has two copies of this, differing only
in the order in which the dedication and the preface are placed.
In Astley's edition of 1743 the original erroneous dedication
"To The Right Honourable Spencer Lord Compton, Baron of
Wilmington, Knt. of the Bath, and one of his Majesty's most
Honourable Privy Council," which had been corrected almost
immediately in 1728 and omitted entirely in 1740, was restored
from the first printed sheets.

In spite of efforts to arouse interest through title-page references to contemporary relations with Spain, the book was
printed only once in the 18th century, and it never became
widely known until after Sir Walter Scott induced Constable to
publish it during Wellington's Peninsular War (1809). Even
Dr. Johnson had never heard of it until he was seventy-five years
old, when Lord Eliot, "after a good deal of enquiry, procured a
copy in London, and sent it to Johnson," after which the Doctor "sat up till he had read it through, . . ."

Copy: BM. *Other copies:* BOD, HW, NLS; BPL, C, COR, H,
HEH, I, IU, JRM, N, NYPL, P, PML, R, RPB, Y

501   ATLAS MARITIMUS & COMMERCIALIS; Or, A General View
of the World, So far as it relates to Trade and Navigation;
Describing All The Coasts, Ports, Harbours, and Noted
Rivers, according to the latest Discoveries and most Exact

Observations. Together with a Large Account of the Commerce Carried on by Sea between the several Countries of the World, As likewise of all Inland Trade by means of Navigable Rivers; The Rise, Progress, and Decay thereof, in its various Branches; with Methods for farther Improvements. To which are Added Sailing Directions For All the Known Coasts and Islands on the Globe; With A Sett of Sea-Charts, some laid down after Mercator, but the greater Part according to a New Globular Projection, Adapted for measuring Distances (as near as possible) by Scale and Compass, and Authorized by Letters Patent under the Great Seal of Great-Britain. The Use of the Projection Justified by Dr. Halley. To which are Subjoined Two Large Hemispheres on the Plane of the Equinoctial; containing all the Stars in the Britannic Catalogue: Of great Use to Sailors for finding the Latitude in the Night. LONDON: *Printed for* JAMES *and* JOHN KNAPTON, WILLIAM *and* JOHN INNYS *in St. Paul's Church-yard;* JOHN DARBY *in Bartholomew-Close;* ARTHUR BETTESWORTH, JOHN OSBORN *and* THOMAS LONGMAN *in Pater-noster-Row;* JOHN SENEX *in Fleet-street;* EDWARD SYMON *in Cornhil;* ANDREW JOHNSTON *in Peter's Court in St. Martin's Lane; and the Executors of* WILLIAM TAYLOR *deceas'd.* M.DCC.XXVIII.

Large fol. Pp. i–[vi] + 1–340 + i–ix + iii–vi + 3–[198] + A List of the Charts + 54 Charts

Notes: Published 3 June 1728. The 1 page address "To the Reader" is signed "April 10, 1728. Edm. Halley." Of the seven copies which I have examined closely, no two are exactly alike in pagination and in the arrangement of the signatures, in tables, and in maps. In the IU copy Defoe's contribution can be limited to the Preface (pp. ii–iii), the chapters of geographical and historical description (pp. 1–340), and perhaps the Errata (p. iv) and the Index (pp. i–ix). In spite of the exceptionally high price announced for the atlas (3 guineas), no less than 432 subscribers are listed in "The Names of such of the Subscribers as came to the Undertakers Hands." The price was raised to 3 pounds and 18 shillings at the time of delivery, be-

cause 45 sheets had been added to the 150 originally promised.
On 28 November 1728 a complete table of contents was offered
gratis to "any Gentleman who has bought the Book." Apparently the atlas as delivered on 3 June lacked any such table.

The atlas was being assembled for William Taylor nine years
before its final publication. In the advertisements at the back of
The Farther Adventures of Robinson Crusoe (20 August 1719)
it was listed as No. 15 among the folios sold by Taylor: "A new
general Atlas, with above 40 large Maps, printed on an Elephant Paper, is in the Press, and in great Forwardness." Nothing was said to indicate that Taylor's maps were to be drawn
according to the new globular projection, which soon became
a source of controversy in the newspapers. But in the proposals
reprinted in *The Post-Boy* for 21 November 1721 two of the
three patentees of that projection were listed among the publishers of the atlas:

"This Day is publish'd, PROPOSALS for printing a complete
SEA-ATLAS, from a true Globular Projection; approved by
several of the Ablest Judges of Navigation and Astronomy, and
warranted his Majesty's Letters Patent under the Great Seal of
Great Britain, granted to John Harris, John Senex, and Henry
Wilson. Containing a Description of all the Ports and Harbours
in the World; the Soundings, Landmarks, Lighthouses, Beacons,
Buoys, and whatever else is necessary to be known for conduct-
ing a Ship in or out of the same: As also an Account of the Sea-
Ports, as to their Situation, what Navigable Rivers flow up to
them; of their Trade, Shipping, Product, Manufactures, Customs, &c. To which will be prefix'd, A General Treatise of
Navigation, wherein the necessary Rules and Tables, for supplying the Use of all other Books of that Kind, both in Theory
and Practice, will be included. The Whole Revised by Dr.
Edmond Halley, Regius Professor of Astronomy. I. To contain about 150 Sheets, printed on a fine large Elephant Paper,
fifty whereof to be Charts engraven on Copper, in several of
which will be Plans of the most noted Harbours in the World.
II. Price to Subscribers to be three Guineas, one to be paid
down. III. The Subscribers Names to be printed, and their
Arms engraven before the Work. Subscriptions are taken in by
J. Senex and T. Taylor in Fleetstreet, W. Taylor in Pater-
Noster-Row, W. Innys at the West End of S. Paul's, Andr.

Johnston Engraver in Round-Court in the Strand, H. Wilson at the Globe in the Little-Minories, and E. Symson in Cornhill."

In *The London Journal* for 14 March 1723–4 these proposals were reprinted as "Lately publish'd" with few changes; the role of Halley was reduced to revising the charts and certifying the whole work, and there were a few alterations in the list of publishers: "J. Senex and Tho. Taylor in Fleetstreet, J. Darby in Bartholomew Close, W. Taylor in Paternoster-Row, W. Innis at the West End of St. Paul's, A. Johnston in Round Court, J. Osborn in Lombardstreet, and E. Symon in Cornhil."

In the atlas as finally issued there were further changes in the list of publishers. Subscribers were listed, but without having "their Arms engraven" in any copy which I have seen.

Copy: IU. *Other copies:* BM, BOD, UL; BPL, COR, F, H, HEH, JCB, LEH, M, N, NO, PTS

502   AN IMPARTIAL ACCOUNT OF THE late Famous SIEGE OF GIBRALTAR: To which are Added, Most Accurate Plans of the Town, and of the Approaches and Camp of the Spaniards. With Many Remarkable Transactions never made Publick before. *By an Officer,* who was at the Taking and Defence of Gibraltar by the Prince Hesse, of Glorious Memory; and served in the Town, during the last Siege. LONDON: *Printed for* T. WARNER, *at the Black-Boy, in Pater-Noster-Row,* 1728.

8°. Pp. [3]–51. Folding map (bay and town of Gibraltar, with a plan of the enemy's approaches)

Notes: Published 16 July. Fictitious attribution to an officer.

Copy: BM. *Other copies:* BOD; BPL, IU, P, Y

A GENERAL HISTORY OF THE PYRATES . . . VOL. II [1728]. [See No. 458.]

503   SECOND THOUGHTS ARE BEST: Or, A Further Improvement Of A Late Scheme To Prevent Street Robberies: By Which Our Streets will be so strongly guarded, and so gloriously illuminated, that any part of London will be as safe and

pleasant at Midnight as at Noonday; and Burglary totally
impracticable: With Some Thoughts for suppressing Robberies in all the publick Roads of England, &c. Humbly
Offered for the good of his Country, submitted to the Consideration of the Parliament, and dedicated to his sacred
Majesty King George IId. *By Andrew Moreton, Esq;* London: *Printed for* W. Meadows, *at the Angel in Cornhil;
and sold by* J. Roberts *in Warwick-Lane,* 1729 [for 1728].
Price Six-Pence.

8°. Pp. [iii]–viii + [i]–vi + [1]–24

Notes: Published 8 October. Attributed to Andrew Moreton,
Esq. An unpaged leaf at the end advertises *Every-Body's Business, The Protestant Monastery,* and *Augusta Triumphans* (all
by Defoe) as "Books written by Andrew Moreton, Esq; and
printed for W. Meadows, at the Angel in Cornhil."

Copy: IU. *Other copies:* BPL, N, R, Y

504   Street-Robberies, Consider'd; The Reason Of their being
so Frequent, With Probable Means to Prevent 'em. To
which is added, Three Short Treatises: I. A Warning for
Travellers: With Rules to know a Highwayman; and Instructions how to behave upon the Occasion. II. Observations on House-breakers: How to prevent a Tenement from
being broke open: With a Word of Advice concerning
Servants. III. A Caveat for Shopkeepers: With a Description
of Shop-Lifts, how to know 'em, and how to prevent 'em:
Also a Caution of delivering Goods: With the Relation of
several Cheats practiced lately upon the Publick. *Written
by a Converted Thief.* To which is prefix'd some Memoirs
of his Life. Set a Thief to Catch a Thief. London: *Printed
for* J. Roberts *in Warwick Lane. Price 1s.*

8°. Pp. [3]–72

Notes: Attributed to a converted thief. Lee dates this 12 November. But it was advertised in *The London Evening Post* for 12
November: "To-morrow will be published" and in *The White-*

hall Evening-Post for 14 November: "This Day was published, . . ." *CBEL* places this tract before *Second Thoughts are best,* apparently on the supposition that it is referred to in the title of *Second Thoughts are best;* but there Defoe had in mind a quite different tract by a rival author, a *Discovery to Prevent Street Robberies.*

Copy: BM. *Other copies:* BOD; BPL, F, HEH, IU, N, T, Y

1729

505 REASONS FOR A WAR, In Order to Establish the Tranquillity and Commerce Of Europe. Pax Quaeritur Bello: LONDON: *Printed for* A. DODD, *and* R. WALKER, *without Temple-Bar;* E. NUTT, *and* E. SMITH, *at the Royal-Exchange; and sold by the Booksellers and Pamphlet-Shops, Mercuries and Hawkers of London and Westminster,* 1729. [*Price Six-pence.*]

8º. Pp. 3–32

Notes: Published 11 February.

Copy: BOD. *Other copies:* NLS, UL; BPL, C, F, H, HEH, JCB, LC, RPB, T, Y

506 THE UNREASONABLENESS And Ill Consequences OF IMPRISONING THE BODY FOR DEBT, Prov'd from the Laws of God and Nature, Human Policy and Interest. Address'd to a Noble Lord. Nemo Tenetur Ultra suum posse. Bracton. LONDON: *Printed, and Sold by* T. READ *and* J. PURSER, *the Corner of Dogwell-Court, in White-Fryers, Fleetstreet; and by the Booksellers of London and Westminster.* 1729. (*Price Six Pence*)

8º. Pp. 3–28

Notes: Published 3 March 1729.

Copy: HEH. *Other copies:* UL; BPL

507 AN HUMBLE PROPOSAL To The People of England, For the Encrease of their Trade, And Encouragement of their Man-

ufactures; Whether The present Uncertainty of Affairs Issues in Peace or War. *By the Author of the Compleat Tradesman.* LONDON: *Printed for* CHARLES RIVINGTON, *at the Bible and Crown in St. Paul's Church-yard,* 1729. (*Price One Shilling.*)

8°. Pp. [2 unnumbered] + [1]–59

Notes: Published 15 March. Attributed to the Author of the Compleat Tradesman. Largely an expansion of No. 499, which is advertised at the end.

Copy: BM. *Other copies:* NLS; C, HEH, IU, R, Y

508   AN ENQUIRY INTO THE PRETENSIONS OF SPAIN TO GIBRAL-TAR. Together with A Copy of a Letter (Said to be sent) to His Catholick Majesty. LONDON: *Printed for* R. WALKER, *at the White Hart without Temple-Bar, and sold by the Booksellers of London and Westminster.* 1729. (*Price Six-pence.*)

8°. Pp. [1]–24

Notes: An approximate date for this tract is suggested by current events in Great Britain. On 18 March 1729 the House of Lords (deeply concerned over the publication of a letter of 1 June 1721 in which George I had expressed his willingness to restore Gibraltar to Spain, subject to the approval of Parliament) resolved that Spain should renounce all claim to Gibraltar. On 19 March the House of Commons was asked to confer with the Lords on the subject. On 25 March a joint resolution was presented to George II, to which he replied at once by promising to secure his undoubted right to Gibraltar. On pp. 2–3 of *An Enquiry* Defoe referred to these events: ". . . as well from the *joint* Address of the British Parliament lately made publick, as from His Majesty's Answer to the said Address." Probably *An Enquiry* was published in early April 1729. BM has a copy of the second edition, published in the same year for R. Walker, "with additions."

Copy: IU. *Another copy:* BPL

509   SOME OBJECTIONS Humbly offered to the Consideration Of The Hon. House of Commons, Relating To THE PRESENT

INTENDED RELIEF OF PRISONERS. LONDON: *Printed for* R.
WALKER, *at the White-Hart, without Temple-Bar,* E. NUTT,
*at the Royal-Exchange, and sold by the Booksellers of Lon-
don and Westminster.* 1729. *(Price 6d.)*

8⁰. Pp. 1–24

Notes: On 21 April the engrossed Bill for the Relief of In-
solvent Debtors passed its third reading in the House of Commons and was sent up to the Lords. Defoe's tract must have
been published somewhat earlier, while the Bill was still under
consideration in the House of Commons.

Copy: UL. *Other copies:* BPL, Y

510   THE ADVANTAGES OF PEACE AND COMMERCE; With Some
Remarks on the East-India Trade. *Printed for* J. BROTHER-
TON *and* THO. COX *in Cornhill, and sold by* A. DODD *with-
out Temple-Bar.* 1729.

8⁰. Pp. 3–40

Notes: Published 22 April. Contains seven very favorable references to *Atlas Maritimus & Commercialis* (No. 501), on which it
is largely based.

Copy: BM. *Other copies:* UL; Y

511   MADAGASCAR: OR, ROBERT DRURY'S JOURNAL, During Fifteen Years Captivity on that Island. Containing I. His Voyage to the East Indies, and short stay there. II. An Account
of the Shipwreck of the Degrave on the Island of Madagascar; the Murder of Captain Younge and his Ship's Company, except Admiral Benbow's Son, and some few Others,
who escap'd the Hands of the barbarous Natives. III. His
being taken into Captivity, hard Usage, Marriage, and
Variety of Fortune. IV. His Travels through the Island,
and Description of it; as to its Situation, Product, Manufactures, Commodities, &c. V. The Nature of the People,
their Customs, Wars, Religion, and Policy; As also, The
Conferences between the Author and some of their Chiefs,

Concerning the Christian and Their Religion. VI. His Redemption from thence by Capt. Mackett, Commander of the Prince of Wales, in the East India Company's Service; His Arrival to England, and Second Voyage thither. VII. A Vocabulary of the Madagascar Language. The Whole is a Faithful Narrative of Matters of Fact, interspers'd with Variety of surprising Incidents, and illustrated with a Sheet Map of Madagascar, and Cuts. *Written by Himself,* digested into Order, and now publish'd at the Request of his Friends. LONDON: *Printed, and Sold by* W. MEADOWS, *at the Angel in Cornhill;* J. MARSHALL, *at the Bible in Newgate-street;* W. WORRALL, *at the Judge's Head in Fleet street; and by the Author, at Old Tom's Coffee-House in Birchin Lane.* MDCCXXIX. [*Price bound Six Shillings.*]

8⁰. Pp. [ii]–xvi + [1]–464. Folding map of Madagascar and 5 plates (facing pp. 12, 61, 222, 345, 418)

Notes: Published 22 May. Like Captain Carleton, Drury seems to have been a real personage; but he was not possibly the author of the major part of the original narrative which the "Transcriber" professedly recast to "put it in a more agreeable Method."

Copy: IU. *Other copies:* BM, BOD, NLS; BPL, C, COR, HEH, I, Y

1730

512 A BRIEF STATE OF THE INLAND OR HOME TRADE, Of England; And of the Oppressions it suffers, and the Dangers which threaten it from the Invasion of Hawkers, Pedlars, and Clandestine Traders of all Sorts. Humbly Represented to the Present Parliament. LONDON: *Printed for* THO. WARNER, *at the Black-Boy in Pater-noster-Row.* 1730.

8⁰. Pp. [2 unnumbered] + [5]–70

Notes: This tract can be dated between 18 February 1730 and sometime before the middle of April—probably in February. It was part of a well-organized campaign to induce Parliament to restrict or forbid the growing encroachment on inland re-tail trade by hawkers and peddlers. On 18 February the House of Commons received a petition on this subject from "certain Manufacturers, Traders, and Shopkeepers, in the City of London." Next day there were similar petitions from 24 other communities; and from 20 February to 15 April there were at least 40 additional petitions of the same sort.

In *The Political State of Great-Britain* for March 1730, of which Defoe was then acting as editor, an abstract of this pamphlet was printed (XXXIX, 315–321) with the explanation: "As this Book tho' Printed, has not been publickly Sold, it may not have fallen into many Hands, . . ." Presumably Defoe's material had appeared successively in three different forms: in a brochure presented to members of the House of Commons on or shortly after 18 February, in a condensed statement in *The Political State* for March 1730, and in the full-length pamphlet sold to the general public by Thomas Warner. I do not recall having seen a copy of the tract in its first form, but Defoe's explanation in *The Political State* implies its existence and its restricted circulation. Very probably some of Defoe's other tracts such as No. 509, which were said to be "Humbly Offered to the Consideration Of The Hon. House of Commons," were printed for private distribution at the door of the House of Commons before being offered for public sale.

An old manuscript note in one of the BM copies reads: "This is one of the clearest and most masterly History in fact [?] of the home Trade I ever read. Not a freeman of London but should have a Copy on his Counter. *M T*."

CBEL assigns to Defoe *A Second Letter From A Hawker and Pedlar In the Country, To a Member of Parliament at London* (1731). If Defoe was actually responsible for that, he would have to be charged with its closely related predecessor, *A Letter From A Hawker and Pedlar In the Country* (1731). But both of these cynical little pamphlets are attacks on the established inland trade which Defoe had advocated all his life and was still defending, and both are quite unlike Defoe in style and temper. In fact, *A Second Letter* appeared months later than any known publication of Defoe's during his lifetime. It was advertised "This Day is Published" in *The Daily Journal* for

2 April 1731—— only 22 days before Defoe's death "of a lethargy."

Copy: BM. *Other copies:* NLS, UL; IU, Y

513   CHICKENS FEED CAPONS: Or A Dissertation On The Pertness of our Youth in general, Especially Those trained up
at Tea-Tables; With The true Picture of a Petit Maitre,
and a Modern fine Lady; Some Hints on Abuses in Education; not forgetting the Insolence and Scorn with which
the generality of young Persons treat their Elders and Bet-
ters. Also A very remarkable Tragical Case, which may
serve as a Warning to Persons in Years, how they give the
Staff out of their own Hands, and leave themselves to the
Mercy of others. *Written by a Friend of the Person injured.*
LONDON: *Printed for* A. DODD *near Temple-Bar, and* E.
NUTT *at the Royal-Exchange,* 1731 [for 1730]. (*Price Six-
pence.*)

8°. Pp. 1–24

Notes: Attributed to a Friend of the Person injured. On 24
October 1730 Defoe published this revision and condensation
of *The Protestant Monastery* (No. 486). If we may trust the title-
pages, prefaces, and newspaper advertisements of the paper
war which followed, certain events occurred in order: Objections to *Chickens Feed Capons* were raised by the family or
friends of the young wife who had been accused by Defoe of
unkindness to her old father. On 14 November Defoe published a second edition with a defensive preface, and on 21
November a third edition (still with a defensive preface). On
28 November a reply to Defoe was published: *No Fool like
the Old Fool.* On 17 December Defoe brought out his fourth
edition, with an advertisement in *The Daily Post* stating that
"There has been t'other Skirmish, or this Edition had been
publish'd sooner." The preface to the fourth edition spoke
contemptuously of *No Fool like the Old Fool,* referred to the
prodigious sale of the first three editions of *Chickens Feed
Capons* (which, as Defoe suggested, might have been partly
due to the book's being bought up in the effort to suppress it),
said that the author had given bond to indemnify his publisher

in case of damages, and threatened that if he met with further provocation he would certainly publish the name of the ungrateful daughter (which he had previously withheld).

It is not clear how much of this is to be taken literally, how much was meant as a jocular advertisement. *The Protestant Monastery* had gone almost unnoticed for four years, whereas *Chickens Feed Capons* (a much slighter reworking of the more sensational part) went through four actual editions in less than two months. Defoe died 24 April 1731. It is clear from the advertisements that *Chickens Feed Capons* appeared no later than 17 December 1730, although all four editions are postdated 1731.

Copy: BM. *Another copy:* BOD

514 THE GENEROUS PROJECTOR, Or A Friendly Proposal to prevent Murder and other enormous Abuses, By erecting an Hospital for Foundlings and Bastard-Children. With a full Answer to all Objections yet brought against that laudable Undertaking. Also to save many Persons from Destruction, by clearing the Streets of shameless Strumpets, suppressing Gaming-Tables, and Sunday Debauches: With a plain Explosion of, and Proposal to amend a growing Abuse, viz. the barbarous Custom of Men's putting their Wives into private Mad-houses, on frivolous Pretences, where they often end their Days in the utmost Misery. Also a Proposal to amend several great Abuses daily committed by Watermen. And necessary Hints for redressing divers other publick Grievances, which call aloud for Amendment. Humbly Dedicated to the Right Honourable Humphry Parsons, Esq; Lord-Mayor of the City of London. And highly worthy the Consideration of the Legislature. LONDON: *Printed for* A. DODD *without Temple-Bar, and* E. NUTT *at the Royal-Exchange,* 1731. (*Price 1s.*)

8º. Pp. [iv]–viii + 9–46

Notes: Published 31 October 1730. This is a revision of *Augusta Triumphans* (No. 498). The preface on pp. vii–viii is a resetting of the first page and a half of the original tract; and pp. 9–44 appear to be unsold sheets, for they are identical with the corresponding pages in *Augusta Triumphans*. But considerable parts of the original (from the middle of p. 4 through p. 8 and pp. 45–63) are omitted altogether. There are certain additions: p. [iv] gives an "After-Thought" about extending Defoe's earlier scheme (pp. 16, 17, etc.) to painting, sculpture, etc.; on pp. v–vi there is a dedication to the Lord Mayor signed "Tokenhouse Yard, October 28, 1730: C. H."; and pp. 45–46 introduce an exposure of the evil practices of London watermen.

Copy: BM. *Other copies:* UL; BPL

515 THE PERJUR'D FREE MASON DETECTED; And yet The Honour And Antiquity Of The Society Of Free Masons Preserv'd and Defended. By a Free Mason.

> For Perjury's a Blast upon the Mind,
> The last Degeneracy of human Kind;
> The utmost Prostitution of the Soul
> That poisons every Part, and damns the whole.

LONDON: *Printed for* T. WARNER *at the Black-Boy in Pater-Noster-Row*. MDCCXXX. [*Price 6d.*]

8°. Pp. 3–22

Notes: Attributed to a Free Mason. A. J. Shirren, Deputy Town Clerk of Stoke Newington, states that "During the last period of his life Defoe was associated with the masonic lodge which met at the 'Three Crowns,' on the corner of Church Street and High Street, and wrote a pamphlet attacking Pritchard the renegade free-mason" (*Daniel Defoe in Stoke Newington*, Stoke Newington Public Libraries Committee, 1960, p. 26). Elsewhere (as in *An Essay On The History and Reality of Apparitions* [1727], p. 43; *Second Thoughts are best* [1729], p. iv; and *The Political State of Great-Britain*, XL, 210–219, 328–382 [for 332]) he seemed rather hostile to the Society. But the position taken in this tract is one which he might have supported at any time in his life. "The Perjur'd Free Mason" had attracted public attention by a professed betrayal of secrets which he could have learned only under a vow not to disclose them. Even if the supposed revelations were true, Defoe held that they were unworthy of credence as coming from a man who had perjured himself by disclosing them. Published 13 November, apparently as a reply to *Masonry Dissected,* which had been reprinted in Read's *Weekly Journal* for 24 October 1730.

Copy: BM

516 AN EFFECTUAL SCHEME FOR THE IMMEDIATE PREVENTING OF STREET ROBBERIES, And suppressing all other Disorders of the Night. With A Brief History Of The Night-Houses. And An Appendix Relating to those Sons of Hell, call'd Incendiaries. Humbly inscribed to the Right Honourable the Lord-Mayor of the City of London. LONDON: *Printed for* J. WILFORD, *at the Three-Flower-de-Luces behind the Chapter-House, in St. Paul's* Church-Yard. MDCCXXXI [for 1730] (*Price 1s.*)

8°. Pp. [6 unnumbered] + 9–72

Notes: The dedication to the Lord Mayor, Humphry Parsons, is signed J. R. Published 15 December 1730. Except the forty-page supplement in the second edition of *A Plan of the English Commerce* (13 January 1731), this was apparently Defoe's last new publication during his lifetime.

Copy: Y

PART TWO

Undated Works Published Posthumously

[In the preceding pages, Defoe's posthumous works have been listed in the order of their actual composition as far as that could be established. The first three following were never completed by Defoe, and they cannot be assigned to any specific year during his lifetime.]

517 THE VOYAGE OF DON MANOEL GONZALES, (Late Merchant) of the City of Lisbon in Portugal, To Great-Britain: Containing an Historical, Geographical, Topographical, Political, and Ecclesiastical Account of England and Scotland; With A curious Collection of Things particularly Rare, Both in Nature and Antiquity. *Translated from the Portugueze Manuscript.* [1745]

Fol. Pp. [9]–208

Notes: Published in Vol. I of *A Collection of Voyages and Travels* in the *Harleian Collection* by Thomas Osborne, London, 1745. In this curiously assembled work, attributed to a young merchant from Portugal and published 14 years after Defoe's death, the bulk of the material is inferior hack-work, much of it cribbed verbatim from Miege, Hatton, and other works of reference. But Chapters I, IX, and X, with the first half of Chapter II (pp. 10–11, 82–110) are to a large extent the work of Defoe, and in places they are strikingly analogous to his *Tour.* Perhaps these pages represent Defoe's uncompleted attempt to prepare for publication a now-lost manuscript of fictitious travels in Great Britain by a supposed foreign observer. Just such a project had been outlined in detail by Defoe as early as 1724 in *The Great Law of Subordination* (pp. 44–

50). Possibly such a manuscript by Defoe fell into the hands of a bookseller who sought to have it expanded for publication. From internal evidence, it would seem that an attempt at completion was undertaken not long after Defoe's death in 1731 (although the compilation was not published until 1745). See my *Defoe in the Pillory and Other Studies* (Bloomington, Indiana, 1939), pp. 72–103.

Copy: BM. *Other copies:* BOD, NLS; H, N, NYPL, Y

518   THE COMPLEAT ENGLISH GENTLEMAN *By Daniel Defoe* Edited for the First Time from the Author's Autograph Manuscript in the British Museum, with Introduction [,] Notes, and Index By Karl D. Bülbring, M.A., Ph.D. LONDON: *Published by* DAVID NUTT MDCCCXC

8°. Pp. [3]–278

Notes: This work was being prepared for the press on 10 September 1729. See Defoe's letter to the printer John Watts (*Letters,* ed. Healey, p. 473).

Copy: BM. *Other copies:* BOD, CU, UL; BPL, COR, H, I, IU, N, T, Y

519   OF ROYALL EDUCACION A Fragmentary Treatise *by Daniel Defoe* Edited for the First Time, with Introduction [,] Notes, and Index by Karl D. Bülbring, M.A., Ph.D. Professor of the English Language and Literature in the University of Groningen, Netherlands [.] LONDON: *Published by* DAVID NUTT MDCCCXCV

8°. Pp. [1]–63

Copy: BM. *Other copies:* BOD, CU, UL; BPL, COR, H, IU, NYPL, T, Y

520   THE LETTERS OF DANIEL DEFOE. Edited by George Harris Healey. OXFORD *At the Clarendon Press* 1955 [Improperly inserted here.]

8°. Pp. xxii + 1–506.

Copy: IU

PART THREE

Periodicals

[*For the following list I have not attempted to indicate where I have examined the journals. Few complete files are to be found in any one library. I have studied the periodicals of the early 18th century in many collections, especially in the British Museum, the Bodleian, the National Library of Scotland, the University of Texas Library, and the Indiana University Library; and I have made use of microfilms and photostats from elsewhere (especially from the Yale University Library).*

For some of these periodicals Defoe wrote almost every line of the text—as for the Review, Mercator, The Manufacturer, The Commentator, The Director, *and* The Citizen. *For* The Universal Spectator (*as for* Fog's Weekly Journal) *he wrote only a single essay. For several journals (such as* Mist's *and* Applebee's) *he was a principal contributor at times, and at intervals he influenced or controlled the editorial policy.*

The list which follows is meant primarily to indicate the names and dates of the journals in which Defoe had some hand, avoiding most of the complexities of the subject.]

521 THE ATHENIAN MERCURY

Occasional contributions at various times in 1690 and 1691.

522 REVIEW

19 February 1704 to 11 June 1713. For a distinction between the six different publications included under this generic name— the first eight volumes of the *Review* proper, the ninth volume of the *Review* (numbered I, but usually known now as [IX]), the Edinburgh edition of the *Review, The Little Review,* the

Supplement, and the *Appendix* to the first volume—see the Facsimile Text Society's reprint: *Defoe's Review Reproduced from the Original Editions, with an Introduction and Bibliographical Notes by Arthur Wellesley Secord,* . . . New York, MCMXXXVIII. See especially I, xvii–xxiii for an analysis of the six different publications.

523 THE LONDON POST, WITH INTELLIGENCE FOREIGN AND DOMESTICK

Defoe had a hand in this from 25 September 1704 to 8 June 1705 (possibly from 27 March 1704 onward). On 3 January 1705 the title was shortened to *The London Post.*

524 THE EDINBURGH COURANT

Contributions from 24 September 1708 to July 1709, and perhaps again for a time after 15 May 1710. Defoe certainly wrote the leading articles from 29 December 1708 to 21 January 1709, summarizing the principal events of the preceding year.

525 THE LONDON POST-MAN

Contributions during Defoe's two long stays in Edinburgh between 1706 and 1708. See *The Boston Public Library Quarterly,* VI [1954], 195–205.

526 THE NEWCASTLE GAZETTE: OR, NORTHERN COURANT

Some connection in December 1710.

527 THE SCOTS POSTMAN

27 December 1709–late in 1710 (?)

528 THE OBSERVATOR

Contributor and collaborator from 19 July to early October 1710.

529 MERCATOR: OR, COMMERCE RETRIEVED

26 May 1713–20 July 1714. Certainly Defoe's throughout, although at times it has been mistakenly attributed to a supposi-

titious W. Brown, to Dr. Davenant, and to others. According
to Boyer's *Political State of Great Britain* (V [1713], 356) this
paper was generally fathered upon Arthur Moore assisted by
Dr. Davenant, but the latter solemnly protested that he had
had no hand in it. On 21 May 1714 Defoe wrote to Harley
(*Letters*, ed. Healey, p. 441) to say that Arthur Moore first set
him upon that work, and undertook the support of it, but later
declined any consideration for it after 25 March 1714; so that
Defoe performed it wholly without any appointment for it, or
benefit by it. The W. Brown named in *Mercator* as the author
or editor was but another pseudonym for Defoe.

530   THE MONITOR

      22 April–7 August 1714

531   THE FLYING POST: AND MEDLEY

      27 July–21 August 1714

532   THE FLYING POST

      Defoe's connection with this journal seems to have been occa-
      sional only. In 1718 he published one letter in it, and in 1724
      two letters. In No. 3597 (22 January 1715) he published the
      remarks on a sermon by Dr. Sacheverell which he later reprinted
      in No. 293 (*The Immorality of the Priesthood*, pp. 61–63).

533   MERCURIUS POLITICUS

      May 1716–October 1720. The editor was said to be "A Lover of
      Old England." A new editor was announced for November and
      the months following.

534   DORMER'S NEWS LETTER

      June 1716–August 1718

535   THE WEEKLY-JOURNAL; OR SATURDAY'S EVENING POST
      [commonly called Mist's WEEKLY-JOURNAL]

      Certainly as early as 9 February 1716/7. Not later than 24 Oc-
      tober 1724. See Nos. 444, 445, 491, 492.

536 THE WEEKLY JOURNAL BEING AN AUXILIARY PACKET TO THE SATURDAY'S POST

25 September–23 October 1717

537 MERCURIUS BRITANNICUS

January 1718–March 1719. Attributed to Walter Campbel in the first monthly issue; thereafter the pseudonym was spelled Campbell.

538 THE WHITE-HALL EVENING POST

18 September 1718–c. 14 October 1720

539 THE DAILY POST

3 October 1719–c. 27 April 1725

540 THE MANUFACTURER

30 October 1719–17 February 1720

541 THE COMMENTATOR

1 January–16 September 1720. No later number known.

542 THE ORIGINAL WEEKLY JOURNAL [Later Called APPLEBEE'S ORIGINAL WEEKLY JOURNAL]

25 June 1720–14 May 1726 (occasional contributions thereafter)

543 THE DIRECTOR

5 October 1720–16 January 1721. No later number known.

544 THE CITIZEN

18 September–17 November 1727. No later number known. First two numbers lost (18 and 22 September).

545 THE UNIVERSAL SPECTATOR, AND WEEKLY JOURNAL

For No. 1 (12 October 1728) Defoe wrote the first leader essay for the editor, Henry Baker, who soon afterward married Defoe's youngest daughter, Sophia (30 April 1729).

546 FOG'S WEEKLY JOURNAL

For the issue of 11 January 1729 Defoe wrote a brief essay on Trade. This served also as an advertisement of No. 474, *The Compleat English Tradesman.*

547 THE POLITICAL STATE OF GREAT-BRITAIN

December, 1729–October, 1730. Soon after the death of Abel Boyer (16 November 1729) Defoe succeeded him as editor for the next eleven monthly issues. With the issue of November 1730 the journal passed into entirely different hands; several of Defoe's projected discussions were abruptly dropped, and the journal suddenly became violently anti-ministerial in tone.

For a student of the canon of Defoe there are three important features of these eleven issues: (1) Defoe quoted freely from his earlier writings and repeated many ideas and arguments he had advanced previously; (2) he gave an abstract and something of the history of one of his own current tracts (*A Brief State of the Inland or Home-Trade,* XXXIX, 315–321); and (3) he gave abstracts of several other writings of his own which have not as yet been found elsewhere. One of these was introduced as follows (XXXIX, 43–44): "We here present the Reader with an Abstract of a Paper handed about in Manuscript upon the Subject of this new Treaty, which Paper being very Curious and not yet Printed, we thought it would be very agreeable to the Publick to contract in this Manner, and to give them so much of it as consists with the Brevity of this Work; the Remainder may as Opportunity presents see the light hereafter." Similar abstracts of otherwise unknown tracts or letters by Defoe were introduced later (XXXIX, 360–364, 443–447, 655–659; XL, 123–127, 192–197).

160a A Brief History of the Poor Palatine Refugees. Lately Arriv'd in England. Containing, I. A full Answer to all Objections made against receiving them; and plain and convincing Proofs, that the Accession of Foreigners is a manifest Advantage to Great Britain, and no Detriment to any of her Majesty's native Subjects. II. A Relation of their deplorable Condition; and how they came to be reduc'd to such Extremities. III. A Description of the Country from whence they came. IV. An Account of their Numbers. V. By what Methods they have been subsisted. VI. How they may be dispos'd of, to the Honour and Service of the Queen's Majesty, the Glory and Profit of this Kingdom, and the Advantage of themselves and Posterities. And VII. An exact List of the Names of the Commissioners and Trustees appointed by her Majesty, for receiving and disposing of the Money to be collected for the Subsistance and Settlement of the said Palatines. In a Letter to a Friend in the Country. London *Printed: And Sold by* J. Baker *at the Black Boy in Pater-Noster-Row.* 1709. *Price 6d.*

8°. Pp. 1–40

Notes: Published sometime in the summer of 1709, presumably just before Defoe went to Scotland in late August as Godolphin's agent. The plan for settling the Palatines in England has close analogues in Nos. 459, 499, and 522. IU has a copy of a Dublin reprint in the same year.
Copy: BM.

Foreword

When the first edition of this checklist appeared in 1960, a reviewer in the *Antiquarian Bookman* quoted with approval the objectives listed on page xii and added: "The voluminous work of Defoe defies usual procedure, and this practical checklist of the 548 entries has a number of new and easy reference features, including for the first time an index of his printers and publishers."

This new edition reproduces the revised text of the second printing [1962], with additional corrections and supplements, an updated list of printers and booksellers, and much new material. Two attributions (Nos. 11 and 364a) have been cancelled. All entries were originally numbered to indicate relative dates of publication. A few belong somewhat earlier or later, but the numbering cannot be altered. Intermediate numbers (like 279a) are assigned to new entries.

It was not expected that the listing of Defoe holdings in selected libraries could be kept up to date; but so far that goal has been approximated for the Bodleian, the British Museum, the Boston Public, the Huntington, the Lilly Library of Indiana, and the Beinecke Library of Yale. For assistance in this (and in other matters) I am again deeply indebted to friends and correspondents at home and abroad—most recently to D. G. Neill of the Bodleian, R. J. Roberts and I. B. Willison of the British Museum, Ellen Oldham of the Boston Public, Mrs. Myron Kimnach (formerly of the Huntington), Geneva Warner and Mrs. James Work of the Lilly Library, Thomas Atteridge III of Syracuse University, and Robert J. Barry, Jr., of C. A. Stonehill, Inc., New Haven.

After my accidental discovery in 1931 that Defoe wrote "Johnson's" *History of the Pyrates*, I was content to trace its multifarious relationship to Defoe's other writings. It seemed sufficient to accept the attributions of Trent and Dottin, and to acquaint myself with every work in their lists to be found in the principal libraries or procured through antiquarian booksellers.

That confidence was gradually dispelled as I began to discover unlisted works which were undoubtedly by Defoe (like *A Letter to a Dissenter from his Friend at the Hague* [1688], identified by Defoe himself in *An Appeal to Honour and Justice*), or when entries in the best current lists proved to be impossible for Defoe. For instance, Defoe's broadside *Declaration without Doors* (No. 108) is quite unlike the imaginary pamphlet suggested to fit that title; *A Letter from Daniel de Foe to Mr. Matthews Printer* [1711] is (after the misleading title-page) perhaps the most libellous attack on Defoe ever published; *A Letter to a Member of Parliament, on the Settling a Trade to the South-Sea* [1711] is specifically dated nearly two months before Defoe agreed very reluctantly to give any support to Harley's favorite project; *A Second Letter from a Hawker and Pedlar in the Country* [1731] loses much of its meaning without the unmentioned first letter, and both are bitter and rather vulgar attacks on the inland trade which Defoe was actively supporting and which throughout his life he regarded as the cornerstone of English prosperity.

Gradually I was forced to undertake the examination of any publication or manuscript between 1680 and 1731 which could reasonably be regarded as Defoe's, and to reconsider every such attribution which had been proposed by responsible writers. Unless I could offer valid objections against an earlier attribution, I accepted it (at least temporarily) on the assumption that my predecessor might have known of evidence which I had not seen. When I have proposed new attributions I have constantly sought for further confirmation—and I have become increasingly skeptical when I have not found it abundantly.

In this I have been aided by many librarians and literary scholars, but it would be of little use to proceed in such an inquiry by seeking a consensus or a poll. For so simple an attribution as that for *Robinson Crusoe* we could find at least a dozen suggested authors; so good a literary critic as the third Earl of

Chesterfield gave it to the Earl of Oxford; so good a natural scientist as the hydrographer of the *Naval Chronicle* gave it to Crusoe himself (as did Defoe); so good a literary historian as Thomas Wright gave it to Defoe's use of the supposititious manuscript of Alexander Selkirk; and a lawyer in the learned city of Ithaca gave it to posthumous publication for no less an author than Francis Bacon.

Very rarely some contemporary of Defoe's showed real knowledge of what Defoe had written (as when John How printed a perfectly accurate list of thirteen of Defoe's early writings—a list which Defoe denounced, and two of whose titles he rejected as spurious). The man who employed Defoe longest and most intimately was Robert Harley, Earl of Oxford; but he had no idea that a defense of Scotland against the ruthlessness of Harley's agents (No. 196) was Defoe's, he probably smiled with Defoe over the common attribution of a Defoe tract to himself (*Letters*, pp. 276–77), and in travels over England his son and heir used Defoe's *Tour* as his guide without guessing at its author. Defoe alone knew all that he wrote, but for various good reasons he chose more often to deny his authorship than to admit it. After a consideration of all the external evidence available, the most promising method of identifying his writings is to trace the continuity of his ideas and style in his known writings. For example:

Perhaps the most central idea in Defoe's mind was expressed in *The True-Born Englishman*: that England had been settled by foreigners, and that

> Fame of Families is all a Cheat,
> 'Tis Personal Virtue only makes us Great.

He liked to call himself "The Author of *The True-Born Englishman*," and he quoted from the poem *by memory* twenty-nine years after it was published. He wrote a poem beginning "Ye true-born Englishmen proceed" and another (after the Union with Scotland) called "The True-Born Britain." He recalled his own family's foreign extraction, and he discussed the anglicizing of foreign names among families from the Continent who had become eminent in England. He was intimate with the Huguenot exiles

(Frank Bastian has suggested that he acquired his working knowledge of French from one of them) and he collaborated with the Huguenot journalist Fonvive in his *London Post-Man*. For twenty years he advocated unrestricted naturalization of foreigners. Among English writers he was almost alone in his vigorous and extremely unpopular support of the swarms of refugees from the Palatinate during the famine summer of 1709. When we discover (in addition) that *A Brief History of the Poor Palatine Refugees* [1709] contains one of his favorite Biblical quotations (rarely used by other writers), and that it is closely analogous to many significant passages in his *Review* and his *Tour* and his *Plan of the English Commerce*, and that it recalls a confidential proposal he is known to have made to Lord Godolphin about settling refugees in England, we can recognize his hand as if from a fingerprint.

No fixed line of progression can be charted for our knowledge of Defoe's authorship, which requires constant reexamination on the basis of available evidence. Occasionally such evidence comes from an accidental discovery, as in the six letters from Defoe to De la Faye which were found in the State Paper Office in 1864 and served to open a vast new area in his journalistic career. More often it comes from long-neglected clues or from careful observation of likenesses and relationships.

It is sometimes suggested that a complete record should be made of all the attributions to Defoe which have ever been proposed, as a means of tracing such discoveries. Aside from being an almost endless undertaking, this would lead to supposed lines of influence which never existed. For example, in 1966 the late R. G. Iványi recognized *The Schism Act Explain'd* as one of Defoe's most characteristic writings (not knowing that George Ridpath had surmised the same thing two and a half centuries before); in the 1950's I assembled abundant evidence to prove that *The Political State of Great-Britain* was edited for eleven months by Defoe (not knowing that Trent had anticipated my judgment in a statement in *The Encyclopedia Americana* which he chose not to reaffirm thereafter). On the other hand, some of the most important influences are not recognized; the Sacheverell researches of the late F. F. Madan remain unpublished, and no outsider could possibly surmise the extent of my profound indebtedness to him in the obscure area where he was the only master and guide.

It is perhaps impossible that any catalogue of Defoe's writings will ever be entirely complete or entirely accurate. The present list is meant to be as nearly so as forty years of investigation, in many places and from many lines of approach, have been sufficient to make it.

Corrections and Additional Notes

3   See *Review*, I, 234.

5   Also N. HEH has two copies, one somewhat trimmed.

7   Also IU, N

10   Signed "D. F., Gent."

12   Also N. A Jacobite pamphleteer in France (in *A Reply to the Answer Doctor Welwood has made to King James's Declaration*) assumed that Welwood, author of the semi-official reply to James's Declaration of 1689, wrote this reply also. But the Jacobite writer was out of touch with affairs in London; an old manuscript note in the HEH copy of his pamphlet reads: "This it is evident, from the many typographical errors has been printed abroad." In No. 12 Defoe seemed to have replaced Welwood as propagandist for King William, apparently with no official authorization.

17   Also N

18   Also HEH, IU

26   Also BM

32   Also Y

33   This tract is referred to very favorably in No. 414.

34   For an earlier version see *Huntington Library Quarterly*, XXVIII, 53–54 (November 1964).

35   Also HEH

36   Also Y

37   Also IU

41   Also IU, and a variant called *The Original Right*. BOD has an uncut copy of *The Original Power*, stitched as issued.

49   Also BPL

50   Mr. Frank Bastian suggests a later date than 1 December; the tract does not seem to have been mentioned so early in the month.

51   Also Y. Published earlier; Tutchin mentioned it in his *Observator* for 6/9 January 1703. The 1703 reprints omit Defoe's postscript.

53   Reissued eight years later with a slightly different title (*Observator*, 24/28 February 1711): "King William's Affection to the Church of England consider'd. S. Popping, in Pater-noster-Row, Price 6 d."

57 Also HEH. BM has an additional copy which reads: *"By the Author of the Shortest Way with the Dissenters."*

68 The IU copy has an unnumbered page attacking a tax on printed news and pp. 3–22 (actually two pages more, because page numbers 7 and 8 are duplicated).

70 Also Y

71 Also Y

74 Also HEH

77 Reprinted in *Poems on Affairs of State* (1716), II, 68–76.

84 Also Y

85 For "De Foe" read "DeFoe."

88 BM has an additional copy entitled *Giving Alms to Charity.*

89 Y has only known copy.

101 Also BOD; Y

102 Also T

104 Also N

105 Read "Practised" for "Practiced."

113 Also Y. Apparently this was the "Remarks &c." which Defoe mailed into the country in the spring of 1706 (*Letters*, p. 115).

116 N has only the Edinburgh reprint.

121 Also BPL

122 Also Y

127 Also BOD; Y. Ostensibly by a Scotsman. JRM copy has a contemporary inscription: "by Mercenary Dan De ffoe."

130 Also Y

131 Also BPL

133 Also Y

135 Also Y

139 Also Y

140 In a hostile list of Defoe's works (*A Looking-Glass for Mr. De-Foe*, B. Bragg, 1709, p. 1) this is called *A Vindication of the Presbyterians in the South to the Kirk in the North.*

143 Also BPL

146 Also BOD

149 Also Y

152 Also Y

155 Also N

156 Professor Henry L. Snyder gives very interesting evidence for attributing this to Maynwaring (*Huntington Library Quarterly,*

XXIX [November 1965]). It undoubtedly passed through the hands of that principal agent for the Whigs, and it was apparently edited by him; but it has marked characteristics of Defoe's style. Ghost writing for public officials was almost as common in Queen Anne's London as in Washington today. Some of Defoe's tracts are still frequently attributed to Harley; and Defoe was partly responsible for such misunderstandings, as in No. 194, p. 69: "I know what a certain Great-man, and now Leader of the Management, has been pleas'd to publish to the World in Print, in his *Essay upon Credit* . . ."

160a   Also Y. Published 11 August 1709. Facsimile reprint (with my introduction), Augustan Reprint Society Publication No. 106 (University of California, Los Angeles, 1964).

161   BOD has George Chalmers' autographed copy. It has no portrait of Defoe and no marginalia. Dr. William Beattie has informed me that NLS has two copies with Defoe's portrait (tipped in, as elsewhere).

164   Also HEH, Y

166   Also Y

167   Also Y

169   Also BPL, H, Y

174   JRM has a very clear photographic copy.

180   JRM has a very clear photographic copy.

182   IU has a variant of BOD.

183   Also Y

184   Also BPL. Y has three copies—the two described here and a variant.

185   Also N, Y. "This Day is Publish'd (*Daily Courant*, 7 August 1710).

186   "This Day is publish'd" (*Daily Courant*, 9 October 1710).

187   "This day is publish'd" (*Daily Courant*, 15/17 August 1710).

188   "This day is publish'd" (J. Baker, *Evening Post*, 15/17 October 1710).

189   Also Y. "Next Monday [i. e., 4 September] will be publish'd" (*Flying-Post*, 31 August/2 September 1710).

190   "This Day is Publish'd (*Flying-Post*, 16/19 September 1710).

192   "This day is publish'd" (*Post-Boy*, 21/23 September 1710).

193   "This Day is Publish'd" (*Flying-Post*, 3/5 October 1710).

194   P. 69 quotes No. 192 approvingly.

195   Also Y. "This day is publish'd" (*Post-Boy*, 21/24 April 1711).

198   Dated 1711 but published in the previous December. "To Morrow will be publish'd" (*Evening Post*, 9/12 December 1710); "Yesterday was published" (*Evening Post*, 12/14 December 1710). Dr. Patricia Köster has identified the pages mistakenly bound in the BM copy from *Reasons for Restoring the Whigs* (1710).

199   Also N, Y. "This Day is publish'd" (*Evening Post*, 20/22 February 1711).

200   Also Y

202   Also HEH

203   Also HEH, N, Y

204   Also N, Y. HEH has some forms of this. Duke has a copy naming A. Baldwin as publisher. "This Day is publish'd" (J. Baker, *Evening Post*, 17/19 April 1711).

205   Also BOD

206   P. 55 refers to Nos. 204 and 207. "This day is publish'd" (*Post-Boy* and *Evening Post*, 12/15 May 1711).

208   Also Y. "This Day is Publish'd" (*Flying-Post*, 28/30 June 1711). "On Saturday last [i. e., 30 June] was publish'd" (*Flying-Post*, 30 June/3 July 1711).

210   Also BPL, H, Y

211   Also BPL, Y

213   Also BOD; HEH

214   Also Y

215   Also BM

216   N lacks p. 47.

220   Also BPL, Y

226   Also Y

228   Also N

232   Also IU

233   Also Y

234   BM, BPL, and Y have copies like BOD. IU has what appears to be a pirated copy.

235   Also BPL

238   Also Y

239   Also N, Y

240 BM has a copy with six unnumbered pages + 1–34.

242 Also Y. IU has another copy entitled "Further Search."

248 Also Y

249 Also HEH

250 Also Y

256 Also BOD; BPL

257 Also Y. "This Day is publish'd" (*Post-Boy*, 8/10 October 1713).

260 N copy for July has ms. note "15. August." BPL and IU lack the August issue. The four parts were reissued in one volume by J. Baker, 1713.

261 Also HEH, IU, Y

264 Also Y

265 Also Y

266 Also HEH

272 Also HEH, Y

274 Also N, Y

275 Also N

278 Also IU

280 IU lacks the first edition, but has two copies of the second and one of the fourth.

281 Reprinted in Dublin, with far more italics for emphasis and with this addition on the title-page: "Written in Vindication of the E——l of Ox——rd. And supposed to be written by his Directions, if not by himself. *LONDON:* Printed for *J. Baker* in Pater-Noster-Row: And Reprinted in *Dublin*, for G. Risk, Bookseller, at the *London* in *Danes-Street*, over-against the Horse-Guard, 1714."
8°. Pp. 3–30.
Copy: HEH

282 IU has two copies of first edition and one of second.

284 Also HEH, N, Y. "Just publish'd" (*Evening Post*, 18/20 November 1714).

285 "The Day is publish'd" (*Evening Post*, 9/11 November 1714).

286 Also Y. "This Day is publish'd" (*Evening Post*, 30 November/2 December 1714).

288 Also HEH, Y. Apparently 286 and 288 were soon offered together at 1 s. instead of 6 d. for each: (*Evening Post*, 30 December 1714/1 January 1715); "The complete Tryals of the Bristol Rioters, before Mr. Justice Powys, Mr. Justice Tracy, and Mr. Baron

Price. With a full and impartial Account of the late Disorders in that City. By a Gentleman who attended the Commission, in 2 Parts, price 1 s." Most of the same material was drawn on for *The Political State of Great-Britain* (VIII, 362–368, 463, 475, 495) and *The Annals of King George, Year the First* (pp. 312–16). See also No. 316a.

289   Also Y

290   Also Y. "This Day is publish'd" (*Flying-Post*, 21/23 December 1714).

291   Actually only 72 pp. 41–72 misnumbered 49–80.

292   Advertisements confusing: "This Day is published" (*Evening Post*, 18/20 January 1715 and *Post-Man*, 20/22 January 1715); but "This day is publish'd, the 2d Edition of, Treason Detected" (*Flying-Post*, 20/22 January 1715).

294   "This Day is publish'd" (*Flying-Post*, 12/15 February 1714–15).

296   "This Day is publish'd" (*Flying-Post*, 21/23 December 1714).

298   Also Y. IU has two copies of first edition.

299   "Tomorrow will be publish'd" (*Evening-Post*, 18/20 January 1715).

303   Also BOD

304   No exact date known. See my discussion in "A Rare Tract by Daniel Defoe" (*Indiana Quarterly for Bookmen* [1945], I, 9–17).

305   Also HEH. The following advertisement appeared in *The London Gazette* No. 5308 (1/5 March 1714–15) and in *The Daily Courant* (7 March 1715): "Whereas there hath been a Pamphlet lately published, Intitled, A Friendly Epistle by way of Reproof [pretended to be] from one of the People called Quakers, To Thomas Bradbury, a Dealer in many Words; wherein are sundry Irreverent Expressions Reflecting upon the King, Princes and Rulers; We the People called Quakers do hereby Advertise all concern'd, That we had no Hand in the said Pamphlet, but do utterly disown it, believing it to have been a Contrivance of some Adversary of Ours, whereby to vent his own Invectives against the Government in our Name, and to Expose us to the Displeasure thereof, and the Censure of Sober People." In No. 310 (published 24 March 1715) the page of advertisements is headed by an emphatic claim that the author of No. 305 was a Quaker: "Whereas there was publick Notice given in a Paper, commonly call'd the London-Gazette, the 5th Day, and in another Paper

call'd the Daily-Courant, the 7th Day of the present Month (by several Ministring Friends, and others, who, have become Back-sliders and Time-servers) That a Book, entitled, A Friendly Epistle, by way of Reproof, from one of the People call'd Quakers, was written by an Adversary, and with an evil Intent against the King, Princes, and Rulers of the Land; and that the said Book contains several irreverent Expressions against the King: This is to inform the People, that the said Notice is entirely false and malicious, and that the said Book was written by a Friend in Unity with the People call'd Quakers; and that he is mov'd to reprove them also in Publick for their Back-slidings. N. B. This Day is publish'd the Fifth Edition of the said Book. Printed for the Author, and sold by the Publisher of this Paper. P. S. The Reason why the Author does not put his Name on the aforesaid Book, is because Friends would ruin him for his Plain-Dealing." But in the next edition of No. 305 (the sixth) the offending passages were toned down.

306   I saw this in the British Museum in 1955–56 but was unable to find it again in 1970 with the assistance of two members of the staff. Perhaps a pamphlet [BM 199 (23) and BOD Pamph. 316 (11)] which was advertised as being published on 1 March 1714–15 (*Flying-Post*, 26 February/ 1 March) is identical with No. 306 except for the title-page: "A/SERMON/ Preach'd/ January 31, 1714/5 BY/ *Henry Sacheverell, D. D./* Rector of St. *Andrew's Holborn/* As it was taken in Short Hand by one of his Parishioners./ To which is added,/ A Postscript containing Notes of another/Sermon, Preach'd on the Twentieth of/ the same Month./ With proper Reflections upon each Discourse/ *LONDON./* Printed and sold by *A. Boulton* without *Temple-Bar,/* and J. Harrison at the Royal-Exchange. 1715./ (Price 4*d*". Probably the Grubstreet pamphlet against which Defoe advertised is to be found in BM b 11/ 1416: "A Sermon Preach'd January 31st, 1714/15. By Henry Sacheverel, D. D. Rector of St. Andrew's Holborn. London: Printed for D. Brown near Fleet-street. 1715."

309   BM, BOD, BPL, and NLS copies agree in their erratic pagination: Pp. [1–6 unnumbered: p. [1] title; p. [2] blank; pp. [3–6] A letter to the publisher]+ 1–322+ 293–444. The text reads consecutively despite almost incredible confusion in the signatures. This confusion explains prefatory complaint about the poor printing—a complaint later echoed by Defoe.

310 "This Day is Publish'd" (*Flying-Post*, 22/24 March 1715).

311 Also HEH, N

314 "This day is publish'd" (*Post-Boy*, 7/10 May 1715).

315 Also Y. "Just published" (*Post-Man*, 22/24 February 1715).

316 "This Day is published" (*Post-Man*, 19/21 May 1715).

317 Also IU. "This Day is Publish'd" (*Flying-Post*, 26/28 May 1715).

318 Also BPL

319 Also BOD; Y (2 variants)

320 "This Day is Publish'd" (*Evening Post*, 14/17 May 1715).

321 Also Y

323 T has p. 3 for p. 1.

325 Also IU

326 Also BOD

327 Also BPL, Y

329 Also Y

330 BPL has only Glasgow (1715) and Dublin (1716) editions. "This Day is Publish'd" (*Flying-Post*, 8/10 November 1715). 2d edition November 19.

331 Also IU, N

331a Also HEH

332 Published in *Flying-Post* 17/20 December 1715. A similarly fictitious reply from Mar to Forster, in exactly the same ironic vein, appeared in the *Flying-Post* for 29/31 March 1716.

333 Certainly Defoe's. "This Day is published" (*Post-Man*, 8/10 May 1716). For the variant *Proper Lessons Written by a Quaker* see *Huntington Library Quarterly*, XXVIII, 46–47 (November 1964).

334 "This Day is publish'd" (*St. James's Post*, 13/15 June 1716).

336 Reprinted in the *Flying-Post* (31 January/ 2 February 1715–16).

337 The address was reprinted without the remarks in the *Flying-Post* (31 January/ 2 February 1715–16).

340 "This Day is publish'd" (*St. James's Post*, 9/11 May 1716).

341 Also Y. "This Day is Publish'd" (*Flying-Post*, 16/18 February 1715–16). Summarized at considerable length in the *Flying-Post* (18/21 February 1715–16).

343 Also Y. Certainly Defoe's.

344 "This Day is publish'd" (*St. James's Post*, 14/16 May 1716).

345 "This Day is publish'd" (*St. James's Post*, 9/11 April 1716).

346 Also HEH, Y

347 Also N, Y

348 Also IU. "This Day is publish'd (*St. James's Post*, 9/11 May 1716).

349   Also Y. "This Day is publish'd" (*St. James's Post*, 20/22 June 1716).

350   Also BPL, Y. "This Day will be publish'd" (*Flying-Post*, 17/19 July 1716).

351   Also BOD; BPL, Y. Except for the proclamations and other quoted material Defoe wrote most of Vols. II and III.

352   Also Y

356   Also HEH, Y. HEH has Dublin reprint also. Cited on p. 3 of No. 359.

357   Also Y

358   Also BPL, N

359   N lacks pp. 57–70. Cited also in No. 533 (August 1717), p. 444.

360   Also Y

363   Also BM. Quoted at length in No. 370 (pp. 59–68).

364   Also BOD; IU

366   Also N. Referred to in No. 533 (April 1717, p. 234) as one of the "virulent Pamphlets" published to authorize a Royal Visitation of the universities. No. 533 was edited by Defoe with an ostensible Tory bias.

367   Referred to (with No. 366) as one of the "virulent Pamphlets" published to vindicate a Royal Visitation.

368   IU has also the original sheets reissued in 1734 by Charles Marsh as *The Ecclesiastical History of Scotland*.

370   Also BOD; IU

372   Also BOD; BPL

373   Also N

378   Also N

379   Also BPL, N

380   Also BPL. Quoted and defended in No. 385 (p. 252). On p. 262 of No. 385 Defoe's controversy with Farbery is summed up briefly.

385   Also BOD; BPL, Y

386   Also Y

387   Referred to in No. 533 (January 1718, p. 24).

389   Also BPL

390   Also BPL

392   Also BPL, IU, Y

393   Certainly by Defoe

394   Also Y

395   Also Y

397 Also Y

402 "Just Published" (*Post-Man*, 20–22 May 1718).

406 Also, HEH, Y

408 Also HEH

409 Also Y

411 Also HEH

412 Also Y

413 Also Y

414 See Nos. 30 and 33.

416 Perhaps published earlier. Quoted or summarized at length in No. 523 (July 1719, pp. 422–448). No. 533 usually appeared in the month following the assigned date.

417 Also Y

418 Also Y

431 Also Y

432 E. Curll's *Catalogue of Poems, Plays, and Novels* (HEH 296374, ca. 1720 or later) advertised this as "The Life and Surprizing Adventures of the Celebrated Mr. *Duncan Campbell*" and listed it under NOVELS.

433 Also BOD; IU, Y

436 Also BOD

437 Also Y

438 Also Y

439 Also N

440 Also HEH, T, Y. The JRM title-page announces the key, but this is lacking in the text.

445 Also Y

446 IU has two copies of both first and second editions.

447 T has two copies.

448 Also IU

450 Also Y

453 Also HEH

454 Also IU, Y

455 Also Y

457 IU has two copies.

458 Also Y

459 The 7th edition (T, 1769) is apparently the first which specifically named Samuel Richardson as a continuator of Defoe's *Tour*.

460 N is not first edition.

461 N is not first edition.

465 IU has second edition (1725) also—apparently identical except for the reset title-page. The second edition also lacks the frontispiece depicting a monument erected for the murdered Englishmen—but this was apparently worn off.

466 Also BOD

467 Also IU

472 Also IU, T

476 Not in IU, which has only the subsequently issued *History of the Principal Discoveries.*

480 Not in IU, which has second, third, and fourth editions. The second is called *The History of the Devil.* The verse quotation should be italicized.

484 Also BM

487 IU has two copies of this: Lilly Library PR3404–.S9–1727 and PR3404–.S9–1727). It has also a copy (1–5185) which seems to be identical except for a substitution at the bottom of the title-page: "*LONDON,* Printed: And Sold by ANDREW MILLER, at *Buchanan's* Head, against St. *Clement's* Church in the *Strand.* MDCCXXVIII." In addition it has unused sheets reissued as *A Compleat System of Magick: or, The History of the Black Art* (PR3404–.S9–1729), with an entirely new title-page outlining the contents under seven headings and concluding: "*LONDON:* Printed for J. CLARKE, at the *Royal-Exchange*; A. MILLER, against St. *Clement's* Church in the *Strand*; H. NOORTHOUCK, under the *Great-Piazza, Covent-Garden*; T. GREEN at *Charing-Cross*; J. PEN, in *Westminster-Hall*; J. Jackson, and *Mrs. Graves,* at *St. James's*; and J. BRINDLEY, in *New-Bond-street*, M.DCC.-xxix. (Price 5 s.)"

489 Also BPL, CH. In addition IU has *A Treatise.*

490 Advertises the second edition of No. 488 and refers to it (in the preface and pp. 1–2) as a work by the same hand.

494 The title-page of *The Secrets* substitutes a quotation from Milton. IU has also the second and third editions of *The Secrets* (1735 and 1738), identical with the first edition except for two new title-pages and the loss of the frontispiece in the 1738 copy.

502 Also HEH

506 See also Nos. 199a and 509.

509 See also Nos. 199a and 506. On the verso of the title-page Y has

a handwritten receipt for 3 s. stamp duty, dated 9 May 1729.

510 Also IU

513 Also HEH

515 An attack on Samuel Prichard (or Pritchard) for his *Masonry Detected* (1730).

532 Defoe's connection with Ridpath's *Flying-Post: or, The Post-Master* seems to have been far more extensive than I had supposed, involving some of the apparent contradictions which appear throughout his journalistic connections—as in his brief share in the *Observator* after Tutchin's death, in the *News-Letter* after it passed from the hands of Dyer and Dormer, in *The Political State of Great-Britain* for eleven months after the death of Boyer, and in his editing *Mercurius Politicus* and *Mercurius Britannicus* as Tory and Whig rivals at the same time.

Unfortunately there is no discovery such as Defoe's letters to De la Faye to explain the complications of his connection here. What seems apparent is that after Ridpath slipped back from his voluntary exile shortly before the death of Queen Anne, he discharged Hurt as his printer because of his secret cooperation with Defoe and attempted to carry on his old *Flying-Post* in rivalry with their new periodical of almost the same name. Hurt and Defoe soon fell afoul of the new Government by printing a letter attacking the Earl of Anglesey, and Defoe escaped prosecution only through lack of evidence. In July 1715 he was arrested on the old charge, but appealed to Chief Justice Parker and soon afterwards was accepted as the Government's chief press representative.

Ridpath had been very active in the arrest of Defoe in April 1713, and he continued occasionally to insinuate that he was a Jacobite; in the *Review* Defoe had condemned Ridpath's flight to Holland, and in No. 405 he made a bantering attack on him as an opponent of Mist's *Weekly-Journal*. But at intervals from late 1714 to 1724 (see No. 464) Defoe seems to have contributed material to the *Flying-Post* (some of which had been or was afterwards printed separately in pamphlets) on such subjects as Dr. Sacheverell, Jacobite riots, the 1715–16 rebellion, the anti-Hanoverian bias of the universities, the eclipse, and Wood's halfpence. These appear as oases in the arid wastes of Ridpathian prose.

Additional Titles

8a A COMPLEAT HISTORY OF THE LATE REVOLUTION, From the
first Rise of it to this Present Time . . . LONDON, Printed
for Samuel Clement at the Lute in *St. Paul's Church-Yard*,
1691.

4°. Pp. 1–80

Notes: Sometimes mistakenly assigned to Guy Miege.

Copy: BM

10a REFLECTIONS UPON THE LATE HORRID CONSPIRACY Contrived
by Some of the French Court, To Murther His Majesty in
Flanders: And for which Monsieur Grandvall, one of the
Assassinates, was Executed. LONDON: Printed for *Richard
Baldwin*, near the *Oxford Arms*, in Warwick-Lane. 1692.

4°. Pp. 1–35

Copy: HEH. *Other copies:* BM; IU

10b A DIALOGUE BETWIXT WHIG AND TORY; Aliàs Williamite
and Jacobite. Wherein the Principles and Practices of each
Party are fairly and impartially stated; that thereby Mistakes
and Prejudices may be removed from amongst us, and all
those who prefer English Liberty, and Protestant Religion,
to French Slavery and Popery, may be inform'd how to
choose fit and proper Instruments for our Preservation in
these Times of Danger. Printed in the Year 1693.

4°. Pp. (i)–xii + 1 unnumbered sheet + 1–28. Since numbers
17–18 are repeated, there are thirty pages with arabic numerals.

Notes: Pp. (1)–xii are headed "To the King." The two unnumbered pages are headed "To the Honest English Protestant
READER." The text proper is headed "A DIALOGUE *between*
Whig and Tory, *&c.*" The IU copy was apparently printed later,
with 1 p. Errata and only 2 pp. instead of 12pp. of the introduc-
duction. The tract was reprinted in 1710 (for S. Popping and T.
Harriman about 22 July) with the prefatory Advertisement:

"The following Discourse was first printed in the Year 1692, but as the same Causes, will always produce the same Effects, 'tis thought not unseasonable to publish it now afresh: and if they who have a regard to the Happiness of their Native Country, of whatever party they be, will peruse it with Minds free from Heat and Prejudice, the Publisher will attain his chiefest aim." At this time Defoe had become a collaborator in *The Observator* and S. Popping was publishing some of his tracts.

Copy: HEH

13a SOME SEASONABLE QUERIES ON THE THIRD HEAD, viz. A General Naturalization. Fol. pp. 1–4. No title-page

Notes: London, c. January 1697. Written in support of the bill for naturalizing foreigners then pending in the House of Commons, this tract is the first in which Defoe spoke of "the Wealth of Nations," and it is clearly related to his other proposals for relieving the Palatines, recruiting soldiers and sailors, and increasing the value of land by intensive cultivation. See "Some Seasonable Queries: A Chapter Concerning the Humanities" (*Newberry Library Bulletin*, VI, 179–186 [December 1965]).

Copy: N

17a SOME QUERIES CONCERNING THE DISBANDING OF THE ARMY. Printed in the Year 1698.

4°. Pp. [2]–12

Notes: See "Defoe Acquisitions at the Huntington Library" (*Huntington Library Quarterly*, XXVIII, 51–52 [November 1964]).

Copy: HEH

19a THE CASE OF DISBANDING THE ARMY At Present Briefly and Impartially Consider'd. Published by John Nutt, near Stationers Hall, 1698.

4°. Pp. 1–10

Notes: Briefer and slighter than Nos. 15, 18, and 19; but a characteristic work by Defoe, developing the same ideas, with many of the same idioms.

Copy: HEH

22a AN ENCOMIUM UPON A PARLIAMENT. [1699] After wide circulation in manuscript, this 105 line lampoon was printed in *Poems on State Affairs*, II, 241–45 (1703). It has been correctly attributed to Defoe by Frank H. Ellis (*Poems on Affairs of State: Augustan Satirical Verse*, 1660–1714 [Vol. 6, New Haven and London, Yale University Press, 1970]) . The lampoon is similar in verse, diction, and spirit to No. 36, but it deals with the English political situation two years earlier.

34a THE PRESENT CASE OF ENGLAND, AND THE PROTESTANT INTEREST.

4°. Pp. 1–4

Notes: No title-page. No colophon except *FINIS.* No indication of publisher or printer, but folded twice laterally as if it had been carried in the pocket of a member of Parliament after it had been distributed gratis at the door of the House of Commons. Defoe's views were expressed more fully in No. 27. See also his many other references to "the Protestant Interest" (as in *Review,* VI, 102–04; III, 271–73; VIII, 269, 271, 446, 679, 727) and to Charles XII, the Palatines, etc. *The Case of England and the Protestant Interest* (4°, pp. 1–4, HEH) seems to be a cheaper verbatim reprint of this except for the slightly different title and the following addition to the last paragraph: "; and in the words of our liturgy, let us offer up our most fervent Prayers to God Almighty, *Give peace in our time, O Lord! because there is none other that fighteth for us but only thou, O God!"* As *The Case of England* has lighter paper and somewhat smaller type, with rather more errors, such as "Protesant" in the title, and as it lacks the creases, it probably represents a later printing—perhaps one intended for wider circulation.

Copy: HEH

37a AN ARGUMENT, SHEWING, THAT THE PRINCE OF WALES, Tho'

a Protestant, Has no Just Pretentions to the Crown of England. With some Remarks On The late pretended Discovery
of a Design to steal him away. LONDON: Printed for A. BALD-
WIN near the *Oxford Arms* in *Warwick-Lane.* 1701.

4°. Pp. [2 unnumbered] + 1-24

Notes: Two previous rumors regarding the conversion of the
Pretender were recalled on p. 11 of No. 324a. See *The Huntington Library Quarterly,* XXVIII, 55-57 (November 1964).

Copy: HEH

144a QUERIES UPON THE FOREGOING ACT.

4°. Pp. 7-8

Notes: Printed as a supplement to *The Copy of an Act lately
pass'd in Carolina* [1707], presumably to be handed out at the
door of the House of Commons. The introductory paragraph on
the first page is also by Defoe. See "Defoe's 'Queries upon the
Foregoing Act' A Defense of Civil Liberty in South Carolina"
*(Essays in History and Literature Presented by Fellows of the
Newberry Library to Stanley Pargellis,* edited by Heinz Bluhm
[Chicago, 1965], pp. 133-155).

Copy: N

199a VOX DEI & NATURAE: Shewing The Unreasonableness and
Folly Of Imprisoning the Body For Debt, From The Laws
of God and Reason, Custom of Nations, Human Policy and
Interest. In a Letter to Sir T— H—, Knight of the Shire, for
the County of ——.*LONDON,* Printed in the year 1711.

4°. Pp. 3-15

Notes: This is addressed to Sir Thomas Hanmer, the very independent representative of Suffolk in the House of Commons, at
a time when the Tories were in power. Later Hanmer, although
a Tory, was instrumental in establishing the Hanoverian Succession. Discussion of arrest for debt, later expanded in No. 506.
See also No. 509, in which Defoe reaffirmed that honest but
unfortunate debtors should be relieved, but pointed out that

credit could not be sustained without the possibility of arrest as a check on dishonest debtors.

Copy: IU. *Another copy:* BM

200a THE QUAKER'S SERMON: Or, A Holding-Forth Concerning Barabbas. LONDON: Sold by *A. Baldwin* near the Oxford Arms in Warwick-Lane, 1711. Price Three Pence.

8°. Pp. 3–24

Notes: See also Nos. 305, 310, 317, 330, 333, 379, 383, 409.

Copy: HEH. *Another copy:* IU, slightly imperfect

219a THE STATE OF THE BRITISH NATION, Relating to a General Peace.

8°. 4 pp. unnumbered

Notes: The colophon reads: *Dublin Printed by G. C at the Old Post Office in Fishamble-street.* A verbatim reprint from the *Review* for 18 October 1711, except for a few very minor changes in punctuation, etc., and the substitution of different advertisements, two of them specifically intended for Dublin.

Copy: HEH

229a SOME QUERIES HUMBLY PROPOS'D UPON THE BILL FOR A TOLERATION to the Episcopal Clergy in Scotland.

Fol. half-sheet

Notes: No date, but internal evidence establishes this as 1712. The bill came before the Commons 29 January, was passed in its first form by the Lords 26 February, and received the Royal assent 3 March. This half-sheet was probably printed for free distribution at the door of the House of Commons. See Defoe's letters to Harley on 24 January, 14 February, and 5 April and many issues of the *Review* between 29 January and 6 May 1712.

Copy: HEH

229b A LETTER FROM A GENTLEMAN IN SCOTLAND, TO HIS FRIEND AT LONDON. LONDON, Printed in the Year 1712.

8°. Pp. 3–16

Notes: Closely related to Defoe's other discussions of the post-Union attack on Scottish Presbyterians, especially Nos. 237 and 368. See discussions of the Greenshields case in Nos. 170 and 202 and in *Review* (VII, 593).

Copy: HEH

279a THE SCHISM ACT EXPLAIN'D; Wherein Some Methods are laid down how the Dissenters may teach their Schools and Academies as usual, without incurring the Penalties of the said Act. LONDON: Printed for A. BELL, at the *Bible* and *Cross-Keys* in Cornhill, 1714. (Price 6*d.*)

8°. Pp. 3–40

Notes: Established as Defoe's by the late R. G. Iványi ("Defoe's Prelude to The Family Instructor" [*Times Literary Supplement,* 7 April 1966, p. 312]).

Copy: Y. *Another copy:* BM

316a AN ACCOUNT OF THE RIOTS, TUMULTS, AND OTHER TREASONABLE PRACTICES; Since His Majesty's Accession to the Throne. With Some Remarks, Shewing The Necessity of strengthening the Laws against Riots; Humbly offered to the Consideration of the Parliament. LONDON: Printed for J. BAKER, at the *Black-Boy* in *Pater-Noster-Row,* 1715. (Price 4d.)

8°. Pp. 1–26

Notes: Advertised in *The Evening Post* (22/24 March 1715): "This Day is publish'd." Pp. 1–4 addressed to Parliament. Pp. 4–26 a succession of ostensible letters (edited or rewritten by Defoe), many of which had appeared in previous issues of *The Flying-Post* and which have close analogues in *The Annals of King George, Year the First* and in *The Political State of Great-Britain.* These letters were at least nominally addressed from Bristol, Chippenham, Norwich, and Reading (23 October 1714), Abergavenny and Birmingham (21 October 1714), Frome (25

October 1714), Taunton (1 November), Chichester (1 December), Hertford (25 January 1715), Leicester (2 February), Beckington (12 February), Cambridge (19 February), and Bristol (7 March). The second letter from Bristol is signed N. W. (possibly "Mr. Wraxall, Mercha" listed by Defoe as a Bristol agent (*Letters*, p. 116). See also Nos. 286 and 288.

Copy: HEH

320a A LETTER FROM A GENTLEMAN OF THE CHURCH OF ENGLAND, to all the High-Flyers of Great-Britain.

8°. Pp. 1–8

Notes: Known to me only in this Dublin reprint. No title-page. The colophon reads: "*Dublin:* Re-printed, and Sold by *Thomas Humes* in *Copper-Ally*, 1716." See *Huntington Library Quarterly*, XXVIII, 45–47 (November 1964).

Copy: HEH

342a HANOVER OR ROME: Shewing The Absolute Necessity of Assisting His Majesty with such a sufficient Force, as may totally Extinguish the Hopes of the Pretender's Open and Secret Abettors. . . . LONDON: Printed for J. ROBERTS, near the Oxford-Arms in *Warwick-Lane*. MDCCXV. Price Sixpence.

8°. Pp. 1–35

Notes: HEH has two copies of the London original and a Dublin reprint by "James Carson, at the Sign of King George in Fishamble-street, 1715. Price Threepence."

Copy: IU. *Other copies:* HEH

365a CHRISTIANITY NO CREATURE OF THE STATE: Or, if it be made One, Reasons Why it should be Abolish'd. Humbly offer'd to the Consideration of our States-Men. In a Letter to a Friend. *Probitas laudatur & alget.* By the Author of the Case of the Protestant Dissenters fairly Stated. Re-printed in the Year, MDCCXVII.

8°. Pp. 2–20

Notes: Known to me only in this Dublin reprint. The title-page identifies the writer as the author of No. 335, one of Defoe's principal London tracts in the previous year.

Copy: HEH

390a THE NEW BRITISH INQUISITION: OR, THE RACKING OF MR. PILLONIERE, To Extort a Confession of Jesuitism from him. Wherein His Communicating with all the Orthodox Branches of the Reformation is justified. *By a Layman of Conscience and Common Sense:* LONDON Printed: And Sold by *J. Roberts* in Warwick-lane. 1718. (Price Six Pence)

8°. Pp. 5–36

Notes: Clearly related to No. 390.

Copy: IU

424a THE FEMALE MANUFACTURERS COMPLAINT: Being The Humble Petition of Dorothy Distaff, Abigail Spinning-Wheel, Eleanor Reel, &c. Spinsters, To The Lady Rebecca Woollpack. With a Respectful Epistle to Sir R— St— l, concerning some Omissions of the utmost Importance in his Lady's Wardrobe. By Monsieur de Brocade of Paris. LONDON: Printed for W. BOREHAM at the *Angel* in Paternoster-Row: 1720.

8°. Pp. 5–23

Notes: This is the previously unidentified original of the tract known only as *The Petition of Dorothy Distaff, etc. To Mrs. Rebecca Woolpack,* which was printed by Defoe in *Mercurius Politicus* for December 1719, pp. 294–303 (actually at least a month later). The fictitious letter from Monsieur Brocade to Sir Richard Steele is dated "Jan. 2, 1720." Closely related to No. 420.

Copy: UL. *Another copy:* BM

Index of Printers and Booksellers

(with Entry Numbers)

Anderson, Andrew (Heirs and Successors of), 129, 156, 157, 158, 159, 161

Applebee, John, 466, 468, 473, 474

Astley, Thomas, 500

Baker, J. 21, 160a, 164, 165, 172, 173, 180, 188, 189, 194, 195, 198, 199, 204, 205, 206, 207, 212, 214, 215, 216, 217, 218, 219, 221, 222, 224, 225, 226, 232, 234, 236, 237, 239, 241, 244, 245, 246, 247, 248, 249, 250, 251, 252, 253, 255, 256, 257, 260, 263, 265, 266, 267, 270, 273, 274, 276, 277, 278, 279, 280, 281, 282, 284, 287, 298, 299, 303, 307, 312, 313, 316a, 318, 319, 321, 322, 331, 331a, 334, 340, 341, 344, 345, 346, 348, 349, 350, 351, 352, 355, 366

Baker, S., 371, 373, 374, 376, 377, 381, 382

Baldwin, Abigail, 20, 24, 25, 31, 34, 37a, 38, 62, 65, 89, 144, 168, 174, 182, 183, 186, 200a, 204, 208

Baldwin, M., 361

Baldwin, Richard, 5, 10a, 12

Ballard, T., 16

Battey, J., 447

Bell, A., 53, 273, 279a, 284, 322, 351, 352, 385, 389, 433, 434

Bell, W., 352

Berington, B., 280

Bettesworth, A., 424, 432, 448, 457, 469, 483

Bettesworth, Arthur (perhaps not identical with the preceding), 501

Bickerton, T., 415, 421, 422, 442

Billingsly, J., 92

Blanford (Blandford), N., 486, 498

Boreham, William, 387, 388, 391, 394, 395, 402, 404, 408, 410, 416, 420, 424, 424a, 425, 428

Boulter, A., 306, 324

Boulter, S., 324

Bowles, John, 479

Bowles, Thomas, 479

Bragg (Bragge), Benjamin, 42, 90, 92, 93, 94, 99, 104, 107, 115, 123, 135

Briscoe, S., 442

Brotherton, J., 363, 424, 435, 446, 448, 451, 452, 462, 510

Brown (Browne), D., 476

Burleigh, R., 326, 327, 338, 343, 357

Burton, 421

Button, Joseph, 195, 309

C., G., 219a

Carson, James, 324a

Chapman, S., 452, 459, 460

Chetwood, W., 424, 446, 451, 452

Chiswell, Ric., 6, 7

Clark, J., (with R. Ford in the Poultry) 389, 487, 494

Clark, John (under the Piazzas, Royal-Exchange), 479

Clay, F., 476

Clement, Samuel, 8a

Index of Titles

(including works by Defoe and works which contain some of his writings)